Aesthetics and Art Theory

An Historical Introduction

Harold Osborne, M.A., is a founding member of the Executive Committee of the British Society of Aesthetics and is editor of the Society's quarterly journal, *The British Journal of Aesthetics.* He is the author of two widely read books: *The Theory of Beauty* (1952) and *Aesthetics and Criticism* (1955); and has edited the recently published *Aesthetics in the Modern World* (1968). He is also a frequent contributor to a number of scholarly periodicals in Europe and America.

Harold Osborne, M.A., is a founding member of the Executive Committee of the British Society of Aesthetics and is editor of the Society's quarterly journal, *The British Journal of Aesthetics*. He is the author of two widely read books: *The Theory of Beauty* (1952) and *Aesthetics and Criticism* (1955); and has edited the recently published *Aesthetics in the Modern World* (1968). He is also a frequent contributor to a number of scholarly periodicals in Europe and America.

Harold Osborne

Aesthetics and Art Theory
An Historical Introduction

E. P. Dutton & Co., Inc. New York *1970*

Contents

Illustrations

Introduction

This book is not a history of aesthetics as a branch of philosophy, nor is it confined to doctrines of art and beauty as these appear in the writings of the great philosophers. It is a study in the history of ideas in a broad sense and it deals with aesthetical concepts as they are manifested in the behavior and assumptions of artists and practical men as well as the formulations of theorists. For ideas are often active in practice long before they become articulate in the writings of professional theorists. Formal aesthetics as we know it was a recent arrival in the history of human thought. But men pondered, speculated, held convictions about the nature of art, the why and wherefore of artistic activity, long before the eighteenth century. Different ages and cultures had their different outlooks on these matters, manifested both in what the artists were striving or expected to do and in the criteria by which their works were assessed. For this reason the remarks of an artist, a moralist or a churchman are sometimes as significant in revealing the implicit aesthetic assumptions of an age as are the more high-powered and recondite formulations of the philosophers—which does not mean that the latter can be neglected either. The field is not a tidy one. In our aesthetical activities, as in many other walks of life, concepts are seldom clear or precise. Men can happily and on the whole successfully work with assumptions which when rendered articulate are seen to be conflicting. Or the assumptions which control their practice may be at variance with the doctrines they consciously profess. Disparity between profession and practice has been particularly characteristic of the modern period since aesthetic concepts have been worked over and become common counters: artists and their public, being generally practical men not always prone to analytical profundity, will sometimes profess the aesthetic doctrines that became current in the time immediately preceding their own without noticing that the assumptions implicit in their own practice are not conformable to these doctrines. The lack of a clear tradition either in theory or in practice along with the doctrinaire repudiation of authority, healthy enough in itself, which is characteristic of the present age have brought about an almost hysterical jangle of confusion about purposes and ends which ultimately can only foster frustration and the dissipation of talent.

Current language of art and criticism with its strong reminiscences of Romanticism is often at odds with the aesthetic outlook of today. In planning this survey of aesthetical ideas I have been guided not merely by academic or historical interest but have had an eye to contemporary relevance. Knowledge of the background of thought, the context of historical development, is necessary today in order to give substance and meaning to the concepts we have inherited and without it the language we use in our commerce with the arts will continue to be a patter of emotional clichés as profitless for descriptive understanding as checks drawn on a bank which has gone out of business. With this in view I have not only presented the ideas of past times in deliberate relation or contrast to contemporary aesthetic attitudes, but in a number of Appendices I have given brief historical portraits of certain key concepts, bringing out the vicissitudes which they have undergone and which have contributed to the character and the content they have acquired. This method will be useful to the general reader as well as the student. Furthermore, the ideas which have been dominant in Western tradition are set over against those which have prevailed elsewhere, particularly in Chinese and Indian aesthetic thought. This too has a value beyond its immediate usefulness in helping us to come to terms with Oriental and other artistic traditions than our own. It is valuable and even necessary if we are to clarify our own conceptual apparatus. For our most stubborn and pertinacious assumptions are precisely those which remain unconscious and therefore uncritical, concepts like creative imagination or expressive communication, and others which we take for granted without realizing that we do so, their pristine novelty and vigor eroded by the platitudinous complacency of middle age. The best and perhaps the only sure way of bringing to light and revivifying these fossilized assumptions, and of destroying their power to cramp and confine, is by subjecting ourselves to the shock of contact with a very alien tradition.

The influence of classical antiquity bulks large in Western tradition. At least until the Romantic Age European art pursued its tortuous course with one eye cocked ever backwards on the classical past of Greece and Rome. New movements of taste and style found their impetus in a new enthusiasm for the ancients. But although admiration for the art of classical antiquity remained a recurring feature of the most vigorous and original periods of European art, the classical has meant very different things at different times according to the accidents of knowledge and discovery, the conscious or unconscious selectivity of artists, and most of all through the different interpretations given to it, the different eyes with which it was seen. The classical renaissance of Carolingian times looked back to fourth- and fifth-century Roman products often seen indirectly through the transforming medium of Byzantine or Christian models. The works of the Pisani in thirteenth-century Italy held echoes of the forms they admired in third- and fourth-century sarcophagi found in the Campo Santo. The new Naturalism which burgeoned in the Gothic sculpture of Reims still went with a new admiration for the antique. But the drawings of classical sculptures done by the French artist Villard de Honnecourt reveal an eye insensitive to volume and translate them into calligraphic linear patterns after the centuries-old traditions of manuscript illumination. So too, classical forms are interpreted as animated linear rhythms by Duccio di Buoninsegna (*ca.* 1255–*ca.* 1318). The influence of classicizing Neo-Attic reliefs in the sculpture of Agostino di Duccio (1418–81) in the Tempio at Rimini is very different from Giulio Romano's modulation of Hellenistic reliefs in the age of Michelangelo and Raphael. Pierre Puget (1620–94) projected the vigorous Hellenistic forms of the Pergamene school into seventeeth-century French sculpture through his knowledge of Roman works from Trajan's time before the discovery of the originals in the 1880s. The famous group of the *Laocoön* was described by the Roman encyclopedist Pliny the Elder (A.D. 24–79) as "a work to be preferred to all that the arts of painting and sculpture have produced." Rediscovered in 1506, this sculpture—which seems so vapid and rhetorical to many people today—made an enormous impact on Michelangelo, was widely popularized through casts and engravings and archaeological speculations such as Jonathan Richardson's *An Account of Some Statues, Bas-Reliefs, Drawings and Pictures in Italy* (1728), and remained the most admired of all works of sculpture until the time of Goethe and Winckelmann. Until the Elgin marbles were acquired for the British Museum in 1816 very few people had any firsthand acquaintance with the classical sculpture of Greece.

From being a living inspiration to the Renaissance the admiration for the antique hardened into an academic doctrine which sought to impose the ancient models on contemporary artists as both the ultimate perfection in art and the standards for representing the ideal beauties of nature. The doctrine was formulated in a much quoted passage by the French painter Charles Alphonse Du Fresnoy (1611–88), author of a verse treatise *De Arte Graphica* which was translated into French in 1668 by Roger de Piles (1635–1709) and into English by John Dryden under the title *The Art of Painting* (1716). He wrote:

> *The principal and most important part of Painting is to find out and thoroughly to understand what Nature has made most beautiful and most proper to this Art; and that a choice of it may be made according to the Taste and manner of the Ancients: Without which all is nothing*

but a blind and rash Barbarity; which rejects what is most beautiful, and seems with audacious Insolence to despise an Art, of which it is wholly ignorant. . . . . Our business is to imitate the beauties of Nature as the Ancients have done before us, and as the Object and Nature of the thing require from us. And for this reason we must be careful in the Search of Ancient Medals, Statues, Gems, Vases, Paintings, and Basso Reliovos: And of all other things which discover to us the Thoughts and Inventions of the Graecians; because they furnish us with great Ideas, and make our Productions wholly Beautiful.

This doctrinaire classicism culminated with the great French Neoclassical critic A. C. Quatremère de Quincy, who, in his book *An Essay on the Nature and Means of Imitation in the Fine Arts* (Eng. trans. 1837), put out the theory that the final perfection of all art is to reproduce not the things we see, since these are always liable to faults and imperfections, but an ideally beautiful nature in accordance with the principles of true beauty which are present in nature itself. He thought that by their intuitive understanding of the principles of beauty inherent in nature though never completely exemplified in actual things, the Greek artists had been able to "correct nature through herself" and to realize the type of "superior beauty" which is the goal of all art. In this way he gave a semblance of reason to the Neoclassicist belief that contemporary artists must take the Greeks as their models and guides.

Yet, as we now see, the Neoclassicists were as blatant as any before them in imposing their individual and one-sided vision of the realities of classical art. If Winckelmann had confined himself to instructing artists with Teutonic ponderousness that "To take the ancients for models is our only way to become great," the damage would have ended when the vogue was past. But his etiolated conception of classical beauty as a "noble simplicity and calm majesty" so established itself in the minds of the many who look with their ears instead of their eyes that until well into the twentieth century it was difficult for most people to see Greek sculpture in other terms than that of petrified Germanic sentimentality. Yet in truth of fact the Romantic Rodin (1840–1917) had a closer affinity with the classical tradition than the Neoclassical Canova (1757–1822). Later on the twentieth-century excitement with prehistoric and primitive artistic manifestations—Negro, Mexican, Sumerian, Egyptian—

brought a broadening and an enrichment rather than a rejection of the classical tradition, which was carried on by many artists as diverse among themselves as Maillol, Despiau, Picasso, Moore, Giacometti, and many more. The widening of our artistic horizons has, however, enabled us to see our own classical heritage from outside, by comparison and contrast with independent cultures and traditions, a thing which was not possible in the earlier stages of European artistic development.

But all this belongs to art history. In the realm of aesthetic theory, which is our concern, the weight of antiquity is heavier, more stifling still. The language we use, the categories by which we seek to express ourselves to ourselves and to others, the conceptual framework which gives practical direction to our commerce with the arts, are all descended from antiquity. Until the Romantic period introduced such new notions as self-expression, creative originality, the value of fictional imagination, and so on—all of which are now in the melting pot—there was hardly an idea in aesthetics which had not been taken over from Greek and Roman antiquity. Today, with the relatively sudden expansion of aesthetic experience as the art of the world is brought within the purview of everyone and our aesthetic horizons have rapidly receded, we urgently need to revise and enlarge our conceptual apparatus. To do this usefully we must understand the background of ideas implicit in the concepts we have.

The aesthetic terminology of the ancients was evolved primarily in the context of their theory of public speaking or rhetoric and then applied in the first place to poetics and secondarily to art. As will be seen, their conception of art was primarily a literary one. *Ut pictura poesis*: a painting is like a poem. It tells a story, points a moral, pictures a belief. Until the rise of photography in the present century cut the ground from under traditional criticism, most writing about the arts consisted of verbal descriptions of subject matter, story, or message. Homage was paid to the technical dexterity with which realism was achieved, but what we now call "aesthetic" criticism—talk about the work of art itself—was little or not at all in evidence. The few aesthetic ideas which were inherited from antiquity—harmony, composition, proportion, concinnity, and the rest—had little practical relevance to art criticism. This is the material from which our own linguistic furniture is constructed. In the presence of works of art we can talk anecdotally about the artists, we can discuss technique and subject matter and details of iconography, we can find means of indicating superficial resemblances of style, and we can express our own feelings in exclamation marks. But when we wish to communicate something about the work of art itself and the qualities which make it a work of art we can only point and grunt. The Chinese were sometimes articulate where we are inarticulate. We cannot take over their conceptual apparatus, though we can see from it where our own poverty is a matter more of historical accident than of the necessity of things. We need to clarify and elaborate our own aesthetic vocabulary while overhauling our language of criticism. For without words in which to clothe them our ideas lack coherence and our thinking and apprehension are muddled.

The study of the background of our ideas and assumptions will help to pinpoint what it is we are lacking, where our need lies, and perhaps help us to see how to set about finding our feet again.

A reasonably dispassionate survey of Western cultural history reveals three basic categories of interest in the fine arts, manifested by social practice and conventions and by the fluctuations of taste as well as the ways in which people have been accustomed to talk about art and artists. With each of these kinds of interest is associated a characteristic group of art theories and critical criteria, though historically these have not been entirely exclusive or rigidly distinct but may often be seen interacting and simultaneously or even sometimes inconsistently assumed.

First there is the pragmatic interest, which gives rise to a large and complicated group of *instrumental* theories of art. In the most general terms this involves a practical interest in the purposes which works of art are considered or intended to serve and the effects which are believed to flow from them. Since through the greater part of human history the so-called fine arts were regarded as handicrafts among others, not distinguished as a class, and since art objects like other products of human industry were designed to serve a purpose recognized and approved by the society in which they arose, this practical interest in the purposes of the arts is the most general and in a sense the most natural of all. The purposes of the arts have been extraordinarily various: works of art have been religious implements, symbols for the glorification of rulers or institutions, memorials, and a hundred and one other things. But until the notion of the fine arts as a class of handicrafts whose sole or main purpose was to serve aesthetic contemplation established itself from the eighteenth century onward, no special group of "aesthetic" attitudes was consciously called into play in talking and thinking about the fine arts. The pragmatic interest in the arts as handicrafts, products of workshop industry, found its earliest and still interesting theoretical expression in the writings of the Greek philosophers, who discussed the arts within the context of a wider theory of Manufacture, and in the Greek socioeconomic theory of the arts. But the attitude of mind which tends to think of the fine arts as one group of human artifacts among others is by no means obsolete or without influence. As an example of its persistence today the art historian George Kubler begins his book *The Shape of Time* (1962) as follows: "Let us suppose that the idea of art can be expanded to embrace the whole range of man-made things, including all tools and writing in addition to the useless, beautiful, and poetic things of the world. By this view the universe of man-made things simply coincides with the history of art."

This sort of criteria which are germane to this pragmatic attitude of interest are: the value of the purpose served or thought to be served by a work of art; the effectiveness of the artwork for this purpose; and the quality of its workmanship. These are not *aesthetic* criteria as we understand the matter today and in this context of ideas the aesthetic motive is not deliberate—which is not to say that an aesthetic motive may not have been active both in the manufacture and in the assessment of artworks long before it was consciously recognized.

Among the uses of the arts to which the highest social importance has often been attached are their uses as instruments of education or edification. The powerful emotional appeal of the arts and the intimate connections which they have often had with moral conventions and with religious belief and ritual have rendered their functions in these fields particularly prominent to theorists. Therefore moralistic theories of art—that is theories which justify, condemn, or assess art products in terms of their educational, edificatory, and propaganda uses and the effects, controlled or uncontrolled, which they are seen to have on human behavior—form a special group of instrumental theories. During classical antiquity the moralistic outlook was predominant in discussions of the literary and musical arts. During the medieval period in the West the moralistic outlook was very prominent with regard to the visual arts also. In modern times a strong interest in the social effects of the arts, judged by political or moral rather than by aesthetic standards, has been characteristic of Marxist theories and of theories such as those of Tolstoy. In one form or another the relation of art and morality has remained a persistent theme of interest and is debated today particularly in literary theory, and in connection with such practical social issues as the rights or wrongs of censorship. Those who participate in all such debates are precluded from making fruitful contact with one another unless there is agreement whether an instrumental or some other basic interest in the arts is to be presupposed for the purposes of the discussion.

A rather separate group of instrumental theories came to prominence during the age of Romanticism and is still prevalent in the language of contemporary art criticism. These theories arose from interest in the arts as a means for the expression of emotion (in a wide and indefinite sense of that word), as a means for the communication of emotion and feeling, and as a means of edification by the vicarious expansion of experience. In the context of these theories art objects are, characteristically, valued and appraised for their effectiveness in furthering these purposes. The criteria which they impose are not aesthetic criteria. Works of art are not the only forms of self-expression, the only ways of communicating emotion, or the only ways of expanding experience beyond the confines of a man's real-life experience. It does not make nonsense to ask of an artifact (a novel, a psychotic's drawing, a volume of photographs) which does any of these things whether it is also a work of art in the aesthetic sense. Even more insidiously than in the case of some other types of instrumental theories, these Romantic modes of interest conduce to the substitution of pragmatic for aesthetic criteria in the theories of art to which they give rise.

The second basic category of interest with which we shall be concerned is interest in the work of art as a reflection of a reality other than itself. Like a mirror, the work of art is assumed to represent, reflect, or somehow copy a section of reality, which is its subject or theme. The characteristic group of theories which presuppose an interest in the subject or theme, rather than an interest in the artwork for itself, we call *naturalistic*. They do not always or necessarily preclude an instrumental intesest; but neither do they imply it. They arise from a different attitude of mind toward the art object. It is not incumbent on naturalistic theories to speculate *why* we are interested in having copies, though suggestions about this have sometimes been given. Aristotle, for example, spoke of a natural human instinct for mimicry which finds an exalted outlet in the arts, and also suggested that our liking for representations derives from an intellectual pleasure in recognizing what they are copies of. Others have assumed that we value copies because they remind us of, or help us to experience vicariously, sections of reality which it is inconvenient to contact directly—the reason that people bring back souvenir postcards from their holidays. Our interest in the subject or theme of a representation may also be an aesthetic one: we may find it beautiful and therefore take pleasure in experiencing its beauty vicariously by means of a statue or painted picture of it. In such case the naturalistic attitude has affinities with the aesthetic interest which is the third basic type. Naturalism as such, however, is the attitude of mind which deflects attention away from or *through* the art object toward that of which the art object is a representation.

The attitude of interest from which Naturalism derives is more restricted than the pragmatic interest which underlies instrumental theories. For example it applies less obviously to the nonfigurative arts of music, architecture, and decoration of the sort which preponderated in Islamic art than to the representational and literary arts—even though in classical antiquity music was regarded as a "mimetic" art. Naturalism as an artistic aim probably emerged with the painting and sculpture of the Greeks in the fifth century B.C., in striking contrast to the still highly conventionalized character of their drama. With regard to the visual arts naturalistic assumptions were basic to the art theory of classical antiquity and continued to be preponderant in the West until about a century ago. By comparison Naturalism has been of comparatively minor significance for Chinese and Oriental art theory. Its importance in Europe from the end of the Middle Ages until about the middle of the nineteenth century accounts for the prominence it must be given in any handbook of aesthetics. Indeed in Western countries artistically unsophisticated persons still tend automatically to assume that it is the job of a picture to provide a reasonably accurate reflection of the external reality which is its subject.

The characteristic criteria of Naturalism are correctness, completeness, and vividness (or convincingness) of representation. We find "correctness" assumed as the standard when the reflected reality can be independently known. It is replaced by "convincingness" when the depicted reality is imaginary or ideal. The technical skill of the artist in representing something in a different medium is usually associated with both these as a secondary criterion of value.

Naturalism of one sort or another expresses the attitude of interest in the subject of the work of art rather than the work itself. The same sort of interest may apply to Realistic art (which represents what is actual) or to Idealistic art (which represents the actual improved and embellished) or to Imaginative art (which represents fancied reality or fiction). Both the Realistic and the Idealistic attitudes have had a strong influence on art theory—and of course on our ways of appraising artworks in practice—from classical antiquity onward into the present day. The value of imaginative fiction for its own sake had little recognition before the Romantic Age. The various sorts of naturalistic art have their different uses and practical effects. Realistic art may teach and inform, as Aristotle noticed. As was recognized in the second half of the nineteenth century, by emphasizing social ugliness and injustice it may touch men's feelings, awaken their conscience, and stir indignation, thus operating as an influence toward social amelioration. Idealistic art may edify and inspire: indeed this has often been alleged as its main function. Thus Naturalism ties up with the moral and practical interest in art and links with instrumental theories. Again, Realism may be thought of as the representation of the actual as it appears to the particular temperament of this or that artist—a version of the theory which also came to the fore in the second half of the nineteenth century—and in this way Naturalism ties in with the Expressionist group of instrumental theories.

The third basic attitude toward works of art, ancient or modern, involves interest in them as furthering deliberate cultivation and enjoyment of aesthetic experience. From this attitude derive *formalistic* theories of art, which express the aesthetic outlook most characteristic of the last fifty or a hundred years. Presupposed in this outlook is belief in a mode of apprehending the world around us which, although not wholly separable from our ordinary everyday commerce with our environment, differs from the latter in the emphasis it lays on direct perceptual or intuitional awareness without consideration of practical implications. This way of commerce with the world in which we live is called "aesthetic experience" or "aesthetic contemplation" and although it has probably been practiced by most peoples at most periods of history, it first began to emerge as a deliberate value to be cultivated in the course of the eighteenth century. But in contrast to the attitudes which prevailed in the eighteenth century the outlook which is more typical of our own day involves an assumption that the exercise of our perceptive powers in this mode of apprehension needs no justification of an instrumental kind; it is worthwhile for its own sake and for the sake of the heightened awareness of the world which it brings.

The value ascribed to aesthetic experience rests not entirely and perhaps not primarily in the knowledge of the world around us which it imparts; it is not a kind of cognition which can be formulated in terms of theoretical knowledge. The value derives partly and perhaps mainly from full exercise of a trained and mature sensibility extended to maximum capacity. It is further recognized that although we can take up an aesthetic attitude toward anything at all, not all things are equally adapted to sustain aesthetic contemplation at a high pitch. Contary to the eighteenth-century preferences for natural beauty, it is characteristic of the contemporary outlook in aesthetics to assume that on the whole art objects are most adapted for expanding and sustaining mature sensibility. Consistently with this works of art are thought of as things created in their own right rather than as copies of other sections of reality, as objects with their own autonomous values rather than as things intended primarily to be bearers of values extraneous to the furtherance of aesthetic experience. The critical criterion germane to this attitude of interest is therefore the aptness of a work of art for appreciation, the degree in which an artwork is adapted to sustain aesthetic contemplation in a suitably trained and prepared observer.

The sort of interest in works of art which we are now discussing invites a *formalistic* theory of art since by definition it is what are called the formal properties of things rather than their practical or scientific significance which make them more or less adapted to aesthetic apprehension. Furthermore attention tends to be directed toward those "emergent" properties of things—sometimes called "field" properties or "gestalt properties"—which belong to rich and closely knit complexes of perceptual material but not to the smaller constituents into which they can be broken up. These qualities are particularly interesting to nondiscursive, aesthetic contemplation. Some advocates of a formalistic type of art theory (among whom I number myself) have thought that fine works of art are the most successful examples of a special class of perceptual objects, called "organic wholes," which by the subtlety and complexity of their emergent properties and the intricate hierarchical relations among them are outstandingly adapted to evoke and sustain aesthetic contemplation.

Many people who have now adopted this characteristic aesthetic outlook believe that the aesthetic motive has been operative throughout history to control the making and appraisal of those artifacts which we now regard as works of art even though it has been latent and unconscious. Though there was no explicit theory of aesthetic experience in classical antiquity or in the Middle Ages or at the Renaissance, works of art were fashioned meet for appreciation; and from the earliest human periods artifacts were made with formal qualities enabling us now to appreciate them aesthetically although these formal qualities—often far from easy to achieve —were redundant to their practical utility or to the religious, magical, or other functions which they were designed to fulfill. This unconscious operation of a natural aesthetic impulse which became self-conscious only recently forms one of the recurrent themes of this book.

Western art theories may therefore be schematized as follows in relation to the basic interests from which they derive.

1. *Pragmatic interest: instrumental theories of art.*
   1) Art as manufacture *handicraft*
   2) Art as an instrument of education or improvement
   3) Art as an instrument of religious or moral indoctrination
   4) Art as an instrument for the expression or communication of emotion
   5) Art as an instrument for the vicarious expansion of experience

2. *Interest in art as a reflection or copy: naturalistic theories of art.*
   1) Realism: art as a reflection of the actual
   2) Idealism: art as a reflection of the ideal
   3) Fiction: art as reflecting imaginative actuality or the unachievable ideal

3. *The aesthetic interest: formalistic theories of art.*
   1) Art as autonomous creation
   2) Art as organic unity

Oriental attitudes to art and the theories which derive from them do not fit well into this scheme. The differences of outlook are sometimes fundamental but owing to the absence of a common conceptual framework are often difficult to formulate in the language which is available. Some knowledge of them nevertheless helps one to see Western attitudes and theories in perspective. For this reason some comparative account of Oriental attitudes—particularly the outlook embodied in Chinese and Indian aesthetics—has been given.

I. The Classical Concept of Art

The making of aesthetic objects has been almost universal through human history. From the emergence of modern man during the Upper Paleolithic age, and the fine efflorescence of cave art in the Aurignacian and Magdalenian periods, there have been comparatively few peoples at any time who did not produce some artifacts which we can now enjoy aesthetically as things of beauty even though we no longer know or subscribe to the values which they once served.

For throughout history works of art were artifacts made to serve some ulterior value and not, as now, made primarily in order to be works of art, to be enjoyed aesthetically as those which have survived from the past can be enjoyed after they have been removed from their context and displayed in museums. If we were to adopt the concept of a work of art suggested by Professor Urmson as "an artifact primarily intended for aesthetic consideration,"[1] we should have to exclude most of the art products we have inherited from the past. As we survey the artworks of the past from the earliest cave art onward we find that, various as their uses were, by and large all works of art were made for a use. A magical fetish, a temple to honor the gods and glorify the community, a statue to perpetuate a man's memory (Greece) or to insure his immortality (Egypt), an epic poem to preserve the traditions of the race, or a totem pole to enhance the dignity of a clan—these were all artifacts, manufactured for a purpose other than what we should now call aesthetic. Their motive was often to serve as vehicles for values which have since sunk into oblivion. They were essentially "utensils" in the same sort of sense that a suit of armor, a horse's harness or objects of domestic service are utensils, though the purpose they served was not necessarily a material one.

This is not to say that the aesthetic impulse was inoperative over the greater part of man's history. In his book *The Biology of Art* (1962), in which he studies the picture-making behavior of the great apes and its relationship to human art, Dr. Desmond Morris argues that from the earliest evolutionary stages man was actuated by aesthetic motives alongside magico-religious or utilitarian purposes. This is borne out by Professor Paul S. Wingert, one of the foremost authorities on primitive art, who shows how in the development of the utilitarian crafts such as textiles, ceramics, basketry, metallurgy, stone carving or wood carving, the aesthetic impulse was at work, inducing primitive men for vanity or esteem, or indeed from sheer pleasure, to give to his artifacts fine craftsmanship, decorative embellishment, and beauty of form redundant to and beyond their purely practical requirements.[2] But the aesthetic function seldom if ever stood alone and autonomous. The now familiar distinction between the "fine arts" and the useful or industrial arts emerged to prominence only in the course of the eighteenth century in Europe, and it was from one point of view an early symptom of the gradual extrusion of "art" from the integrated

---

[1] J. O. Urmson, "What Makes a Situation Aesthetic?" Reprinted in *Philosophy Looks at the Arts*, ed. Joseph Margolis (1962).
[2] Paul S. Wingert, *Primitive Art* (1962).

Drawing for sculpture by Villard de Honnecourt, thirteenth century A.D. *Details of musculature, etc., are seen as flat linear pattern. Courtesy of the Trustees of the British Museum, London.*

structure of society. In past ages there was no concept of "fine art"; all art was an art of use. And when in the past men judged their works of art they appraised them for the excellence of their workmanship and for their effectiveness in achieving the purposes for which they were made. This attitude is articulated with the utmost conciseness in Plato's dialogue *Hippias Major*, in which occurs the proposed definition of beauty as "effectiveness for some good purpose."

The ancient Greek—and Roman—concept of art is illuminating because it makes articulate this attitude, which predominated over the greater part of human history. In contrast to ours their attitude to the arts was eminently practical and there was little conscious aestheticism in antiquity at least before the rise of connoisseurship in the age of Augustus (44 B.C.–A.D. 17). As has been said by E. E. Sikes, a writer on Greek literature: "To the Greeks of the fifth

"Hercules as Fortitude*" by Nicola Pisano,
the most prominent figure of the classicizing
renaissance of the thirteenth century. Detail from
the carved pulpit in the Baptistery, Pisa,
ca. A.D. 1260. The Mansell Collection
of Photographs. Photo: Alinari.*

century, the formula of *L'art pour l'art* (art for its own sake) would
have been either monstrous or simply unintelligible." The arts were
appraised just as any other products of human industry—by their
effectiveness in promoting the objects for which they were made.
Moreover the fine arts, as we now call them, were more closely
integrated into the life of the ancient city state than they are in the

The Lamentation of Christ (Maestà) *by Duccio di Buoninsegna,*
thirteenth century A.D. *Opera del Duomo, Siena. The Mansell Collection*
of Photographs. Photo: Alinari.

modern community, where an aesthetic approach is still restricted
and the elevation of the arts onto a cultural pedestal has weakened
their direct influence in the life of the majority by widening the gap
between uncultivated and what we call "refined" taste. Life in
ancient Greece was lived far more on the social plane than it is with
us. Private occupations and preoccupations played a relatively small

Laocoön. *Engraving from Montfaucon's* L'Antiquité expliquée, *1719–24. Knowledge of works from late classical antiquity was disseminated in this form. Courtesy of the Courtauld Institute of Art, London.*

Massacre of the Britons by Hengist's Party at Stonehenge *by John Flaxman, 1783. Wash drawing. An example from the Neo-Classical school. Courtesy of the Fitzwilliam Museum, Cambridge.*

part in the total existence of the average Greek of the classical age. Their art too was primarily social in function. Poetry was not made to be read at home by the few who happen to like it. The national epics were bible and textbook in the educational system. Poetry was sung at all social gatherings, public and private, and at all religious ceremonies, and was an essential adjunct of the great athletic contests. Drama was performed under state auspices at national religious festivals which were attended by the whole citizen body. Music was an essential concomitant of poetry. It was ubiquitous in all social and religious events, in peace and in war, for recreation and in the most serious activities of a man's life. It formed part of the accepted educational curriculum. Great statues and paintings were commissioned and bought by cities rather than individuals. Poetry and the arts were, quite simply, the most important influence in ancient Greece for molding the life of the individual and the structure of society. Therefore the Greeks assessed works of art by the nature of the influence they were thought to have. The only other criterion commonly applied was that of craftsmanship. In an age without machine industry people were keenly conscious of standards of workmanship. Works of art, like other products of human industry, were appraised for the level of craftsmanship they displayed.

The philosophers were mainly interested to discuss the arts in relation to their educational function and their social impact. They judged by results. Was a work of art effective for its purpose and was the purpose a good one? Where technical and moral criteria clashed, the latter had precedence—as, for example, when Plato proposed to bowdlerize Homer not because certain passages were unpoetical but because he thought that the more poetical they were the stronger and therefore the more dangerous was their influence (*Republic*, Bk. iii, 387b). The distinction between the aesthetic qualities and the total effect of a work of art did not come readily to the Greek mind if at all.

Summary. Works of art are regarded as artifacts made for a purpose. They are regarded as successful according to their effectiveness for their purpose and the estimation of that purpose. This attitude tends to obscure aesthetic criteria and substitutes for them technical

The Toilet *by Picasso,* ca. *1925.*
Lithograph drawing. Recovery of the Greek line.
Author's collection.

Artek furniture, ca. *1933,*
designed by the Finnish architect
Alvar Aalto and his wife, Aino Marsio.
Courtesy of Danasco.

Totem pole in the traditional style of the Haida Indians,
British Columbia.

efficiency on the one hand and on the other hand moral or social appraisal of effects. It is opposed to the modern belief in independent or "autonomous" aesthetic standards by which works of art are to be appraised.

A SOCIOECONOMIC THEORY OF ART

For these reasons it has been maintained that the Greeks had no word for "art" or "artist" in our sense and that they lacked the concept of it. Before the age of machine production manufacture was synonymous with workshop industry. The artist was regarded as a manufacturer among others at a time when a high premium was set upon craftsmanship. He was commonly spoken of as a craftsman (*technites*) or artisan (*demiourgos*). Thus Plato speaks of the sculptor Phidias as an "artisan" at the top of his profession and therefore an authority on what is right and appropriate in making a sculpture of the gods (*Hippias Major*, 290b). No difference of category was recognized such as is nowadays assumed between a creative artist and an artisan who is skilled in the techniques of his craft. The idea of creativity (in the modern, Romantic sense) in connection with the arts was absent from Greek philosophy. Equally foreign to their mentality was the idea of art as an "expression" of the artist's personality.

For this reason the general theory of art in Greek philosophy was subordinate to their theory of manufacture, which has been called "one of the greatest and most solid achievements of the Greek mind." The theory was based on the twin ideas of function and technique. The competent artisan must of necessity know the "good" which is the end or object of his craft (i.e., shoes in the case of the cobbler, health in the case of the physician, statues in the case of the sculptor. In the *Republic* (Bk. x, 601d), Plato put forward as a truism the general proposition that "the virtue and beauty and rightness of every manufactured article, living creature, and action is assessed only in relation to the purpose for which it was made or naturally produced." Throughout his sociological writings Plato emphasized the idea of specialization. Each artisan is a specialist in the "good" of his particular craft. It was the task of the philosopher-statesman—the supreme "artist"—to evaluate these several "goods"

Research Tower, Johnson Wax Center,
Racine, Wisconsin, 1949–50, Frank Lloyd Wright, architect.
Courtesy of the United States Information Service.

"Lily and Pomegranates" wallpaper designed by *William Morris* ca. *1870.*
Courtesy of the Victoria and Albert Museum, London.

of the particular crafts according to their usefulness in a planned society. The notion of the "kingly" art of the statesman was developed in his *Republic* and *Politicus*: the training of a body of good citizens each completely and expertly performing a useful function in a planned society. Plato had difficulty in fitting those artisans whom we would now call "artists" into this scheme both because they did not easily accord with his idea of specialization and because the social value of the "ends" of their particular crafts was not clear to him. A cobbler is an expert in the making of real shoes, a carpenter in tables and chairs. But a painter produces imitations or unreal copies of shoes, chairs, tables, and all visible things, without being an expert in anything. If you assume that the value of any manufacture is its usefulness, then the usefulness of a painted shoe is less than that of a real shoe. So too the poets described anything and everything, having expert knowledge of nothing. It was largely on this ground that Plato was unable to reconcile himself to the use of the poets for instruction in the education of the young and regarded their works as inferior to technical and scientific handbooks.

At a time when their handicrafts had achieved a very high level of formal beauty and taste, it is clear that the Greeks had reached hardly the most distant intimation of aesthetic appreciation as a distinct value or "good" to be cultivated for its own sake. In the case of fine art, as Professor W. D. Ross says in his book *Aristotle* (1923, p. 217) : "Its use might be supposed to be aesthetic contemplation, but there is no clear evidence that Aristotle thought of this as an end in itself."[3] This purblindness is oddly illustrated in various discussions of the "beauty" of artifacts. In the *Hippias Major* the pompous polymath Hippias is brought with difficulty to admit that if "appropriateness to purpose" is the criterion of excellence, then a wooden soup ladle is finer than a gold one because better adapted to its job. In the *Memorabilia* Xenophon represents

---

[3] A possible exception and perhaps the only explicit recognition in Greek literature of aesthetic enjoyment (apart from aesthetic appreciation of the physical beauty of the human body) as an end in itself is a statement by Aristotle in the *Politics* that music is a proper leisure-time occupation of a free citizen. Aristotle's discussion in the *Poetics* of the appreciation of tragedy does not seem to imply a recognition that it is an aesthetic enjoyment in the modern sense.

Socrates as arguing that a serviceable manure basket can be a beautiful thing and a badly fashioned gold shield an ugly thing, that those houses are most "beautiful" which are warm in winter, cool in summer, and burglar proof. (In ancient Athens householders were menaced by thieves who operated by digging a hole through the house wall.) Xenophon adds the curious and unexplained note: "Paintings and colored decorations of the walls deprive us, he thought, of more pleasure than they give." But in the argument itself efficiency is the one criterion: a thing may be called beautiful (*kalon*) with reference to one purpose and the reverse with regard to another. It does not enter into consideration whether the wooden spoon or the golden spoon is better shaped (the purpose of a spoon is to eat with, not to be contemplated with pleasure) or whether Socrates' manure basket or country house is so fashioned as to be good to look at. Such theorizing becomes inexplicable if we translate the word concerned—*to kalon*—as "beautiful." And a similar perplexity arises if we treat the Greek *techne* as equivalent to "art." The discussion shows that the Greek concepts of "art" and "beauty" were different from ours.

The Greek word *techne* (from which we derive "technique") denoted a skill or craft. But it was thought of not merely as manual skill cultivated in accordance with nonspecifiable rules of workshop tradition; it was regarded rather as a branch of knowledge, a form of practical science. For the Greeks were alive to the desirability of converting inherited techniques into systems of rules and methods which could be communicated and taught, rather as the growth of factory industry in modern times caused the old skills of craftsmanship to be reduced as far as possible to specifiable systems of industrial know-how. In the classical statement, therefore, Aristotle defines *techne* (translated "art") as "a capacity to make or do something with a correct understanding of the principle involved." In the order of knowledge *techne* came after "science," the theoretical knowledge of principles and causes such as belongs to mathematics and philosophy, and "practical wisdom," whereby we place in order of value the several "goods" of the various crafts and professions. Memory, by which man differs from the animals, makes possible the accumulation and transfer of experience from generation to generation; and from inherited experience illuminated by understanding comes *techne*. *Techne* is always directed to some ulterior end (the end of medicine is health, etc.) and is not pursued for its own sake. "Science" on the other hand is the pure love of knowledge for its own sake. What we do not get is a suggestion that there may be value in the cultivation of experience, including aesthetic experience, for its own sake.[4] This was one of the prominent ideas of the Romantic Age.

In the *Ethics* (Z, 4) Aristotle distinguished two classes of *techne*, the crafts by which we *do* something (*prakton*), and those by which we *make* something (*poieton*). Examples of the former would be agriculture and medicine, of the latter sculpture and shoemaking. In the *Metaphysics* (981b 17) he distinguished the crafts which are directed to life's necessities from those which are directed to the occupation of leisure. The latter were regarded as "wiser" than the former because their branches of knowledge do not aim at any utility. Leisure occupations may be either a form of play (*paidia*) or of recreation (*anapausis*) (*Eth.* 1127b 34); but neither of these is an end in itself—their values are derivative (*Eth.* 1176b 30), restoring a man's powers for work. In the *Politics* (viii, 5) Aristotle enumerates uses which music may serve in education, as a legitimate pastime and as a recreation from toil. He distinguishes from these the higher delight in music as an ideal employment of leisure to be indulged in for its own sake and as such he considers it a constituent in the supreme goal of happiness. This, as has been noted, is the closest approach in classical Greek writing to the modern notion of a self-justifying aesthetic experience.

The tendency to think of the fine arts in terms of a general theory of production appears very clearly in Plato when in the *Symposium* (205c) he discusses the word *poiesis* (from which "poet" derives), a word which originally means "making" or "doing" in the widest

---

4 The Greeks sometimes spoke of the arts which we call "fine arts" (excluding architecture) as "pleasure-giving" arts—crafts whose function was to produce sources of pleasure. Aristotle spoke of the "proper" pleasure of tragedy as distinct from the characteristic pleasures evoked by other arts. But whereas there was a clear and explicit recognition that the pleasurable exercise of reason in doing philosophy was an end in itself, self-justifying, there is nowhere such specific regonition of self-justifying aesthetic pleasures.

sense. "Every cause," he says, "for a thing passing from not being to being is *poiesis,* so that manufacturing activities in all branches of industry are forms of *poiesis* and all artisans and craftsmen are *poietai* (poets). Yet they are not called poets but are given other names, and out of all *poiesis* that part which has to do with music and verse alone is distinguished by being called by that name which really belongs to all. For this alone is commonly called poetry and those who concern themselves with this one part of *poiesis* are called poets." The argument is to the effect that despite the distinction of names artists and poets are on all fours with other manufacturers as regards their productive activity. Plato's formal classification of the fine arts is set out in the *Sophist* (265). He distinguishes divine making (*poiesis*) as the making of something out of nothing (i.e., creation) and the human making of one thing out of something else. Both divine and human *poiesis* may be either a making of real things or a making of images and appearances. The gods created real things (men, animals, plants, and so on) from nothing, and they create images of these things as in dreams and mirages. In the products of the industrial crafts human beings create real things; but in poetry and painting and the other "pleasure-giving" arts they create simulacra or images of real things. These images give the appearances of things without the reality and they are therefore in their essence an illusion and a deceit. So the activity of the artist is a "kind of game lacking in seriousness" (*Republic,* Bk. x, 602b) .

It is perhaps inevitable that philosophers who make discussions of the fine arts subordinate to a social or economic theory of industry in general will come to the point where they are hard put to it to find reasonable justifications for the esteem in which the arts are so often held or to produce reasons that they should not be dismissed as trivial redundancies to the serious concerns of life.[5] Since the time of the Greeks this kind of outlook, though rarely overtly ex-

---

[5] Although Plato himself was a literary artist of no mean ability, and although it is abundantly apparent throughout his works that he had both knowledge of the arts and a sincere, if somewhat conservative, appreciation of them, yet as a *philosopher* he repeatedly repudiates their importance in human life and society, calling them a kind of "play" without serious import (e.g., *Statesman,* 288c; *Sophist,* 234a; *Republic,* 602b; *Phaedrus,* 276c-e, *Laws,* 889d) .

pressed, has had a far deeper influence on the character of European thinking about the arts than in any other of the major cultures.

Summary. A sociological approach which subordinates the theory of art to a theory of manufacture or industry tends to belittle the importance of fine art and to treat it as a social frivolity. Some modern sociological theories of art aim only at factual generalizations about the vagaries of taste, the sort of things people at various times and places have in fact regarded as beautiful and the criteria of artistic judgment which they have in fact applied. Greek theory, insofar as it was sociological in its approach, shared with modern Marxist theories the wish to *assess* artistic activities in terms of the contribution they are thought to make to society and the realization of a wider ideal of social value.

APPENDIX I

THE SOCIAL POSITION OF THE ARTIST

The theory of art which dominates any period of history can seldom be found fully articulate in that period. It is implicit in practical attitudes toward works of art and in the social situation of the artist. When, for example, art is regarded as a craft or a branch of workshop industry the position of the artist in society and the esteem in which he is held will correspond with the social attitude toward workmen and artisans. In connection therefore with the socioeconomic attitude which is exemplified in much Greek art theory, we shall give a brief review of the social standing of the artist as it has varied with the changes which the concept of art has undergone from classical antiquity to William Morris.

Greek society was founded on an aristocracy of citizens superimposed upon a body of foreign-born artisans and merchants with a slave population to attend to the rougher types of manual work and domestic services. The conception of the dignity of toil did not enter into Greek philosophy. It was considered beneath the dignity of a free-born citizen to undertake manual labor, rather as in Victorian times "trade" was beneath the dignity of a gentleman. Thus artists, who were regarded as a class of draftsmen workers, held no high place in the social scale. Arnold Hauser in *The Social History of Art* (1951) quotes Plutarch (1st century A.D.) as saying: "No generous youth when contemplating the *Zeus* of Olympia or the *Hera* of Argos, will desire to become a Phidias or a Polycletus," and Seneca (1st century A.D.) : "We offer prayers and sarcifices before the statues of the gods, but we praise the sculptors who make them." Classical scholars point out that this picture is somewhat exaggerated. Phidias was the friend of the great statesman Pericles. The painter Apelles and the sculptor Lysippus were court artists to Alexander the Great. The surviving anecdotes represent some of the more famous Greek artists as eccentrics, men of enormous wealth, and notable for arrogance. By and large, however, the artist in antiquity was treated as a workman and this remained his position throughout the Middle Ages. Poetry and the theory (but not the practice) of music were ranked among the "Liberal Arts," pursuits proper for an educated man and a gentleman; sculpture and painting belonged to the "sordid arts" and their practitioners were classed among the manual workers or artisans and were often members of the craftsmen's guilds. In Brussels they were associated with the goldsmiths, in Bruges with the butchers, in Florence with apothecaries and spice-grocers *(speziali)*. In the course of time artists organized confraternities of their own. The Florentine self-governing Compagnia dei Pittori, dedicated to St. Luke, dates from 1339. The theoretical basis of this grading received its classical formulation in a commentary of St. Thomas Aquinas on the *De Anima* of Aristotle, in which he says: "Every art (i.e., branch of knowledge) is good and not only good but honorable. Yet in this regard one art excels over another. . . . Among good things some are praiseworthy, namely those which are useful in themselves . . . the theoretical arts are good and honorable; the practical arts are only praiseworthy." As a very broad generalization the "practical arts" were considered to be those which involve a manual skill and the "theoretical arts" those which were thought of as belonging to the mind, as depending on the exercise of reason or the acquisition of scholarship.

A change in the social position of the artist took place during the Renaissance when the concept of the artist as scholar or scientist came to the fore. One of the main purposes of Leonardo's influential book *Paragone,* with its elaborate comparisons between painters and poets, was to prove that painting and sculpture were "theoretical arts," affairs of the intellect rather than manual crafts. This accounts for the emphasis which was placed on such things as perspective, mathematical theories of proportion, and the paraphernalia of historical and classical learning held to be necessary for a historical painter. From this time prominence was given to the "philosophical" content of the visual arts and to the predominantly intellectual nature of appreciation. It was this which imparted a rationalistic and intellectual bias to art theory for centuries to come. The emergence of the conception of "fine art" in the eighteenth century encouraged the divorce of the artist from artisans and craftsmen in utilitarian fields.

Toward the end of the nineteenth century the Arts and Crafts Movement in England attempted to bring about an artificial restoration of the medieval situation and at the same time gave practical significance to various sociological theories of art whose ramifications extended importantly into the twentieth century. The prime inspiration of the movement came from William Morris, who gave practical effect to ideas which he derived largely from Ruskin. Morris' philosophy was based partly on an idealization of the Middle Ages, which he shared with Ruskin, Pugin, the Pre-Raphaelite brotherhood, and many other artists and thinkers of his time, and it was partly an attempt to escape from the sordidness of the early industrial era by putting back the clock and finding an alternative to factory production. Morris did not go all the way with Ruskin in the latter's belief that since good art must result from high moral purpose and since a machine has no conscience, machine industry is incapable of producing artworks. But he did adopt as the core of his socialistic doctrines the belief that the root of social evil in his day was to be found in the separation of work from joy and of art from craft. For him it was the social system, and the conditions of labor resulting from mass production, rather than the machine in itself which "made life grow uglier every day." He therefore repudiated the idea of "fine art" as a thing apart in the category of luxury articles and defined art as "man's expression of his joy in labor." Insisting that aesthetic activity should be coextensive with the whole of man's life, he made it his endeavor to reintroduce the ideal of universal craftsmanship. His medievalism fitted into this scheme of social reform because of his belief that the Middle Ages more than any other period in European history exemplified the fusion of art with life and that universality of craftsmanship in which he saw the salvation of contemporary society.

In fact his doctrines were much more than a turning back. There is all the difference in the world between a society where an artist is a craftsman who happens to be an expert at making pictures or sculptures instead of shoes or furniture and a society such as Morris longed for, in which all craftsmen will have the attitudes of the artist. The artist is, by and large, a man with a vocation. He finds fulfillment in his art and if he does not achieve joy and happiness in its practice, at least is not happy without it. In general an artist will continue to practice his art even when economic conditions dictate otherwise. All this is not true of the craftsman or the artisan generally. Moreover, as we have seen, in classical antiquity and during the Middle Ages the artist-craftsman did not apply conscious aesthetic standards to his work but regarded himself as an honest artisan putting his best workmanship into a job done for a purpose. When the aesthetic standards implicit in the concept of fine art have become articulate they cannot be imposed universally on craftsmen of all kinds. Only a presumption in favor of functionalism could once more bridge the gap.

From a practical point of view Morris' movement was doomed to failure since there was never any real economic possibility of reintroducing studio industry on a large scale in place of factory production or in any way stemming the advance of mass production by machinery. Yet the movement had considerable influence, particularly abroad. In Austria it led to the establishment of the Werkstätte and in Germany was an ancestor of the aesthetic trend which crystallized in the Bauhaus. Instead of Morris' idea of universal craftsmanship the new aesthetic self-consciousness found expression in attempts to improve the aesthetic standard of machine-made goods by using artists to design prototypes for mass production. In Germany the architect Behrens was employed in 1907 by the German General Electric Company to design objects of daily use which would not only be functionally efficient but also finely and harmoniously shaped. The Finnish architect Alvar Aalto, in collaboration with his wife Aino Marsio, designed the once popular Artek furniture. It was one of the central aims of the Bauhaus to reunite art and craft and to train artist-craftsmen who would introduce the principles of good aesthetic design into the products of industry, adapting design to the new materials of the modern age and the new methods of manufacture. Somewhat similar aims inspired the Omega Workshops founded in England by Roger Fry in 1913.

This idea of designing for industrial processes, always conceived in a fairly close if not always clearly defined relation to the artistic doctrine of Functionalism, stands at the opposite pole from the theory of "applied art" which prevailed around the middle of the nineteenth century. The latter sought to select out the "best" in the way of ornament or decoration from all times and all styles, then to superimpose it on machine products without fundamentally changing their design. The idea of adding or *applying* decoration to manufactured goods in order to make them more "artistic" and more attractive was opposed by the "functionalist" idea, which repudiated everything that could distract the eye from functionally efficient design.

APPENDIX 2

FUNCTIONAL THEORIES OF BEAUTY

The habit of mind which regards works of art as artifacts made to serve a purpose, culminating in the Greek theory of art as part of a wider theory of industry or manufacture, implies a *functionalist* theory of art which recognizes no fundamental distinction between the fine and the useful arts. If this is combined with a conscious connection between art and beauty, it leads naturally to a functionalist theory of beauty. This may therefore be a convenient place for a review of the various forms which Functionalism has taken.

The functionalist theory of aesthetics is the theory that if a thing is made to function well, if its construction is well suited to the job it has to do, then that thing will be beautiful. It is a theory with a very long history and one which was very popular, particularly in connection with architecture and the useful arts, during the early decades of the present century. Unfortunately the theory is by no means unambiguous. It can be interpreted in several different senses, which have not usually been kept distinct. The main meanings which the theory has borne are the following:

1) By definition adaptation to purpose is part of the meaning of the word "beautiful." Hence when we call anything beautiful we *mean* that it is well made for a particular purpose but we do not necessarily imply that it is good to look at or that it has beauty of appearance in the aesthetic sense.

2) Instances of purposive design such as teleology manifested in nature or functional adaptation are called "beautiful" because apprehension of this sort of purposiveness gives us intellectual delight such as we get from a neat chess problem or an elegant mathematical proof. This beauty of intellectually apprehended purpose does not, in the theory, necessarily involve perceptual beauty of appearance.

3) On the other hand it may be held that functionalism in the sense of suitability for an intended purpose is a guarantee of visual beauty.

4) Or it may be held that suitability for a purpose is a guarantee of beauty only on the condition that the suitability is visible and apparent (i.e., "streamlined" form).

5) Suitability for purpose is a *condition* of anything being beautiful but is not in itself a guarantee of beauty.

It will therefore be apparent that there is in the various forms of functionalist theory an implied antithesis between visual and intellectually apprehensible beauty. The first sense of Functionalism goes back to classical antiquity. As we have seen, Plato in the *Hippias Major* discussed the definitions of beauty as "suitability" and "utility" (i.e., efficient adaptation for an approved purpose). These definitions are further discussed by Aristotle in the *Topica* (102a 6 and 135a 13). In the *Memorabilia* of Xenophon Socrates is made to argue that human bodies and all things which men use "are considered beautiful and good with reference to the objects for which they are serviceable." In these discussions visual beauty, attractiveness of outward form, does not enter into point. The discussions are elucidating the implications of the Greek word *kalos* ("beautiful"). It is *not* maintained that if a thing is well designed to serve the purpose for which it is intended, it will therefore be beautiful in appearance. Indeed it is expressly stated in the *Memorabilia* that one and the same thing may be *kalos* with reference to one purpose and not *kalos* with reference to another.

We find a modern parallel to this attitude in the definition of the beautiful as anything which is considered a good example of its kind, a definition put forward explicitly by the French aesthetician Charles Lalo (1877–1953). This concept of beauty was satirized by Thomas De Quincey in his essay "On Murder as One of the Fine Arts" (1827), where for example he mentions that a doctor may speak of a "beautiful ulcer": he does not mean that the ulcer is beautiful to the eye but that it is an excellent example of a typical ulcer and that in recognition of this we may take intellectual delight. A variant of this concept (No. 4 above) would be if it were held that a thing is beautiful if it is *manifestly* a good example of its kind.

Aristotle was very much alive to the intellectual pleasure derivable from recognition of teleological adaptation but clearly distinguished it from visual beauty of form. In his book about natural history, the *De Partibus Animalium* (645a), he says that he proposes to write about all sorts of animals, even the most ignoble. For although these are repugnant to the senses, nevertheless by revealing the craftsmanship of Nature to intellectual contemplation they give untold pleasure to those who are philosophically inclined and able to recognize causal links. "It would indeed be strange and paradoxical," he adds, "if we took pleasure in looking at their likenesses through our appreciation of the technical skill of the artist and did not derive even greater contentment from the sight of the objects, if that is we are capable of discerning their teleological causes."

During the eighteenth century evidences of teleological adaptation, order, and regularity in nature, interpreted as signs of divine purpose, were closely linked with the notion of beauty. The philosopher Thomas Reid (1710–96) distinguished between an "instinctive" and a "rational" sense of beauty and connected the latter with our apprehension of design or adaptation to purpose:

> *The works of nature have a beauty which strikes even the ignorant and inattentive. But the more we discover of their structure, of their mutual relations, and of the laws by which they are governed, the greater beauty, and the more delightful marks of art, wisdom and goodness we discern. Thus the expert anatomist sees numberless beautiful contrivances in the structure of the human body, which are unknown to the*

ignorant. Although the vulgar eye sees much beauty in the face of the heavens and in the various motions and changes of the celestial bodies, the expert astronomer, who knows their order and distances, their periods, the orbits they describe in the vast regions of space, and the simple and beautiful laws by which their motions are governed, and all the appearances of their stations, progressions and retrogradations, their eclipses, occultations and transits are produced, sees a beauty, order and harmony reign throughout the whole planetary system which delights the mind.

The intellectual idea of beauty which came to prominence at the Renaissance persisted during the eighteenth century even though the first intimations of the Romantic connection of beauty with feeling and emotion were in the air. It manifested itself in the priority given to natural beauty over the beauty of art and specifically in the importance assigned to intellectual appreciation of the orderly system of the laws of nature or of teleological adaptations in the organic world. Although the eighteenth-century interest in purposive order as evidence of divine teleology was a far remove from the medieval idea of a *mathematical* order and "concinnity" symbolizing the Divine Nature, both in their aesthetic applications favored an intellectualist concept of beauty. Kant's concept of "purposiveness without purpose" gave a new turn to the theory.

The distinction between this intellectual beauty and visual beauty of outward appearance was not usually maintained. Burke, in his *Philosophical Inquiry* (1757), uttered a word of caution when he wrote: "It is said that the idea of a part's being well adapted to answer its end is one cause of beauty, or indeed beauty itself. . . . In framing this theory, I am apprehensive that experience is not sufficiently consulted." The French encyclopedist Diderot was less cautious. In his *Essai sur la peinture* (1775) he said: "The beautiful human being is he whom nature has fashioned for the purpose of fulfilling as easily as possible the two great functions: individual self-preservation and the propagation of the species . . ." It is interesting that this functional theory of human beauty was refuted long ago in a Socratic dialogue *The Banquet,* attributed to Xenophon, in which Socrates maintains that it would be ludicrous to suppose that he was more beautiful than the handsome youth Critobulus because his protuberant eyes commanded a wider angle of vision, his simian nostrils were better adapted to snuff the air, and so on. The Greeks had a highly developed sensibility for the visible beauty of the human form and in that regard only put visible beauty before functionalism. In the eighteenth century the painter Hogarth, who wrote a once famous *Analysis of Beauty* (1772), agreed that in useful objects fitness for purpose is an aesthetic quality: "When a vessel sails well, the sailors call her a beauty; the two ideas have such a connection." But he distinguished this intellectual beauty from the visual beauty which appeals to the eye and to the senses, proposing as a general formula for the latter his serpentine "line of beauty" which, he thought, combined the maximum of variety with unity. In the third of three philosophical *Dialogues* the idealist Bishop Berkeley (1685–1753) argued against the idea of sensuous beauty and sought to reduce the "fugacious charm," the *je ne sais quoi* of the early French aestheticians, to intellectual appreciation of order or teleological adaptation. Order, symmetry, and proportion, he argues, exist only in relation to purpose—they mean one thing in a horse, another in a chair or dress. The charm of symmetry and proportion appeals therefore ultimately to the mind which appreciates the perfection of an object in terms of its purpose. "Forasmuch as without thought there can be no end or design; and without an end there can be no use; and without use there is no aptitude or fitness of proportion, from whence Beauty springs."

It was sometimes debated whether a man who came across a mechanism such as a watch would recognize it as a beautiful example of adaptation although he did not know the purpose which it served, and this sort of consideration no doubt prompted Kant's metaphysical theory of beauty as "purposiveness without purpose." In our own time we may think of some of the "ready-mades" of Marcel Duchamp, complicated mechanisms which do not aspire to visual beauty but seem to be examples of intricate mechanical adaptation though serving no purpose at all. It is perhaps significant that these objects were constructed in the context of an "anti-art" theory, debunking the traditional aesthetic values of fine art.

The modern philosophy of Functionalism goes back at least as far as the 1840s when the American sculptor Horatio Greenough spoke in a letter to Emerson about the relation of form to function. The idea was later taken up by the architect Louis Sullivan, who in *Kindergarten Chats* (1901) originated the famous phrase: "Form follows function." This was amplified by Frank Lloyd Wright as follows: " 'Form follows function' is but a statement of fact. When we say 'form and function are one,' only then do we take mere fact into the realm of thought" ("On Architecture," *Selected Writings, 1894–1940*). Functionalism was preached as a new aesthetic creed after World War I by Le Corbusier (e.g., *Towards a New Architecture,* 1927), who defined a house as a machine made for living in, and for a decade enjoyed a considerable vogue. It was argued with almost moral fervor that in architecture and the industrial arts extraneous ornament must be eschewed, the form must reflect the purpose and in order to be beautiful any object need only be designed most obviously and most economically to suit the purpose for which it was intended. Architecture which exposed its materials without concealment and which was functional in this sense was called "honest" architecture. On the other hand the cult of "streamlining" gave rise to a mannered style which looked *as if* it were functional whether it was well adapted for use or not.

During the 1930s the term "functional" was used to describe the severely utilitarian designs for furniture and domestic equipment which became popular under Bauhaus influence. In 1938 Moholy-Nagy could still say: "In all fields of creation, workers are striving today to find pure functional solutions of a technical-biological kind: that is, to build up each piece of work solely from the elements which are required for its function" (*The New Vision*). But the "modern" movement in architecture and industrial design rested on a false assumption, the assumption that by making a thing functional in this sense so that it will be visibly adapted to its purpose one can ensure that it will have aesthetic quality, that its outward appearance will be beautiful to the eyes and the senses. A note of warning was sounded by Herbert Read as early as 1934 when in his book *Art and Industry* he declared: "That functional efficiency and beauty do often coincide may be admitted. . . . The mistake is to assume that the functional efficiency is the cause of the beauty; *because* functional, *therefore* beautiful. That is not the true logic of the case."

The inadequacy of Functionalism as a complete aesthetic theory has been proved by the avalanche of tedious and sordid structures which have disfigured the modern environment, demonstrating by sad experience that design can be adapted to function and economically planned without achieving either beauty or dignity. The experience led in the 1940s and 1950s to a new philosophy of design, and its relation to aesthetic requirements. In the new philosophy "design" denotes the planning of any artifact whether for use or for show. To this extent the gap between the useful arts and the fine arts is bridged. Design involves the manipulation or adaptation of any material so as to obtain an intended result and avoid unwanted results. In *The Nature of Design* (1964) David Pye analyzed the six accepted conditions which must be satisfied by any design intended for use. Four "requirements of use" are given as: (1) the design must correctly embody the essential principle of arrangement; (2) the components of the artifact must be geometrically related in whatever particular ways best suit the particular result intended; (3) the components must be strong enough to transmit and resist such forces as the intended result imposes; (4) access must be provided. In addition there is the requirement for availability and economy and the aesthetic requirement that the appearance must be acceptable.

The theory of Functionalism assumed that the requirements dictated by use and economy automatically determined optimun design from the aesthetic point of view also. It is now understood that these nonaesthetic requirements act as limiting conditions only. They restrict possibilities as to appearance and may serve as a guide to planning, but they cannot determine optimum appearance. The view was stated as follows by P. H. Scholfield in his book *Theory of Proportion in Architecture* (1958) :

> *The attempt was often made by philosophers and critics to reduce the theory of proportion entirely to a theory of fitness. In fact, however, it is the common experience of designers in practice that when the requirements of fitness have been met, a good deal of choice usually remains between proportions which appear pleasant and those which appear unpleasant.*

In view of this new philosophy courses on Basic Design came into vogue in the art schools about the middle of the century for practitioners of the fine arts and for students of the commercial arts. There was conceived the new art of the "designer" and instruction was given with a view to turning out designers for employment in industry and manufacture. The modern "designer" has little or nothing in common with the ancient and medieval artist-craftsman since he is concerned primarily with planning the appearance of objects to be machine-made by others, whereas the old artist-craftsman was not primarily concerned with the aesthetic quality but with the workmanship and utility of objects made by himself or his assistants. On the other hand the modern commercial designer has little in common with the traditional practitioner of the fine arts since he lacks the element of craftsmanship which has usually been important to the latter. The modern architect perhaps stands nearer to this new conception of "designer" than to the older concept of the "master builder" or "works manager."

Summary. Intricate, economic, or elegant adaptation to purpose may be appreciated intellectually and may be regarded as a branch of intellectual beauty. It is not any longer believed to insure that a thing so designed will have a beautiful appearance. In the useful arts (but not presumably in the fine arts) suitability to purpose is a limiting condition which does not insure beauty of appearance.

Some philosophers hold that if a thing *looks as if* it were well designed for an approved purpose, it is beautiful in virtue of that fact whether or not it is really so designed. J. O. Urmson, for example, says: "If a thing looks to have a characteristic which is a desirable one from another point of view, its looking so is a proper ground of aesthetic appreciation."[6] For example if an airplane, a sports car, or a racehorse, an object intended for speed, *looks* speedy, it is therefore beautiful and to be appreciated aesthetically. This is not a doctrine which many would follow.

6 "What Makes a Situation Aesthetic?"

II. Naturalism 1

In Greek visual art from the sixth to the fourth century B.C. there occurred for the first time a cycle of techniques whose primary motivation derived from the impulse to produce convincing facsimiles of the visible appearances of things instead of forms and characters which they were known to have. In technical language there emerged a "naturalistic" rather than a "conceptual" art. The gradual mastery of naturalistic representation has been traced in some detail both in sculpture from the stiff formalism of the archaic *kouroi* to the lifelike semblances produced by Phidias and Praxiteles, and also in the graphic art of vase painting through the discovery of foreshortening and the illusory depiction of three-dimensional space by perspective techniques. An excellent presentation of this development of the techniques of naturalism will be found in

Rhys Carpenter, *Greek Art: A Study of the Formal Evolution of Style* (1962). While this is not the only or even perhaps the most important aspect of Greek art which has interest for the twentieth century, it is the aspect which was most revolutionary in its time.

Art historians used to interpret the art of Egypt and Mesopotamia and the other artistic cycles of the Middle East as blundering attempts to achieve the naturalism which was finally realized and perfected by the Greeks. We now understand that they were aimed at something different. For example Egyptian mortuary art was intended to create a "magical" surrogate of reality, a body which the Pharaoh could inhabit after physical death and a vehicle for his continued existence in enjoyment of the good things of life, which were also depicted in murals or images. Such an art aspired to a rational ideal of truth independent of time and space, representing things in what were deemed to be their objectively true forms. The last thing desired was to reproduce the accidental and changing appearances of objects as they vary for this or that observer. For example Plato, who was an admirer of the principles of Egyptian art, objected to the perspective distortion practiced in Greek monumental sculpture in order that the proportions of a figure should *appear* correct to a spectator standing far below it.

There have been other periods of naturalism in art, for example the Mochica in pre-Columbian Peru. But historically Greek naturalism is important because it determined the main character of European art in antiquity and because, after a break during the Middle Ages, the tradition was revived at the Renaissance and retained its predominance until the present century. Historians whose interests are closely wedded to the European tradition in art speak in glowing terms of this Greek achievement. For example, Professor Gombrich in *Art and Illusion* (1960) took the view that: "It needed the extension of our historical horizon and our increased awareness of the art of other civilisations to bring home to us what has rightly been called the 'Greek miracle,' the uniqueness of Greek art." Other historians have tended to regard the naturalism which found its first flowering in classical Greek art and its continuance in the European tradition as an exception, if not an aberration, from the general course of world art. For example Osvald Sirén, a leading authority on Chinese art, in a book on *Essentials in Art* (1919), describes the special character of the Western tradition in art as follows:

The test of art that is most generally applied in the Western World undoubtedly is fidelity to nature. We Westerners have done our best to bind art down to the world of material phenomena, we have made fidelity of reproduction the highest virtue in painting and sculpture, and have considered that the perfection of art lay in the artist's power to create illusive imitations of nature.

Robert Byron and David Talbot Rice, authorities on the Byzantine period, write in similar terms of Western naturalism. "Times have been when artists have fallen to accepting the natural world without inquiry and reproducing it. Such was the misfortune of Antiquity and . . . of Europe from the sixteenth to the nineteenth centuries. The twentieth preens itself on its evasion of this blind alley."

What has been called the "retreat from likeness" or the "dehumanization of art" in the twentieth century may be interpreted in part as an escape from the tradition of naturalism toward an older conception of art. But the revolt from naturalism has left us in the twentieth century with new puzzles and perplexities about the obvious connection of art with the reality of the world about us and an understanding of the naturalistic impulse from its beginning among the Greeks is a useful, perhaps a necessary, preparation for the solution of these perplexities.

If we define aesthetic naturalism as the ambition to confront the observer with a convincing semblance of the actual appearances of things, the criterion of success becomes illusionistic verisimilitude. In the admiration evoked by a work of art great prominence is given to the artist's skill in making it appear not to be what it is but rather the reality of what it represents. This attitude to art may often be reflected more vividly in critical commonplaces and in popular anecdotes than in formal art theory.

A considerable fund of popular stories about the Greek artists has been preserved for us, mainly by Pliny, who probably derived from them an anecdotal *Lives of Painters* and a *Lives of Sculptors* written in the fourth century B.C. by Duris, a historian and ruler of Samos. Such stories, surviving through the ages, tell us as much or more than formal criticism about what the average educated man expected works of art to be like, what standards he applied and what qualities he admired in artists. The anecdotes of Duris fully confirm the fascination exerted by illusionistic representation, as if painting were regarded as a sort of conjuring trick or optical legerdemain, and the admiration for technical skill on the part of the artist.

Apelles painted a horse so realistically that live horses were deceived and neighed. Parrhasius painted a heavy armed soldier in a race so realistically that he seemed to sweat as he ran, and another laying down his arms whose panting we seem to hear. In a competition with Parrhasius Zeuxis painted grapes so lifelike that the birds flew to peck at them. Thereupon Parrhasius painted a curtain across his own picture which deceived even Zeuxis into asking to have it drawn so that he could see the picture. Another Zeuxis story, borrowed by Shakespeare, runs as follows: Zeuxis painted a boy carrying grapes so realistically that the birds flew down and pecked the grapes. Thereupon Zeuxis confessed failure, because if he had painted the boy as realistically as the grapes, the birds would have been afraid to approach. The value placed upon meticulous accuracy of detail is illustrated by an anecdote of Apelles, who used to exhibit his pictures beside the public thoroughfare and conceal himself in order to listen to the comments of passersby. On one occasion he heard a shoemaker censure his representation of a boot because it had one latchet too few. Apelles then remedied the fault and exhibited the picture again. The shoemaker, seeing that his criticism had borne fruit, got above himself and began to criticize the leg. Thereupon Apelles, coming out from hiding, took him to task with the words: "Sirrah, remember that you are only a shoemaker and therefore meddle no higher, I advise you, than with the shoes." From this story comes the proverb *ne sutor supra crepidam* (cobbler, stick to your last). The ancients admired anything in the nature of a *tour de force*. Polygnotus, for example, painted a famous picture of a warrior with a shield in such a way that you could not tell whether he was mounting or descending a ladder.

At the Renaissance likeness again became a commonplace of appreciation and Vasari in his *Lives of the Most Eminent Painters, Sculptors and Architects* (1550) includes anecdotes rivaling those of Pliny and Aelian: that the strawberries in a fresco by Bernazzone were pecked at by peacocks and a dog in a picture by Francesco Monsignori was attacked by a real dog, and so on. He tells of Giotto that when still a boy and studying under Cimabue he once painted a fly on the nose of a portrait on which Cimabue was working and did it so realistically that Cimabue took it for a real fly and tried to brush it away. The raconteur Boccaccio, author of the *Decameron,* wrote of Giotto that "he was of so excellent a wit, let Nature, mother of all, operant ever by continual revolution of the heavens, fashion what she would, he with his style and pen and pencil would depict its like on such wise that it showed not as its like but rather as the thing itself insomuch as the visual sense of men did often err in regard thereof, mistaking for real that which was but painted."

To us this seems extravagant if not incomprehensible. The pictures of Giotto and his followers no longer seem to us markedly illusionistic. It is for other, more lasting aesthetic qualities that we still admire them. Little or nothing of classical Greek painting has survived, but from such relics as there are of provincial Greek painting in southern Italy there is every reason to suppose that the pictures of the famous Greek artists would not have seemed to us to be strikingly illusionistic. They seemed so to their contemporaries, as did the pictures of Giotto, in contrast to what had gone before. The significance of the stories is their indication of new standards of judgment, new ways of looking at graphic art, which come to the fore in periods when naturalism is prominent. It often happens that accepted attitudes and beliefs, the raw material of inarticulate philosophy, are reflected in the sort of legends and anecdotes which obtain currency. Their truth is not in point; the significant thing for our purpose is the kind of story that is told.

Greek legend attributed the origin of sculpture to the mythical Daedalus, who was the first to make statues with the eyes open and representing figures in motion. The lifelikeness of his work was a commonplace of Greek and Latin literature. In the *Hecuba* (ii. 836–40) and in a surviving fragment from the lost play *Euristheus* Euripides alludes to the myth that his statues seem to move and to see. In a play named *Daedalus* the great comic poet Aristophanes referred to the story that, whereas older sculptors fashioned images without sight, Daedalus first opened the eyes of his statues so that they had the appearance of being alive and moving and speaking: "And so they say that one of the statues made by Daedalus had to be tied by the foot to keep it from running away." In Plato's dialogue *Meno* Socrates alludes to the story as well known (97d), and the comic poet Plato mentions a wooden *Hermes* by Daedalus which could walk and talk. The earliest literary references to naturalism in art emphasize the same qualities: the technical skill of the craftsman in producing a simulacrum, an illusion in the sense of *trompe l'oeil,* particularly an illusion of life. Homer in the *Iliad* (xviii, 548) ends a long description of a chased shield made by the metal-working god Hephaestus for Achilles with a scene of ploughing: "And behind the plough the earth turned black, as a field does when ploughed, although it was wrought of gold: a very marvel of craftsmanship." In the *Odyssey* there is a description of a gold buckle with a chased design on its face: "a hound holding down a dappled fawn and tearing it as it struggled to escape. Everyone admired the craftsmanship, the hound ripping and throttling the fawn, the fawn lashing out with its feet as it sought to escape and the whole thing wrought in gold." Euripides, in the fifth century, makes Admetus in his play *Alcestes* plan to commission a portrait-statue to console him for the loss of his dead wife: "I shall find a clever sculptor to carve your likeness and it shall be laid on our bed; I shall kneel beside it and throw my arms around it and say your name Alcestis! Alcestis! and think that I hold my dear wife in my arms." The story of the legendary king of Cyprus who fell in love with a marble statue is preserved in a fragment from the poet Alexis, uncle of the more famous Menander, and by Philemon, a poet of the New Comedy. The story was told by Ovid and was referred to by Lucian.

The theme of the artists' skill in producing a life-semblance persisted throughout classical antiquity. Vergil typically speaks of "softly breathing bronzes and living faces wrought from marble" (*Aeneid* vi, 847). By the fourth century A.D. it had become a rhetorical commonplace as in the critical descriptions of Callistratus.

Of a *Bacchante* by Scopas, a fourth-century sculptor famous for his rendering of emotions, he writes as follows:

> *It was a statue of a Bacchante made from Parian marble and yet transformed into a real Bacchante. For the stone, while retaining its own nature, seemed to transcend the limitations of stone; although one was really looking at an image, the craftsmanship of the artist had transformed the imitation into reality. You could see that despite its hardness the stone had softened into the semblance of femininity and though it had no power of movement, it knew how to dance the Bacchic dance and to respond to the impulse of Bacchic frenzy. When we looked on the face we stood speechless, so visibly apparent upon it was the appearance of sensibility, although sensation was lacking . . . though void of life, it nevertheless held the vitality of life.*

Of a bronze *Eros* by Praxiteles he wrote:

> *You could see the bronze take on the softness of flesh and a gentle plumpness. It was supple without effeminacy and though it retained the proper colour of bronze, it held the appearance of a healthy bloom. Though it lacked the actual power of movement, it was ready to display movement and while firmly fixed on a pedestal it deceived the beholder into thinking it had the power of flight. It was exultant to laughter and the glance it shot from its eyes was both ardent and honeyed. . . . As I gazed on this piece of craftsmanship I was ready to believe that Daedalus had even done a dancing group in motion and had conferred sensation on the gold, while Praxiteles had all but put intelligence into his likeness of Eros and had fashioned it to cleave the air with its wing.*

The representation of emotion or character by direct visual imagery instead of symbolically by traditional conventions has always exercised a particular fascination in a period of naturalism and has seemed to contribute notably to the impression of "liveliness" to which a naturalistic art aspires. The Greeks called this "imitation of the soul." It is interestingly brought out in two conversations which Xenophon reports (*Memorabilia*, Bk. III, Ch. x), the one between Socrates and the painter Parrhasius and the other between Socrates and the sculptor Cleito. In the former Socrates gets Parrhasius to agree that the painter can "imitate" a cheerful or sad expression, a friendly or unfriendly look, or qualities of character such as "nobleness and generosity, meanness and illiberality, modesty and intelligence, insolence and stupidity," which show themselves in the looks and gestures of men whether they are still or whether they move. In the conversation with Cleito Socrates opens with the truism (as it was regarded) that a "lifelike appearance" in statues is what "most attracts the beholders through the eye," and then makes the, to us, equally obvious point that the sculptor "makes his statues appear more lifelike by assimilating his work to the figures of the living." He then advances to the point that "the representation of the passions of men engaged in any act" arouses a certain pleasure in the beholder and reaches the conclusion that "a statuary, therefore, must express the workings of the mind through his forms."

All this seems quite elementary to readers who have inherited two thousand years of naturalistic presuppositions, but it was no doubt novel and exciting in Socrates' day. A similar interest in the direct visual representation of emotion, rather than by conventional symbolism, is apparent in the art criticism and commentary of the Renaissance, when a new efflorescence of naturalism took place after it had been partially held in abeyance during the Middle Ages. It was for this quality in his painting that Giotto was hailed not only as the greatest realist of his day but as the greatest painter who had lived, the reformer who brought the art of painting back to the true path which had been lost. It was for this quality that Masaccio and Botticelli were held in their day to be more "lifelike" than Giotto, Raphael and Leonardo than Botticelli. Alberti thought that the depiction of emotion and mood was the most essential and most difficult task of the painter and wrote at some length about it in his *Della Pittura* (1546). Leonardo, who said that "that figure is most admirable which by its actions best expresses the spirit which animates it," filled innumerable notebooks with studies of the physical manifestations of emotion drawn from the life and even made a special study of the gestures and facial expressions of the dumb since these are more vivid than the expressions of people who can communicate vocally. The representation of the physical signs of emotion was later systematized in the Academies. In his treatise *On the Art of Painting, Sculpture and Architecture* (1584) Lomazzo discussed "the movements which may be produced in the body by the different emotions of the soul" and attempted a classification of all possible human emotions and the gestures and facial conformations by which they are expressed. Le Brun, the founder of the French Académie, published in 1698 a *Méthode pour apprendre à dessiner les passions*, which had enormous influence. A long series of physiognomic studies bearing on the depiction of emotions by graphic means culminated in the important work of Sir Charles Bell, *The Anatomy and Philosophy of Expression as Connected with the Fine Arts* (1806). This was superseded by Charles Darwin's study *The Expression of the Emotions in Man and Animals* (1872), since when there has arisen doubt about the extent to which facial appearance can communicate emotion unambiguously.

It is inherent to the outlook of naturalism that attention is deflected from the work of art toward the subject represented. The work of art becomes as if it were transparent and we look through it at that which it represents. We do not see a beautiful statue but a beautiful body skillfully "imitated," or the signs of emotional experience presented. When the Greeks devised ideal proportions for the human figure they were thought of as "vital statistics" in the modern sense: the ideal proportions for the living body. The sculptor's job was to produce an image of such a body in bronze or marble. Given equal ability in the artist, the better subject makes the better picture. Thus in his conversation with Parrhasius Socrates assumes that "people look with more pleasure on paintings in which beautiful and good and lovely characters are depicted" than on those in which "the deformed and evil and detestable are represented." Startlingly naïve as this now seems, it nevertheless expresses in the simplest and most direct terms the attitude of mind which underlay the doctrine of the "Grand Manner," as formulated for example by Sir Joshua Reynolds (1723–92), who recommended to the painter a noble and dignified theme and spoke slightingly of the Dutch *genre* painters because of their choice of vulgar or commonplace subjects. A reversal of taste in the twentieth century has brought conventional nobility and grandeur, whether Romantic or academic, into disrepute and has created a predilection for the startling and the stark. Sentiment has been confused with sentimentality; loveliness, grace, and charm in the subject matter are either eschewed or prove themselves beyond the resources of all but a Picasso or a Moore. Facile charm is now most readily acceptable in the abstract, nonrepresentational work of art. Through all these manifestations of changing taste with regard to the subject matter of art we must recognize the continuing operation of that naturalistic habit of mind which leads us to regard the work, whether wholly or in part, as a reflection or mirror, an "imitation," of that which it represents. It is an advantage of classical antiquity that such attitudes, which later become confused and embroiled, are stated with naïve and stark simplicity in their most elemental form.

The habit of mind which regards a work of art as "transparent"—an imitation or replica of some part of the actual world which it represents—has led to a type of descriptive criticism which exerts itself to give an account in words not of the artwork but of the scene, incident, or object which the artwork represents. Often the critic will preen himself on going beyond what is represented and will describe what seems to him to be suggested by the picture. From Homer to the nineteenth century this has been the predominant tone of Western art criticism. Describing the shield made by Hephaestus for Achilles in the *Iliad* the poet says in part:

> *Next he showed two beautiful cities full of people. In one of them weddings and banquets were afoot. They were bringing the brides through the streets from their homes, to the loud music of the wedding-hymn and the light of blazing torches. Youths accompanied by the flute and the lyre were whirling in the dance, and the women had come to the doors of their houses to enjoy the show. But the men had flocked to the meeting-place, where a case had come up between two litigants about the payment of compensation for a man who had been killed. The defendant claimed the right to pay in full and was announcing his intention to the people; but the other contested his claim and refused all compensation. Both parties insisted that the issue should be settled by a referee; and both were cheered by their supporters in the crowd, whom the heralds were attempting to silence.*

Such interpretative embroidery on the actual representation remained a striking feature of much Western anecdotal criticism. The

Sumerian cylinder seal of aragonite, ca. 2500 B.C.
Courtesy of the Trustees of the British Museum, London.

descriptions of ancient pictures which survive in Pausanias and
Lucian tell us much about the scene and story, little about the
pictures. So Euripides describes the statues which adorned the sterns
of ships (*Iphigeneia in Aulis,* 230f) and Apollonius of Rhodes
elaborates on the mythological scenes which decorated the mantle
of Jason (*Argonautica,* 1, 730f). This style of criticism became a
literary *genre* in the *Imagines* of Philostratus (third century A.D.),
which were admired by Goethe. In describing a picture of the
youthful Narcissus who fell in love with his own reflection in a pool
he writes as follows:

> *The painting has such a high regard for verisimilitude that it even
> shows drops of dew dripping down from the flowers and a bee settling
> on the petals—whether a real bee has been deceived by the painted
> flowers or whether we are to be deceived into thinking that a painted
> bee is real, I do not know. But let that pass. As for you, however,
> Narcissus, it is no painting that has deceived you, nor are you engrossed
> in a thing of pigment, or wax; but you do not realise that the water
> represents you exactly as you are when you gaze on it, nor do you see
> through the artifice of the pool . . . but acting as if you had met a
> companion, you wait for some move on his part.*

The famous formula *ut pictura poesis* which Horace took over
from the Greeks, with its implications that poetry and painting are
simply two different means of presenting a slice of reality in con-

vincing "imitation," has dominated European thinking for centuries and has been revived again and again in different contexts. From Leonardo to Lessing, whose important work *Laokoon* was published in 1766, it was a favorite topic of debate to compare and contrast the aspects of reality which could be most vividly represented visually by painting or through words in literature. At the end of the eighteenth century Archibald Alison published his *Essays on the Nature and Principles of Taste* (1790), in which he developed at length the thesis that aesthetic enjoyment of a work of art consists precisely in the indulgence of a controlled stream of ideas and images triggered off by the subject matter of the work in exactly the same fashion as, he thought, we would appreciate the natural objects portrayed or described. Even in the nineteenth century, when critical descriptions tended to be more closely related to the work, they were usually in the main descriptive of the subject. The modern critic and aesthetician André Malraux has acutely remarked that Stendhal's writings in praise of Correggio might be applied word for word to a great actress (*Les Voix du Silence*, 1951, p. 93). He speaks not of the picture but of the woman depicted in the picture. And this is true of most European criticism until the perfection of commercial photography cut the ground from under descriptive criticism. One of the results of this concentration of attention on the thing represented has been a failure to develop a terminology suitable for talking about the work of art as distinct from the actualities of nature which the work "imitates." This poverty of vocabulary has become particularly noticeable in the twentieth century when critics have begun to concern themselves with the aesthetic qualities of the artwork instead of its representational content. When one makes contact with a different critical tradition, such as the Chinese, which has talked about the artwork as a thing in its own right and not merely a reflecting mirror, the difference is brought home to us by the extreme difficulty we have in finding any linguistic equivalents for even the most ordinary of their terms.

Within the ambit of naturalism, if we do give attention to the artwork itself, the only criterion we shall have for assessing it as distinct from the reality mirrored by it, will be Plato's standard of *correctness* and the craftsmanly skill of the artist. This was very

Limestone statue
of Assur-Nasir-Pal II from
Nimrud, ca. 860 B.C.
Courtesy of
the Trustees of the British
Museum, London.

Limestone statue of
Nen-kheft-ka from
Deshasheh,
ca. 2750 B.C.
Courtesy of the Trustees
of the British Museum,
London.

Marble Greek kouros of
the early fifth century B.C.
Courtesy of
the Trustees of the British
Museum, London.

patent indeed to the writers of antiquity. Illustrating a rather recondite point of "correctness" in relation to musical performances Plato takes an example from visual art.

> *Now suppose that in this case too a man did not know what the various bodies represented were. Could he possibly judge of the rightness of the artist's work? For example, could he tell whether it shows the members of the body in their true and natural numbers and real situations, so disposed relatively to one another as to reproduce the natural grouping—to say nothing of colour and shape—or whether all this is confused in the representation? Could a man, think you, possibly decide the question if he simply did not know what the creature depicted was?*

The answer is that naturally he could not *(Laws,* 668). Aristotle *assumes* that pictorial art is "imitation," recognizes that we take pleasure in pictures of things which are not themselves beautiful, and draws the consequence that our enjoyment of pictures is an intellectual pleasure in recognizing the likeness. In a famous passage of the *Poetics* he asserts that everyone enjoys "imitations," as is proved by the facts.

> *For we enjoy looking at accurate likenesses of things which are themselves unpleasant to look at, as for example forms of the nastiest animals or corpses. The reason for this is that learning is highly pleasurable not only to scientists but also to the rest of mankind in the same way, although to a more limited extent. That is why people enjoy seeing illustrations, because in studying them they gain knowledge and make inferences about the class of thing to which each belongs. Because if the observer happens not to have seen the object before, the illustration will not cause him pleasure as an "imitation" but by virtue of its workmanship or its colour or some other such cause.*

Aristotle is here treating pictures in the same manner as illustrations in a scientific textbook of anatomy or botany (it has even been suggested that this is the sort of picture he had in mind) and seems to confuse two things: the pleasure of learning something new and the pleasure we take in recognizing an accurate representation. We learn something new when we do *not* know all about the original (e.g., the musculature of the human body) and relying on the illustration we learn from it what we did not know before. We delight in an accurate representation only when and to the extent that we are familiar with the thing it represents and can compare the two. Aristotle, however, makes the same statement in the *Rhetoric* (1371b4):

> *And since learning and admiration are pleasant, it necessarily follows that things connected with them are pleasant, for example works of imitation such as the arts of painting, sculpture and poetry and everything which is well imitated even if the object which is imitated is not pleasant. For the pleasure does not lie in the object but the inference that the imitation and the thing illustrated are the same so that an act of learning takes place.*

Why we should enjoy pictures of ugly subjects remained a fascinating problem to antiquity and after four centuries Plutarch repeated the view that although an ugly thing cannot make a beautiful picture, yet a clever and accurate representation of an ugly thing by a skilled craftsman may give us pleasure. He instances a representation of Jocasta's corpse by the metal worker Silanion and compares our delight in the imitation of a squealing pig by a clever ventriloquist.

The problem, or the pseudo-problem, of our ability to enjoy a beautiful representation of an ugly or harrowing subject is peculiar to the naturalistic outlook, which assumes that the work of art is "transparent" and that we respond not to it but to the reality reflected in it. Aristotle's suggestion that our delight comes from intellectual recognition of the correctness of the representation, or from admiration of the craftsman's skill, is not acceptable to modern thinking.

It is significant, however, that these implications of naturalism were a recurrent dilemma. Typical of the Renaissance outlook is Dürer, who said: "And a man is held to have done well if he attain accurately to copy a figure according to life, so that his drawing resembles the figure and is like unto nature." And he adds: "In particular if the thing copied is beautiful, then is the copy held to be artistic and, as it deserveth, it is highly praised." For the eighteenth century Edmund Burke, who, in his *Philosophical Enquiry into the Origin of Our Ideas of the Sublime and Beautiful* (1757), eloquently voices the sentiments current in his day, put the matter almost in the same language as Aristotle. He assumes the "trans-

*Gravestone of Theano
from Athens, ca. 450 B.C.
Photo: Hirmer Fotoarchiv.*

*Equestrian group from the
pediment of the Parthenon,
ca. 440 B.C.
Courtesy of
the Trustees of the British
Museum, London.*

Group of three goddesses from the east pediment of the Parthenon, ca. 435 B.C.
Courtesy of the Trustees of the British Museum, London.

Maid carrying ceremonial jar (loutrophoros hydria) for symbolic bridal bath at a wedding. Detail from Athenian red-figure pottery, fifth century B.C.
Courtesy of The Metropolitan Museum of Art, New York, Rogers Fund, 1907.

parent" view of the art object which is symptomatic of a naturalistic outlook. "If I make a drawing of a palace, or a temple, or a landscape, I present a very clear idea of those objects; but then (allowing for the effect of imitation which is something) my picture can at most affect only as the palace, temple, or landscape would have affected in the reality" (Part II, sec. iv) . Of imitation he says:

Herein it is that painting and many other agreeable arts have laid one of the principal foundations of their power. And since by its influence on our manners and our passions it is of such great consequence, I shall here venture to lay down a rule, which may inform us with a good degree of certainty when we are to attribute the power of the arts to imitation or to our pleasure in the skill of the imitator merely, and when to sympathy or some other cause in conjunction with it. When the object represented in poetry or painting is such as we could have no desire of seeing it in reality, then I may be sure that its power in poetry or painting is owing to the power of imitation, and to no cause operating in the thing itself. So it is with most of the pieces which the painters call still life. In these a cottage, a dunghill, the meanest and most ordinary utensils of the kitchen, are capable of giving us pleasure. But when the object of the painting or poem is such as we should run to see if real, let it affect us with what odd sort of sense it will, we may rely on it that the power of the poem or picture is more owing to the nature of the thing itself than to the mere effect of imitation, or to a consideration of the skill of the imitator however excellent (Part I, sec. xvi) .

Burke offers a choice. When the subject of a painting is attractive we take pleasure in the subject as if it were the real thing, disregarding the artwork. When the subject is commonplace or ugly, we admire its representation as a *tour de force*. This is of course impossibly naïve. But the dilemma remains inherent in the outlook of naturalism and subsequent attempts to reach a solution are one of the most important guides to aesthetic thinking. Reynolds, the advocate of the Grand Manner, accepted, as we have seen, most of the consequences of naturalism. "If deceiving the eye," he said, "were the only business of art, there is little doubt, indeed, but that the minute painter would be more apt to succeed." Therefore, he thought:

The painters who have applied themselves more particularly to low and vulgar characters, and who express with precision the various shades of

Front panel of the "Ludovisi Throne," showing Aphrodite rising from the sea, ca. *460* B.C. *Terme Museum, Rome. Photo: Hirmer Fotoarchiv.*

passion as they are exhibited by vulgar minds (such as we see in the works of Hogarth), deserve great praise; but as their genius has been employed in low and confined subjects, the praise which we give must be as limited as its object.

But the dictates of the Grand Manner maintained no lasting hold upon taste. Artists and their followers have been on the whole men with a lively inclination to observe and depict the heterogeneous manifold of natural forms in all their variety and diversity: the ugly, the grotesque, the commonplace, and the vulgar have attracted their interest as objects of representation, and the high-toned preference for lofty and elevated themes hardly survived outside the Academies. The new emphasis which the Romantic movement placed on the "characteristic" rather than the "beautiful" deflected attention from the problem as such. The problem also loses importance with the popular theories of art as a mode of communication and a means of self-expression—both of which are repudiations of naturalism to be discussed in their place. The "social realism" of the nineteenth century—the philosophical im-

petus of Courbet and Daumier among artists, Zola among writers—
and the revolutionary realism of the twentieth century Mexican
school of Orozco and Siqueiros—gave a positive function to the
representation of human misery and oppression, social ugliness in
general, for the arousal of men's conscience and the betterment of
human conditions.

Surely one of the most curious and pathetically inadequate attempts to cope with the problem directly was that of Sir Charles
Eastlake (1793–1865), President of the Royal Academy and Direc-
tor of the National Gallery, a teacher of considerable authority in

*Greek bronze mirror depicting Aphrodite showing Eros how to use a bow
and arrow, fourth century* B.C. *Louvre Museum, Paris. Photo: Giraudon.*

his day, who evolved a theory of *gradations of distinctness* and conceded that representations of the ugly, the unpleasant, and the ignoble may be permitted in pictures but only on condition they are less distinctly portrayed than their opposites. "The sense must never be shocked; distinctness requires beauty, and unpleasant forms require to be partially concealed." Like the philosopher Kant, Eastlake was not prepared to allow the representation of what is ugly or disgusting in sculpture because the three-dimensional form is too naturalistic to allow aesthetic transformation of the observer's response.

The habit of mind which leads to naturalism in the visual arts invites particular stress in literary criticism to be laid on the power through words to bring scenes and situations vividly and convincingly before the imagination. In antiquity, from Aristotle to Longinus as also by Roman theorists such as Cicero and Quintilian, great importance was attached to this power both in poetry and in rhetoric. But this quality of vivid presentation never became a universal criterion of literature in quite the same way as "correctness" in the visual arts, and literary criticism, though often strongly moralistic, retained a sense for style and structure. It rarely went so far as naturalistic criticism of painting in regarding the artwork as completely "transparent" to the disregard of its own formal and structural properties. One may see an analogy between vividness of presentation in the literary arts and the quality of "immediate presence" in the visual arts, a quality which was a standard criterion for Chinese criticism though more rarely understood in the West (see p. 124). It links with naturalism but is not identical with "correctness." It is very emphatic in much of Chardin's work. But it is also evident in the "metaphysical" compositions of Chirico, the dream scenes of Tanguy and the fantasies of Hieronymus Bosch. Vividness and convincingness are not directly or uniquely related to correctness in the mirror-reflection sense of that word.

APPENDIX

THE CONCEPT OF MIMESIS

Naturalism as it has been described was the main impetus for the technical developments in classical Greek painting and sculpture and was the main criterion of practical criticism. Paintings and sculpture were admired for their naturalism, and artists won fame for their skill in producing naturalistic artworks. In the realm of theory the concept which seems most closely to express the idea of naturalism was *mimesis*. The notion expressed by the word *mimesis* is very difficult to pin down. It was not identical with our concept of naturalism. *Mimesis*, for example, was applied equally to music and to the literary arts and drama, although to our way of thinking these are not "naturalistic" in quite the same sense as the visual arts. Aristotle as a matter of course and without argument defined what we should call the "fine arts" (excluding architecture) as the *mimetic* arts; yet it would certainly be strange to use the word "naturalistic" in this way. None the less *mimesis* and naturalism have fairly close links and from one point of view it would not be wrong to regard *mimesis* as the first and still rather vaguely articulated precursor of the emerging concept of naturalism. *Mimesis* was central in discussion of the arts throughout antiquity and it has remained of importance as an aesthetic concept up to the present. We shall therefore give a brief indication of its application when it first appeared in philosophical discourse.

Basically the Greek word means "imitation" (it is the root of "mimic"), but it had such a diverse range of applications in the ordinary language, reflected in philosophical discourse, that no one English equivalent can cover them all without gross distortion of English usage. In his *Preface to Plato* (1963) Professor E. A. Havelock calls *mimesis* the most baffling of all words in Plato's philosophic vocabulary and "a truly protean word." In its narrowest aesthetic use it is applied to a group of handicrafts roughly corresponding to what we think of as the "fine arts" and these are marked off as the "mimetic" crafts. Poetry and drama are included among them; architecture is excluded (the architect makes real buildings and not imitation buildings); and music is regarded as the most "mimetic" of the arts on the ground that it "imitates" the emotional dispositions and ethical attitudes of men. Owing to this lack of correspondence between the scope of the Greek and English terms it will be better here to retain the Greek word *mimesis* and gradually to make its implications plain by showing the complex of contexts in which it is commonly employed.

At the most elementary level *mimesis* meant simple mimicry.[1] In his book *Aristotle's Poetics* (1956) Humphry House gave the example of a child walking behind a pompous person in the street and mimicking his gait. Aristotle says (*Poetics* 4) that all men have a natural instinct for *mimesis* from childhood—indeed man differs from the other animals in being the most prone to mimicry and he learns his first lessons through imitation—and "it stands to reason" that this instinct for imitation is one of the causes of the poetic arts. But we are on less familiar ground when in the *Cratylus* Plato argues that words "imitate" the things they name just as paintings and music "imitate" objects and moods. In his metaphysical dialogues Plato sometimes used *mimesis* to express the relation in which particular empirical things stand to the general concept under which they fall. (Thus a visible figure of a triangle in a textbook "imitates" the general Idea or formula of a triangle; a good action "imitates" the general notion of Goodness; and so on.) In another sense, when Aristotle says, as he often does, that art "imitates" nature (*Physics* ii, 2; *Meteorologica* iv, 3; *De part. animal.* iv, 10), he means by "art" manufacture in general and does not imply that works of fine art (as distinct from useful artifacts) are copies or reproductions of natural objects. (This was made clear in S. H. Butcher's *Aristotle's Theory of Poetry and Fine Art*, 1895.) Aristotle thought of nature as a complete teleological system working out certain immanent and intelligible purposes. Man, as a part of nature, could apprehend these purposes through reason and could cooperate in furthering the ends to which natural processes are directed. Human planned production or *techne* was an instance of nature at work, an example of a natural process enlightened by the rationality of nature become explicit in human understanding. Thus Aristotle can say (*Politics* vii, 17): "All handicrafts and all education complete where nature falls short." He illustrates this from the arts of agriculture and cookery as well as the fine art of sculpture.[2]

---

[1] The most thorough discussion of the Greek word *mimesis* and cognate terms is *Mimesis and Art* (1966) by Göran Sörbom, who believes that the paradigm of the concept is to be found in the type of primitive dramatic performance known as "mime."

[2] The idea occurs in a rather more elementary form in a fragment of the philosopher Democritus (Diels 154 a), where he says that men learned the crafts

In this wide sense *mimesis* is not an aesthetic term and has no special connection with the fine arts. In the narrower sense mentioned above the concept is used to mark off the arts of painting, sculpture, poetry, music, and dance from the useful or industrial arts. Yet even in the narrower, aesthetic sense the concept is singularly elusive. It is not easy to know what property, indicated by the word "mimetic," was supposed to be common to this group of handicrafts and to mark them off from other crafts. Nor is it clear how this property, whatever we suppose it to be, links with the wider applications of *mimesis*. Plato *(Laws,* 667) proposes "correctness" as the criterion for all mimetic or representational art. Yet it is not easy to think of a notion of "imitation" in which correct correspondence or verisimilitude applies in the same way to music and dance rhythms as to naturalistic painting or sculpture. Even in its application to poetry the concept is applied in two senses. Although all poetry is said to be mimetic as an art form, in the third book of the *Republic* and to some extent in the tenth book Plato differentiates between mimetic and nonmimetic species of poetry. He calls that poetry mimetic where the poet makes the characters speak in their own person: that is tragedy and epic poetry when the characters use "direct speech." But in narrative poetry proper, he says, "the poet himself speaks and does not attempt to mislead us into thinking that anyone else is speaking. . . . And if the poet never concealed himself, his whole poetry and narrative would be free from *mimesis.*" The same duality occurs in Aristotle. In the third chapter of the *Poetics* he distinguishes three modes of *mimesis;* narrative poetry without impersonation; dramatic poetry, which uses impersonation throughout; and mixed narrative and impersonation. In chapter 24 he praises Homer because he uses narrative sparingly and adds: "The poet should speak in his own person as little as possible; for he is not an 'imitator' in virtue of that."

In nonphilosophic Greek language *mimesis* was current also with the sense of a thing's being an exact replica or photographic reproduction of something else. For example in a fragment from a lost play of the dramatist Aeschylus (P Oxy., 2162), a group of Satyrs carry painted portraits of themselves and are lost in admiration for

---

from watching the instinctive behavior of animals; weaving and sewing from the spider, building from the swallow, song from the nightingale and the swan.

their verisimilitude: "Could this image, this masterly reproduction, be more like my looks—all it lacks is a voice." Again when describing the customs of the Egyptians the historian Herrodotus mentions that at a certain stage of rich men's banquets they would carry around an exact representation of a corpse in a coffin to remind the revelers of what they would be after death. It is in this sense of an exact replica or a lifelike reproduction that the word came to be adopted as a key term of the rather crude form of naturalistic theory of visual art which originated with the Greeks and has dominated Western thinking about the visual arts.

In modern literary discussion the term "mimesis" has frequently been used in connection with the controversy whether works of literature are to be aesthetically appraised by formal qualities alone or whether they are also to be judged by the quality of their truth, by their commitment with ordinary life situations and the criteria and standards which are applied in life.

III. Naturalism 2

We have described Naturalism in terms of the habit of mind which deflects attention from the artwork as such and looks through it, as if through a mirror or transparent window, toward the slice of reality which it "imitates" or reproduces, assessing the artwork either by the natural standards applied to its subject or by the standards of accuracy, skill, and vividness with which it reflects that subject. This description must now be amplified. The subject represented by the work of art need not be a part of the actual world: it may be an imaginary object, a part of an imaginary world. The work of art may modify or distort the actual world without loss of convincingness. It may reflect general truths about the world rather than individual particulars; or it may aspire to depict an ideal world or a world of absolute truth above and beyond the actual world we know. While still retaining the naturalistic character of a mirror through which the attention of the beholder fixes upon the object represented, the work of art may nevertheless be a distorting mirror or an idealizing projector. Thus both realism and idealism are modifications or types of artistic naturalism.

It was a commonplace of Greek criticism that some painters (e.g., Polygnotus) depicted men better than the average and others (e.g., Pauson) worse than they are. A similar distinction was applied to poetry and drama. Tragedy, says Aristotle (*Poetics* 48a9), tends to represent men better and comedy represents them worse than the average. Other artists (e.g., Dionysius) represent them as they are. We still have critical terms distinguishing such *genres* of art.

<h2 style="text-align:center">REALISM</h2>

When the reality represented in the artwork coincides with the actual world of experience we call that art realistic. This is the most logical and useful, and perhaps also the most general, relation to establish between the much abused terms "naturalistic" and "realistic." We call any art realistic when it is naturalistic and when it shows the actual world as if through a plate-glass window, neither better nor worse than it is. Owing to the tenacious impulse to idealize, the word "realist" has sometimes been applied particularly to artists who instead of choosing conventionally beautiful subjects have emphasized the reality of ugliness in the world. Thus Courbet was called a realist because he depicted the common man without beautification and Caravaggio because he painted St. Matthew with dirty feet. The German movement *die neue Sachlichkeit* in the 1920s was motivated by such a desire to mirror the ugliness or banality of the world as it is without false idealization. A somewhat similar spirit infused the English Camden Town School in the 1930s. There are various other shades of meaning which it will be advisable to distinguish at the outset. In a more specific sense "realistic" is sometimes used as the opposite of "abstract." Thus the apples of Cézanne are said to be more abstract and so less realistic than those of Chardin or Zurbarán, and Zurbarán less realistic than Jan van Huysum. Again "realistic" may be used as an opposite not of "abstract" but of "distorted." For example much of the painting of Salvador Dali would be called realistic in the sense that it is the reverse of abstract, being painted with almost Pre-Raphaelite meticulousness of detail, but in so far as the objects are distorted from their actual appearance—the watch strap melts and runs like wax—it is not realistic. Sometimes, again, the term "realism" is applied to art which pictures the individual actuality rather than the general type. In this meaning of the words Greek portrait sculpture until well on into the Hellenistic period is said to be "idealized" and Roman sculpture realistic. In this sense Copley is more realistic than Philippe de Champaigne. The term "social realism" has been used of art movements, particularly a movement in the second half of the nineteenth century, which have concentrated upon a realistic depiction of ugliness, misery, or poverty either in support of a political theory or in the interests of social amelioration, to arouse men's conscience, to stir up indignation or pity, etc. More recently the term "socialistic realism" has been applied to art which is produced within the ambit and with the approval of Marxist theory as interpreted by the Soviet Union or satellite countries.

The term "Verism" denotes an extreme form of realism in the sense of individuation, as manifested for example in some Roman portrait sculpture. It is properly applied to the sort of art which will include every detail to the last wrinkle and wart and pimple whether or not they contribute to the general impression of character type. It would not be correctly used of the detail in Jan van Eyck's *Arnolfini* group or of the well-known picture of Domenico Ghirlandaio in the Louvre where he depicts with horrifying detail an old Florentine senator afflicted with elephantiasis caressing his grandson. In these pictures the detail is germane to the sentiment of the whole composition rather than included for its own sake. In modern times the term "Verism" has been rather loosely applied to a movement of German social realism initiated by George Grosz (b. 1893), Otto Dix (b. 1891), and Max Beckmann (1884–1950). The term "Veristic Surrealism" has also been applied to that branch of the Surrealist movement which has attempted to depict the unreal world of dreams and imagination with pseudo-photographic accuracy and illusionistic convincingness. Its chief representatives have been Salvador Dali, Max Ernst, and René Magritte.

Sometimes "realism" is used loosely of a conceptual art (such as the analytical form of Cubism) which aspires to reproduce things as they are known to be rather than to mirror their appearances. The word is also used of an art which tries to reflect the appearances of things illusionistically in contrast with an art which indicates them by conventional schemata. Common to most of these uses is the implied naturalistic attitude. The work of art called "realistic" is regarded naturalistically as a reflecting mirror through which is presented a selected slice of reality. By calling it "realistic" we imply that the reflected reality is thought of as actual rather than imaginary, and that it is reflected by and large as it is rather than being deliberately idealized or burlesqued.

ANTI-IDEALISM

There is no single recognized term for the kind of art which, like a distorting mirror, reflects the world as uglier than it is. Satire, caricature, burlesque, pornography may all do this incidentally to other purposes. There is no conventional term of criticism which appropriately characterizes an art such as that of Francis Bacon, who said of his work: "I would like my pictures to look as if a human being had passed between them, like a snail, leaving a trail of the human presence and memory trace of past events as the snail leaves its slime" (in *The New Decade* exhibition catalogue, Museum of Modern Art, New York, 1955). The present century has seen a strong wave of anti-idealistic art; there has been a tendency in many movements to emphasize the more unattractive feature of the environment in deliberate opposition to conventional idealization. But it is still doubtful whether an artist would make it his predominant aim to show the actual world as worse than it is unless it were in furtherance of some other purpose.

The term "Idealistic" in the language of art history and criticism has acquired a composite meaning from three interwoven strands of ideas which it is important to distinguish: Perfectionist, Normative, and Metaphysical Idealism.

PERFECTIONIST IDEALISM

The term is applied to art which reflects for preference nature at its best and most attractive, but attempts to improve and perfect nature by eliminating the inevitable imperfections of individual things. The earliest statement of this concept occurs in a conversation between Socrates and the painter Parrhasius recorded by Xenophon in the *Memorabilia*. "And when you would represent beautiful figures," says Socrates, "do you, since it is not easy to find one person with every part perfect, select out of many the most beautiful parts of each, and thus represent figures beautiful in every part?" Parrhasius accepts that this is his method. The concept, naïve as it is, gave rise to the equally naïve anecdotes already referred to of painters such as Zeuxis who used a number of beautiful models in order to produce a work which combined the beauties of all without the imperfections of any. The idea was taken over solemnly by such Roman writers as Cicero and Quintilian. It was again popular at the Renaissance. It was referred to with approval by Alberti in his *De Pittura* (1435) and the philosopher Francis Bacon (1561–1626) echoes it in the words: "There is no excellent Beauty that has not some strangeness in its proportions," and therefore the artist must "take the best Parts out of Divers Faces to make one Excellent." It was repeated by Sir Joshua Reynolds, although it was hardly consistent with his other precepts for the Grand Manner.

It is, of course, not a practical technique to select out a number of "excellences" from different examples, copy them exactly, and put them together to produce a single supremely excellent figure. These stories must be regarded as a lively anecdotal expression of the awareness that artists have not, or not always, been content simply to copy individual objects in nature, but have sought, and have sometimes achieved, a more perfect beauty than is found in particular natural things. Cicero expressed this notion when he said in the *Orator* that the great painter does not necessarily work from a model but copies an image which he has formed in his mind of the ideally beautiful figure. Even in order to choose out the most beautiful of a number of models the artist must have in his mind an "idea" of a most beautiful figure, at any rate in the sense that such an idea is implicit in the standards by which he chooses. And if having chosen his model he "improves" it in accordance with his idea instead of copying meticulously the actual figure before him, the same thing applies. Such an idea is an "ideal." Greek sculptors worked out canons of proportion for the most perfect human figure and the same idea was prevalent at the Renaissance. Dürer said he had examined between 200 and 300 figures in the attempt to work out ideal proportions of beauty. Yet such ideal art is still naturalistic, since the ideal proportions are regarded as an ideal type for the actual human body of flesh and blood. The artist simply reproduces the ideal in stone or in paint and the observer is invited to look *through* the work of art to this ideal of perfect human beauty.

This ideal beauty has been conceived in two ways, which have often coalesced. On the one hand it is thought of as a class type and on the other hand it has been conceived metaphysically in the context of Plato's Theory of Ideas. Both have had a lasting influence on Western art and theories about art.

NORMATIVE IDEALISM

The artistic ideal has often been thought of as a general class type in the sense of a norm, or a general truth, as distinct from the variable individual instances of any class. At its crudest the artist depicts "a fish" not this or that particular fish; the poet speaks of "the finny tribe," and so on. The stock text to which most theories of artistic universality go back occurs in the ninth chapter of Aristotle's *Poetics*. He says:

> *From what has been said it is clear also that it is not the poet's job to tell what actually happens but the kind of things that could happen, the kind of things that are possible according to probability or necessity. The difference between the historian and the poet is that the former tells what has happened and the latter the sort of things that might well happen. For this reason poetry is a more philosophical and serious thing than history. For poetry tells of universal truths, history of particular occurrences. By "universal truths" we mean the kinds of things a certain type of person will say or do according to probability or necessity, which is what poetry aims at—tacking on the names afterwards.*

What Aristotle is saying is that literature as distinct from "history"—by which he means journalism—gives us an insight into the typology of human nature, showing us not simply a matter-of-fact record of accidental events but the sort of thing men with this or

NATURALISM 2 · 85

that character will naturally or inevitably do in given circumstances. This statement follows his equally important declaration that a work of art must be a unified structure with a completeness of its own in which all the constituent parts and events are so selected and arranged in relation to each other and to the whole that none can be removed or changed without "disjointing and dislocating" the whole. Such a beautiful and unified whole cannot be made simply by recording a slice of actuality. The poet must select and construct. But he must do so in accordance with the laws of "probability and necessity," the laws which are embodied and manifested in external nature but which are not fully exemplified in the chaotic world of particular things and events.

Aristotle is here refuting Plato, whose philosophy was based on the notion of two separate realms, a realm of essential truths or universal Ideas apprehensible only by the mind and a world of particular things, apprehensible by the senses, which imperfectly "imitate" or embody the Ideas. Plato rejected the visual arts from his ideal State partly on the ground that they can offer only imperfect and illusory "imitations" of particular sense objects, which are themselves imperfect imitations of the Ideas. Although Plato's repudiation of most of poetry in the *Republic* was dictated primarily on moral grounds, he did maintain also that poetry is "unphilosophical" because it presents accounts of particular things and does not offer the mind a scientific knowledge of general principles. Aristotle's answer has had an enormous influence on literary aesthetics through the centuries. It has also had its effect on the theory of the visual arts, most strikingly at the Neoclassical revival.

Plato is rejecting a realistic art of naturalism on principle, because (he argues) the mere reproduction of things as they are is without positive value and simply takes us one stage further from the true reality of essences. Aristotle's reply (he is speaking primarily of poetry and drama) is a defense of normative idealism within the general concept of naturalism.

The first theoretician of Neoclassicism, the German art historian J. J. Winckelmann (1717–68), probably did more than any other one person to stultify for later generations a just appreciation of Greek art by his emphasis on its "noble simplicity and serene grandeur." In his *Thoughts on the Imitation of Greek Works in Painting and Sculpture* (1755) he wrote: "The general dominant distinctive mark of the Greek masterpieces is in the last resort a noble simplicity and a quiet grandeur as much in the posture as in the expression. As the ocean depths remain ever still however furiously the surface rages, so the expression in the figures of the Greeks through all the agony shows forth a great and unshaken soul." This sort of thing would have raised as many eyebrows in Aristotle's day as it does in our own. But Winckelmann also proclaimed that in the sensuous beauty of Greek statues there was reflected more perfectly than in any actual human beings the fundamental principles of beauty in nature and that these principles of physical beauty had affinities with spiritual beauty in the human soul. On this doctrine he based his advice that the modern artist should model himself on the Greek and thus recover the Greek insight into the fundamental and universal principles of natural beauty which are but very imperfectly manifested in the world of actual things. Goethe in his early years was influenced by this doctrine, believing that the different ideal characters of the gods and heroes in ancient art were mirrored in the ideal forms given to their faces and bodies, that this lost vision and ideal of the Greeks would be recovered by correlated measurements of many perfect statues and that the lost tradition of the Greek artists could thus be reduced to a system and handed down from master to pupil. The Neoclassical doctrine was formulated most completely by the French critic A. C. Quatremère de Quincy in *An Essay on the Nature and Means of Imitation in the Fine Arts* (Eng. trans. 1837), in which he maintained that by an exceptional gift of insight the Greeks had discovered once for all the perfect principles of natural beauty and that modern artists could do no better than discover nature through the eyes of the Greeks. His theories influenced the painter Ingres, who put the matter most succinctly with his statement that by his insight into the universal laws of natural beauty Phidias had been able "to correct nature through herself."

When applied to visual art the doctrine of "universal truth" as distinct from the individual and accidental as the aesthetic ideal is apt to degenerate into a demand for the norm in the sense of an average: a kind of a composite photograph composed from innumerable memory images superimposed. No theoretical justification for such a criterion in painting or sculpture has ever been advanced. Yet some portraits—portraits by Rembrandt, Greco, Picasso, certain portraits of Fayium and Japan—and in some still lifes by Chardin or by Morandi the observer seems to experience the impact as of a unique personality and yet at the same time, within the same experience, he has a sense of a general truth displayed to him embodied in the particular individual. This aspect of the aesthetic experiencing of some artworks has not hitherto been explained by art theory, though the experience is fairly well attested.

METAPHYSICAL IDEALISM

The Greeks were, then, familiar with the notion that the artist may improve on the world of actuality and that he does so in virtue of a mental picture or a composite image derived from sense experience but more perfect than any individual thing actually seen. The metaphysical doctrine that an artist may obtain an intuitive vision of ultimate reality, the universal Ideas of Plato, and "imitate" this reality in his artwork originated with the Neoplatonists. It was perpetuated in a theological form during the Middle Ages and was revived with tremendous vigor during the Renaissance. To Plato himself such a theory would have been an absurdity. He talks of beauty in connection with the ultimate reality of the Ideas but it is not the beauty of visual art, not a beauty which can receive sensible form. It was a fundamental premise of his philosophy that ultimate Being—the truths of the Ideal world—are apprehensible by reason only; the senses can mediate only imperfect approximations to the true nature of the Idea. The work of art, being apprehended through the senses, could not, in Plato's philosophy, reflect the true nature of things and works of visual art were regarded by him as but a copy of a copy. "But art does not deal in truth. It is content to represent the data of sense which are themselves a distorted image of reality. It is three removes from truth." On two occasions in the *Republic* (484c and 500e) Plato *compares* the way in which the philosopher gazes with the eye of the mind upon absolute truth with the way in which the artist fixes his gaze on his material model. (Failure to understand the semantics of this led to a curious misconception of Plato's statement that the most beautiful forms are the regular geometrical shapes. He does not by this statement mean that a visible circle drawn by a compass is more beautiful to look at than a painting by Parrhasius and he does not in some curious way anticipate modern abstract painting. He is speaking of intellectual beauty and referring to the fact that the regular solids have mathematical formulas apprehensible to the mind. Misunderstanding on this point caused Francis Hutcheson and other eighteenth-century writers on art to indulge in solemn discussion whether the circle or the oval or some other geometrical figure is ideally most beautiful.) The point of Plato's comparison is to illustrate the way in which the mind apprehends directly—"sees," as it were—a theoretical truth or an intellectual concept. He does *not* suggest that truth can be embodied concretely in visible artworks.

The theory that great art "imitates" an ultimate reality which exists beyond the empirical objects of the world of sense perception was first formulated by the semimystical Neoplatonist Plotinus (third century A.D.). The essential of Plotinus' philosophy derives from a desire to escape from the material world and find union with a divine Being, who is pure existence without form or matter. He held that the phenomenal world is a creation of the soul and has no real existence; reality belongs to the spiritual world contemplated by reason. Plotinus found the principle of beauty in the unconscious yearning of the human soul for the Primal Being, the One. Art is not imitation of the phenomenal world in an ordinary sense but is the creation of a beauty which the soul recognizes "from an ancient knowledge" and through which it aspires to union with the divine.

> *We must recognise that the arts give no bare reproduction of the thing seen but go back to the Ideas from which Nature itself derives and, furthermore, that much of their work is all their own; they are holders of beauty and add where nature is lacking. Thus Phidias wrought the Zeus upon no model among things of sense but by apprehending what form Zeus must take if he chose to become manifest to sense* (Enneads, *V.8.1*).

The most influential statement of the Neoplatonic theory of art at the Renaissance was in a lecture delivered by Giovanni Pietro

*Portrait bust of
Alexander the Great by
Lysippus, fourth century* B.C.
*Hellenistic idealism.
Istanbul Museum.
Photo: Hirmer Fotoarchiv.*

Bellori to the Academy of St. Luke at Rome in 1664 and published as a Preface to his *Lives of Painters, Sculptors and Architects* in 1672. Bellori presented the true artist as a seer who gazes upon eternal verities and reveals them to less favored mortals. It was this gift of intuition, he thought, which differentiates the true artist from the mere mechanic who slavishly copies appearances. He also suggested that the artist could cultivate his gift of intuition by the study of ancient marbles, in which the "ideal" was first revealed. The artist who was considered to exemplify this doctrine most perfectly was Poussin, whose achievement was ranked in French academic theory of the seventeenth century almost on a level with that of the ancients. The doctrine provided the philosophical justification for the Grand Manner and was used to confound the realists who followed Caravaggio and the realistic painting of the

Portrait bust of Cicero,
late first century B.C. *Roman realism.*
The Lateran Museum, Rome.
Mansell Collection of Photographs.
Photo: Anderson.

Panel of a mummy-case from Roman
Egypt, with portrait of a Greek boy
painted in encaustic technique,
second century A.D. *Courtesy of the*
Trustees of the British Museum, London.

Netherlands. In the eighteenth century it was supported by
Reynolds against those who preferred to rely on the appeal to
sentiment and emotion and even the controversies of the nineteenth
century, such as that between the followers of Ingres and Delacroix,
were fought around the banner of "ideal beauty."

Among modern philosophers Schopenhauer developed most fully
a theory of the Neoplatonic type. Schopenhauer rejected the "perverse and senseless" opinion that an artist can create a beautiful
form by collecting together in one image the beautiful "points" of a
number of models. He saw that in order to recognize this or that
feature in a particular model as beautiful and another feature as
defective the artist must already have before his mind an ideal type
of beauty which he employs as a standard in judging particular
instances. He claimed that the true objects of aesthetic perception
are Platonic Ideas, that is "the permanent essential forms of the

world and all its phenomena." While he sometimes spoke of these Ideas in an Aristotelian way as generic types, he believed that they could not be found empirically—for example, by examining and comparing a representative selection of actual human figures as Dürer tried to .do—but only when selection was made under the guidance of an already existing ideal from which valid principles of preference were derived. Schopenhauer therefore thought of art as a form of *knowledge*, an intuitive, direct vision of metaphysical essences, which are real in a more ultimate way than the actual objects of the phenomenal world and are in some manner imperfectly and partially embodied in the world of sense perception. He believed that a vision of this reality behind appearances is obtained when we look at particular things of ordinary sense perception with the "disinterested contemplation" of the aesthetic consciousness, which puts them outside the practical context of everyday life interests dominated by our voluntary purpose and concerns, and concentrates upon them as sense-objects in their own right. He gives the following example:

> *If I contemplate a tree aesthetically, i.e. with artistic eyes, and thus recognise not it but its Idea, it becomes at once of no consequence whether it is this tree or its predecessor which flourished a thousand years ago, and whether the contemplator is this individual or any other who lived anywhere at any time; the particular thing and the knowing individual are abolished with the principal of sufficient reason, and there remains nothing but the Idea and the pure subject of knowing.*

Schopenhauer thus understood aesthetic awareness as pure perceptual interest in an object for its own sake without concern for causal connections, utility or use, and held that in this form of awareness we achieve a kind of identification between the observer and the object of contemplation. And having in this way achieved an intuitive vision of the significant reality of the Idea above and beyond the perceptual object, the artist in Schopenhauer's philosophy embodies his vision in his artwork and communicates to others who appreciate the work of art he has made a similar revelation of the new reality he himself has seen. Thus Schopenhauer thought of the creative artist as a person endowed with the faculty for perceiving by direct intuition the true character of things and a gift of embodying his vision in concrete form so as to enable others to share it. This explains why it is that great art, while "imitating" the ordinary things of experience, shows them in a strange and novel light, imparting to them a new and deeper significance which cannot be explained in the theoretical language of reason and science.

This theory of Schopenhauer's might be thought to provide a theoretical basis for the character of universality which we have noticed belongs to some great portraits and still lifes. But it does so—if it does so—at the expense of sacrificing the impact of concrete individuality which is equally germane to their greatness.

In the importance he attaches to the *perceptual* aspect of aesthetic experience and in his theory of the revelatory character of great art Schopenhauer anticipated important elements in twentieth-century aesthetic thought. He failed to do full justice, however, to the creative function of the artist. As the philosopher Heidegger has claimed, Van Gogh in his picture of two old boots conveys a revelatory intuition of the nature of a boot as a human instrument, a utensil, and thus imparts something fundamental about the significance of a boot. But (according to the most general aesthetic doctrine now current) he does not only do this. In his pictures of a kitchen chair he does not only body forth the Platonic Idea of a chair. Much more than that he creates a *picture,* which is a chair or a boot in a system of spatial and coloristic relations contained within the boundaries marked out by the frame. It is the present tendency to emphasize the aesthetic importance of these formal properties which belong to the artwork as a whole, not simply to this or that object represented *in* the artwork. This points to the essential difference between the naturalistic outlook, even though it be idealistic naturalism, and the outlook of contemporary aesthetics.

Those who hold to a formalistic theory of art nowadays commonly maintain that a picture or a statue cannot be regarded as a work of the highest quality merely because it is a good representation of an object, real or ideal, or because it makes apparent some recondite metaphysical significance of the objects which it depicts. According to the antinaturalistic trend of contemporary theory (which may or may not be justified) any work of art must be regarded as a newly created object, not merely as a mirror reflecting

Head of Buddha, Ghandara,
second–third century A.D.
Courtesy of the
Trustees of the British
Museum, London.

Head of Buddha, Khmer,
twelfth century A.D.
Courtesy of the Trustees of
the British Museum, London.

Ceramic portrait statue
of a prisoner, Mohica
(Peruvian) , ca. A.D. 200.
Kemper Collection.

Self-Portrait *by Jean Chardin,*
1775. Louvre Museum, Paris.
The Mansell Collection of
Photographs. Photo: Alinari.

Isabel Cobos de Porcel
by Goya, 1806. Courtesy of
The National Gallery, London.

the things it represents, and its excellence must be assessed by criteria which apply to the new creation which it is as distinct from the things which it reflects.

It is interesting that many of the leaders of abstract movements in twentieth-century art have been attracted toward a revelatory theory of art and have believed that abstract works of art body forth a vision of ultimate verities or reflect a metaphysical reality beyond the world of the senses. Although in common with the trend of the time their attitude to their art has been in the main non-naturalistic, this element of Idealistic naturalism has often remained and they have felt that their works were not only new creations complete in themselves but could convey an emotional revelation of a reality beyond themselves. Kandinsky, who has been called the founder of Abstract Expressionism, recorded in his *Reminiscences* (1913) in words recalling Schopenhauer's account of aesthetic experience that the most ordinary objects seen aesthetically revealed to him their hidden face and being.

Not only the stars, moon, woods, flowers of which the poets sing, but also a cigarette butt lying in the ash-tray, a patient white trouser button looking up from a puddle in the street, a submissive bit of bark that an ant drags through the high grass in its strong jaws to uncertain but important destinations, a page of a calendar which the conscious hand reaches to tear forcibly from the warm companionship of the remaining block of pages—everything shows me its face, its innermost being, its secret soul, which is more often silent than heard. Thus every still and every moving point (= line) became equally alive and revealed its soul to me.

In 1938 he wrote in the magazine *XXme Siècle*: "This art creates alongside the real world a new world which has nothing to do with *external* reality. It is subordinate *internally* to cosmic laws."

Malevich, one of the originators of Suprematism, a movement

Detail from Las Meniñas *by Velasquez, 1656. Prado Museum, Madrid. The Mansell Collection of Photographs. Photo: Alinari.*

which in some respects anticipated the Neoplasticism of Mondrian and the Constructivism of Gabo, maintained in *The Non-Objective World* (1927) that true art is nonrepresentational—"No more likeness to reality, no idealistic images, nothing but a desert!"—but must be an expression of pure plastic feeling. Yet he believed that this abstract art embodies absolute values, since, presumably, "pure" feeling unadulterated by perceptual imagery of actual things must be supposed to bring us into contact with a metaphysical idea. "Nothing," he said, "but the expression of the pure feeling of the subconscious or superconscious (nothing, that is, other than artistic creation) can give tangible form to absolute values." It is doubtful, however, whether *as theory* these views take us much further than the artist's excitement with what he was doing and the personal satisfaction he derived from it.

As an alternative to metaphysical values Piet Mondrian, who like Kandinsky was addicted to the tenets of theosophy, alleged in *Plastic Art and Pure Plastic Art* that in his own work the principles of universal beauty for the first time came into their own. He argued that our response to any figural art, any art that is which represents external things, is necessarily vitiated by our individual and subjectively variable reactions to those things. Only when art is freed from any suggestion of representation do we achieve a universal and unvarying response according to what he called the "fixed objective laws of plastic composition." What distinguishes the abstract from the figural artist, he said, "is the fact that in his creations he frees himself from individual sentiments and from particular impressions which he receives from outside, and that he breaks loose from the domination of individual inclinations within him." These "objective laws" governing response to the elements of compositional design apart from representational significance he believed to have become progressively determinate as the history of art has developed and he regarded them as the true essence of art. He also claimed for them a metaphysical significance, declaring that "they are the great hidden laws of nature which art establishes in its own fashion. It is not necessary to stress the fact that these laws are more or less hidden behind the superficial aspects of nature." He also declared that the "fixed laws of plastic composition" by which he worked were subordinate to a fundamental law of equivalence

Mrs. Thomas Boylston
by John Singleton Copley, 1766.
Courtesy of
the Fogg Museum of Art,
Harvard University.

Head *by Modigliani,* ca. *1913.*
Courtesy of
The Tate Gallery, London.

Daniel-Henry Kahnweiler
by Picasso, 1910.
Courtesy of
The Art Institute of Chicago.

"which creates dynamic equilibrium and *reveals the true content of reality.*" It has not been proved empirically, however, that response to geometrically abstract nonrepresentational art of the sort produced by Mondrian, van Doesburg, and Ben Nicholson is "universal" in the sense of not being subject to variation from one person to another. Many attempts have been made, but none have yet been successful, to show that there are abstract "elements" of design which command unvarying response from all men alike. Still less can it be explained what is meant by saying that such abstract compositions connect with hidden natural laws or reveal a recondite reality.

Even the German Expressionists, who gave primacy to self-expression among the many other functions which have been attributed to art, often tended to combine or confuse this doctrine with a revelatory theory and to assume that by expressing the deeper aspects of the Self they were in some way obscurely revealing or discovering a metaphysical reality beyond the Self. Thus Max Beckmann (1884–1950) said in the course of a lecture delivered at the New Burlington Galleries in 1938:

What I want to show in my work is the idea which hides behind so-called reality. I am seeking for the bridge which leads from the visible to the invisible, like the famous cabalist who once said: "If you wish to get hold of the invisible you must penetrate as deeply as possible into the visible." My aim is always to get hold of the magic of reality and to transfer this into painting—to make the invisible visible through reality.

In concluding we must again emphasize that both Realism and Idealism, as described, fall within the ambit of the naturalistic outlook which, starting with the Greeks, has dominated the greater part of Western art theory. In both theories the work of art is regarded as a mirror reflecting a reality other than itself. The interest is concentrated not on the artwork but on that which is reflected or revealed through it. For art theory the contrast of certain nonnaturalistic theories (Oriental or contemporary European) with naturalism is far more important than the contrast between realistic and idealistic naturalism. Some contemporary artists, not habituated to analytical thinking, have attempted to combine the nonnaturalistic view that their art creates a new reality, independent and to be judged by its own standards alone, with the not easily reconcilable view that it is revelatory of a metaphysical reality behind the world of appearances. But this seems in the last resort to be no more than a confusion of incompatibles.

SYMMETRY AND PROPORTION

The idealistic theory of beauty has been traditionally associated with doctrines of proportion. Although he was not himself prepared to accept without reservation the view that beauty consists in proportion, Plotinus made it clear that such a view was general in his day. "Practically everybody," he said, "asserts that visible beauty is produced by symmetry of the parts toward each other and toward the whole." The Greeks had a natural bent for mathematical ways of thought and evolved various canons of proportion for the ideal human figure. Unfortunately, these canons have not survived. Vitruvius is the only ancient writer who has given actual data of the Greek notions regarding ideal proportions, applying them both to the human body and to architecture. He defines proportion as "the metrical coordination throughout the whole work of a module and the whole" and symmetry as "the appropriate harmony resulting from the members of the work itself and the modular correspondence resulting from the separate parts in relation to the appearance of the whole figure." His words had enormous importance for architects and theorists in later centuries, but they are obscure and the aesthetic implications of the Greek theory which lay behind them cannot now be recovered. The key passage about the Greek theory of ideal proportions is a statement made by the physician Galen (ca. A.D. 129–99) about the famous "canon of Polyclitus." Polyclitus, the most famous sculptor of antiquity after Phidias, was thought to have laid down a canon of ideal beauty and to have embodied it in his statue of the *Doryphorus* (Spear-Bearer). The only words which can with reasonable probability be attributed to him are the statement: "The beautiful comes about little by little, through many numbers." Galen says of his canon: "Chrysippus . . . holds that beauty does not consist in the elements but in the symmetry of the parts, the proportion of one finger to another, of all the fingers to the hand . . . in fine, of all the parts to all others, as it is written in the canon of Polyclitus."

This appears to have been a canon of anthropometry—ideal proportions for a living human body, which the sculptor had simply to "imitate" or reproduce in stone. Even so the meaning of the passage has been differently interpreted. If it means that the ideal proportions were expressible in terms of fractions or multiples of one part of the body taken as a module (the interpretation given by Erwin Panofsky in *Meaning in the Visual Arts*), this canon has little or no bearing on aesthetics since such proportions could equally well be expressed in inches or any other measure. But the language attributed to Chrysippus is consistent with the view that the canon was conceived as a true proportion, that is a relation among ratios, and that it enjoined a single consistent ratio of parts to parts and to the whole. Such a canon might have aesthetic significance, as the ancient tradition seems to have supposed, by helping to insure a principle of organic unity throughout the whole artwork. There may be reason to conjecture that some such principle underlay the Greek theory of "symmetry," but that in practical studio tradition it was transformed for convenience into numerical fractions.[1] Similar practical rule-of-thumb schemes, some elementary and some very complex, were used in Byzantine and medieval art, both for the drawing of figures and for the construction of cathedrals. In the fifteenth and sixteenth centuries an intense interest in proportion led to the search for new canons. In Florence the humanists, led by Brunelleschi, regarded themselves as the heirs to the classical tradition and sought to rediscover the underlying principles of classical proportions. The first canon was produced by Alberti's ingenious system of measurement which he called *Exempeda*. Both Leonardo and Piero della Francesca studied proportion in relation to perspective and Leonardo produced tables of equine as well as human forms. Dürer was obsessed throughout his life by the search for ideal proportion. He tells us that the Venetian Jacopo de'Barbari had showed him the figure of a man

---

[1] This is the case with the practical indications given by Vitruvius, since he expresses his ideal proportions in terms of common fractions of a total length or common multiples of some part used as a module.

and a woman "which had been drawn according to a canon of proportion," and that he thereafter read Vitruvius and embarked on investigations of his own to discover the principle of ideal proportion.

The long interest in proportion was partly influenced by a quasi-metaphysical belief, whose origin is traditionally ascribed to the philosopher and mystic Pythagoras (sixth century B.C.), that proportion has a cosmological significance and is inherent in the structure of the universe. Pythagoras is credited with the discovery of the simple mathematical relations which govern the stopping of a resonant string to produce the main musical intervals and also with showing that the three main intervals can be expressed in terms of the three main types of proportion, arithmetic, geometric, and harmonic. The Pythagoreans conceived numbers spatially as if they were identifiable with simple geometrical figures, and believed that so conceived they belong to the essence of all things and that the ultimate forms of reality can be expressed as numerical ratios. Plato extended the theory to incommensurable relationships and in the cosmological myth of the *Timaeus*, by his theory of the five regular solids, incorporated the irrational numbers into the ultimate elements from which the universe was thought to be constructed. His conception of beauty was connected rather with the rational intelligibility of such a system than with the empirical arts. He said in the *Timaeus* (28) :

> We must first, I believe, make the following distinction—what is that which is Existent always, having no Becoming, and what is that which is always Becoming and never Existent? The former is apprehensible by thought with reasoning since it is always the same, the latter is the object of opinion through a-logical sensation, since it comes into being, changes, perishes and is never really existent. . . . When the artificer of anything in fashioning its shape and nature keeps his gaze upon that which is unchanging and uses a model of this kind, everything so fashioned must necessarily be beautiful. When he gazes on that which has become, using as his model that which has becoming (i.e. things subject to change, things which can come into and pass out of existence, that is things of the perceptual world), what he fashions is not beautiful.

Plato thought that the visual arts belonged to the latter class and therefore spoke poorly of them. Plotinus and later thinkers believed that the true artist, like God the creator, could use as his model the eternally existent Idea. For example Cennino Cennini (b. *ca.* 1370), whose *Craftsman's Handbook* stands on the border between the Middle Ages and the Renaissance, said:

For painting we must be endowed with both imagination and manual skill to discover unseen things concealed beneath the shadow of natural objects and to fix them with the hand, presenting to plain sight what did not appear before to exist. And painting justly deserves to be enthroned next to theoretical knowledge and to be crowned alongside poetry.

Julius Caesar Scaliger (1484–1558), father of the more famous classical scholar, declared that the poet is another god, for he can create what ought to be. And the Platonist Girolamo Fracastoro of Verona, who is chiefly remembered as the author of the poem *Syphilis sive Morbus Gallicus,* one of the earliest accounts of syphilis, wrote in his *Naugerius sive de poetica dialogus* (1555): "The poet is like the painter who does not seek to imitate this or that particular feature, nor things as they happen to be with all their defects in them; but having contemplated the universal and most beautiful idea framed by the Creator, the poet creates things as they ought to be." In connection with the visual arts it was believed that there exist ideal proportions, intellectually apprehensible, and that these express the nature of Diety as manifested in the creation of the world, although they are embodied only imperfectly in the actual world of perceived things. This was the basis of the statement by St. Thomas Aquinas that "due proportion or harmony" was one of the ingredients of beauty, and it remained the basis of Renaissance belief when quite elaborate mathematical investigations, including the Fibonacci series, were undertaken in the hope of discovering a formula of beauty.

The idea of a mathematical and cosmic norm of beauty continued to be influential until the eighteenth century, when the classical notion of aesthetic experience as form of a rational or intellectual intuition began to give place to a notion of beauty based on subjective feeling and sentiment. But although the idea of mathematical proportion was foreign to the outlook of the Romantic Age, it did not completely disappear. About the middle of the nineteenth century the Golden Section—which had been called the "Divine Proportion" and endowed with mystical properties by Luca Pacioli, a friend of Leonardo and Piero della Francesca and the foremost mathematician of his day—was once more given prominence as the universal key to beauty in nature and art by a German, A. Ziesing. Ziesing's work was repeated more scientifically and with better understanding by Sir Theodore Cook in *The Curves of Life* (1900) and interest has continued in attempts to find principles of form common both to aesthetic constructs and to natural forms such as organic growth, crystalline structures, and microscopic or astronomical formations. The interest has given rise to studies such as those reflected in a symposium *Aspects of Form* published with a preface by Sir Herbert Read in 1951. Ziesing's theories attracted the attention of the psychologist Gustav Theodor Fechner (1834–87) and following his lead a good deal of time and effort has been devoted in experimental aesthetics to the attempt to prove empirically that there exists a general instinctive aesthetic preference for objects which embody a mathematical principle of proportion such as the Golden Section. Modern artists have from time to time been attracted by proportion as a principle of composition. Chirico in particular gave much attention to it and about 1912 a splinter group of the Cubist movement was formed with the name *La Section d'Or*. The divisions of Le Corbusier's *Modulor*, intended to facilitate harmoniously proportioned design, were based on the Golden Section, which Le Corbusier believed to be exemplified in the ideal (or average) proportions of the human body. The modern revivals of the theory of proportion do not, however, think of aesthetic experience as a form of intellectual delight in the intuition of theoretical relationships but regarding beauty as an affair of the senses and of feeling, seek to find some empirical mathematical basis for constructing forms which will appeal to the senses as pleasant.

IV. The Aesthetics of Chinese Pictorial Art

Throughout classical antiquity and the Middle Ages the artist was ranked as a manual worker and an artisan in a social framework which did not recognize the dignity of manual labor. An amateur artist would have been as strange a thing as an amateur bricklayer. In China, by contrast, from the Han dynasty (*ca.* 206 B.C.–A.D. 220) onward, painting, poetry, and music were regarded as pursuits worthy of the gentleman and scholar in a social structure which accorded very high prestige to scholarship and culture. The Confucian gentleman-scholar believed that the cultivation of good relations between man and man was the supreme aim of life and cherished the virtues of rightness, decorum, sincerity, and wisdom. The administrative classes and the gentry were recruited by state examinations in which painting and the other arts figured prominently. Good social order was regarded as a reflection or embodiment of the Tao, conceived as a quasi-moral order of the universe. Mai-mai Sze, in his Introduction to his translation of the *Mustard Seed Garden Manual of Painting* (1679–1701), has pointed out that in the traditional Chinese view painting is

> *not a profession but an extension of the art of living, for the practice of the* tao *of painting is part of the traditional* tao *of conduct and thought, of living in harmony with the laws of* Tao. *Under such circumstances, Chinese painting has usually been an expression of maturity: most of the great masters first distinguished themselves as officials, scholars, or poets, and many were expert calligraphers, before they turned to painting . . . in acquiring the education prescribed by the* tao *of painting a painter underwent rigorous intellectual discipline and intensive training of memory. He acquired a store of knowledge crowned by the essence of Chinese thought—the ideals and ideas of painting comprehensible to all who had the same training as well as to all whose education came through custom and hearsay. The ancient wisdom moulded his character and nourished his innermost resources.*

In the first chapter of *Li Tai Ming Hua Chi* (845) on the origin of painting Chang Yen-yüan wrote:

> *Painting promotes culture and strengthens the principles of right conduct. It penetrates completely all the aspects of the universal spirit. It fathoms the subtle and the abtruse, serving thus the same purpose as the Six Classics, and it revolves with the four seasons. It originated from Nature and not from any decrees or works of men.*

The conception of painting as cultivation of the Tao is expressed in the following passage from the *Analects* of Confucius, quoted at the beginning of the *Hsüan-ho hua-p'u*, the Catalogue of the Imperial Collection of Paintings (1119–25):

> *Direct your endeavours towards the* Tao, *support yourself upon its active force, follow selfless humanity and indulge in the arts. As to these arts, a scholar who is striving for the* Tao *must never neglect them, but he should merely take a delight in them and no more. Painting is likewise an art. When it has reached the level of perfection one does not know whether art is* Tao *or* Tao *art.*

This idea of painting as an activity which at once brings the artist into unity with and makes manifest the cosmic principle of Tao lies at the root of Chinese thinking about art, whether it is described as the cultivation of character, the expression of personality, or the search for the essence of things. It is essentially a non-naturalistic conception of art. The Chinese painter was not concerned, except incidentally to the pursuit of other aims, to "imitate" the appearances of things or to represent things ideally as he would like them to be or as they "ought" to be or even to reveal some metaphysical reality behind the appearances of things. The cultivation and practice of painting were thought of as a ritualistic activity creating an embodiment of the cosmic force of order which infuses all reality, human society, and the individual personality. While the Western artist typically aimed to produce a replica of reality, actual, imagined, or ideal, the Chinese artist—although he might in fact do this—made it his first aim to bring his own personality into keeping with the cosmic principle so that the Tao would be expressed through him, and thus in his painting he would act in unison with the natural order and his work would be imbued with and would reflect the Tao. The basic attitudes and the deeper implications reflected in apparently simple statements in Chinese on art are so different from those chiefly familiar to the West that they are not easily formulated in the language to which we have become habituated.

The difference in outlook explains the different character which Chinese writing and thinking about the arts assumed. Until recently in the West art criticism was for the most part either technical or devoted to description and appraisal of the artist's subject matter or it was concerned with divers ulterior functions—educative, propagandist, decorative, devotional, and so on—which works of art have been made to serve. These themes appear in Chinese art criticism also, but they never took a central or preponderant place. Chinese art criticism was also largely technical, but the terms and categories of Chinese technical criticism were different from those with which we are familiar in Western criticism. In the West the categories and concepts as well as the criteria of criticism derived from the naturalistic interest in a lively and convincing representation of some subject matter other than the work of art itself. While this interest is not absent from Chinese criticism, it is kept subordinate to the demand that the work of art shall embody

in its own structure and rhythms the spirit of the Tao which vital-
izes all nature, organic and inorganic alike. Because of this the
language and the concepts of Chinese criticism differ from those
which we use and some considerable effort may be needed to bring
them into connection with the art from which they are derived and
to grasp what they are about in terms of the categories with which
we are more familiar.

Since the attitude of naturalism has not had much influence in
Oriental art and theory, the sort of criticism which we now call
"aesthetic"—criticism arising from a concern with the work of art
itself as an object for contemplation—arose somewhat earlier in
China than in the West. We find it in the *Ku Hua P'in Lu* (Record
of the Classification of Painters) by the portrait painter Hsieh Ho
about A.D. 500, which was continued early in the sixth century by
the critic Yao Tsui in the *Hsü Hua P'in Lu*. Works on the aesthetics of calligraphy preceded those on the aesthetics of painting,
and throughout Chinese critical literature the aesthetic principles
of calligraphic brushwork constituted the core of appreciation in
painting. The Six Canons of Painting, which with varying interpretations and modifications from one generation to another dominated Chinese criticism through the centuries, were already formulated by Hsieh Ho and are thought to have come to him from an
earlier time.

During the Han dynasty Chinese ideographic writing emerged as
a fine art in its own right and the earliest aesthetic and stylistic
classifications are to be found in critical works on the techniques of
calligraphy. The Shuo Wen dictionary (*ca.* A.D. 100) formulated
the six categories of ideographs based on the manner in which the
characters are formed as distinct from the styles of brushstroke used
in writing them, and Chang Huai-kuan in the T'ang period (A.D.
618–906) established a classification of the ten styles of writing
which had grown up through the centuries. A refined appreciation
of the aesthetic qualities of calligraphy preceded and set the standard for the aesthetic of painting. From a very early period painting
and calligraphy were regarded as allied arts, virtually identified by
the gentleman-painters and *literati*, the painters of bamboos, plants,
etc. The two arts used the same equipment, depended on the same
techniques, shared the same aims, and were appraised by the same

standards. Monochrome painting, whose excellences lay in the subtle variation and blending of tones and the appropriate style of brushstroke, was perfected to a very high level and it was a common saying that "if you have ink, you have the Five Colors."

The Chinese connoisseur cultivated a uniquely subtle sensibility to the intrinsic qualities of line and the physical skills involved took years of practice and self-discipline to perfect. As time went on the styles of brushstroke were elaborately classified: *luan ma ts'un,* brushstrokes like tangled hemp; *ho yeh ts'un,* brushstrokes like the veins of the lotus leaf; *chieh so ts'un,* raveled rope strokes; *tsuan tien,* dotting tufted stroke, and so on. The minute classifications both of brushstrokes and for the use of ink tones seem tedious to those who are outside the esoteric tradition and unable themselves to appreciate the subtleties on which these classifications are based. But they bear witness to the delicacy of appreciation which was general among educated persons in China throughout the centuries. Calligraphy in the Oriental sense—the embodiment of Tao in the manipulation of the brush—has little in common with such "calligraphic" styles as International Gothic or *art nouveau.*

Two things stand out as most important for understanding the aesthetic concepts implicit in Chinese critical writing about the visual arts. The first is the very large extent to which the language of Chinese appreciation and criticism is rooted in the aesthetics of calligraphy in the Chinese and not the Western sense of that term. The second is the fact that when Chinese writers speak about emotion and expression in painting they connect these things with calligraphic techniques rather than with subject matter. This is so directly opposed to the Western naturalistic tradition that something more needs to be said about the mental shift which is necessary for understanding Chinese ideas and appreciative attitudes. In the West technique has typically been regarded as an instrument only, an instrument which provides the artist with the mechanical equipment for communicating his message, expressing his personality, embodying emotional appeal through the choice and manipulation of subject matter. It was hardly before the various Post-impressionist movements which stemmed from Gauguin, Denis, the Symbolists, and the Fauves, that "abstract" color and form began to be used deliberately for emotional significance apart from subject and theme. And it has been a misfortune of Western art and aesthetics that such abstract expressionism has lacked an inherited tradition of expression and the experienced and sophisticated appreciative public which such a tradition alone creates. In the Chinese tradition the emotional appeal of a painting, its expressive content, the personality of the artists, reside in the technique of the brushstroke. The most "emotional" paintings for the Chinese connoisseur are paintings in which the subject matter for the Western beholder is most neutral—paintings of bamboos, lotus plants, birds, flowers, etc. Whereas in the West figure drawing has always been primary, dramatic and emotional situations a basic theme of naturalistic representation, and pure landscape a late and secondary development, in China landscape was early and basic. It was a truism of Chinese criticism that a painter who had mastered the art of landscape could draw the human figure, that the bamboo offered more subtle possibilities of expression than dramatic or anecdotal scenes. The same principles of emotional expression through brush technique which are developed primarily in bamboo or still-life painting are fundamental in more elaborate landscape pictures. It is the rhythm and the quality of the stroke, the technique of the brush, which embodies the spirit of Tao.

One further point must be made before we proceed to an account of Chinese aesthetic concepts as expressed in the Six Canons of Painting. In the West, owing to the prevalence of a naturalistic attitude, specifically aesthetic criticism started late and in consequence of this European languages are weak in aesthetic terms. When we are confronted with a painting and wish to indicate the qualities which render it a rewarding object for aesthetic contemplation, we can only use indirect language and hope to be understood. In the absence of a tradition of precise aesthetic terminology an expressive wave of the hand or a gesture of the fingers accompanied by inarticulate grunts communicates more to the connoisseur than pages of verbal exposition. Chinese criticism avails itself of a more extensive and articulate vocabulary of aesthetic terms which are supported by a long and familiar background tradition of appreciation which has been enriched but not substantially changed over some eighteen centuries. But this vocabulary has no precise equivalents in our language. It is a constant exasperation for students of Chinese—and Indian—aesthetics that there exists in European languages no terminology by which to translate the most basic terms, and lacking the vocabulary the very concepts are difficult to conjure up. The aesthetic language of the East is based on ancient habits of appreciation which differ in some important respects from those which have been most prevalent in the West. In approaching Chinese aesthetics one must therefore remain constantly alert to reject inappropriate associations with the naturalistic outlook of the West and every translation which is proposed must be hedged round with cautions and qualifications.

It is not entirely accidental that an interest in Chinese aesthetic ideas has appeared in some recent art movements of the West. If we may make a very approximate suggestion as a guide to the adjustment in outlook called for, it could be said that Mondrian's search for objective laws of plastic composition would not be very alien to the Chinese habit of mind. But whereas Mondrian thought it necessary to eschew representation and restrict himself to geometric design in the attainment of these laws, the Chinese assumed that the objective rules and rhythms are embodied in all things as the principle of their growth or structure and the representational artist must identify himself with them.

THE SIX CANONS OF PAINTING

First Canon. Ch'i yün sheng tung. Spirit resonance which brings life movement.

Ch'i is a key word in all Chinese theory of art. It is an elusive term, easily suggestive of mystagogy in translation, yet in the context of Chinese writing both prosaic and sufficiently precise. In origin it was the principle of vital energy which pervades the whole of animate and inanimate nature (Chinese thought has never made an absolute distinction between organic and inorganic, spiritual and material) and it was conceived quasi-materialistically as something between animal magnetism and mental energy in a human being. In a human being *ch'i* also expressed character and personality insofar as a person had brought himself into consonance with the principle of order, the Tao, which infuses the cosmos and is reflected in civilized society. Since this is a principle of orderliness and ritual propriety, *ch'i* carried moral implications. In *The Way and Its Power* (1935) Arthur Waley wrote:

> *Closely associated with the art of the mind is the art of nurturing* ch'i, *the life spirit. Fear, pettiness, meanness—all those qualities which pollute the "temple of the mind"—are due to a shrinkage of the life spirit. The valiant, the magnanimous, the strong of will are those whose* ch'i *pervades the whole body, down to the very toes and fingertips. A great well of energy must be stored within, "a fountain that never dries," giving strength and firmness to every sinew and joint.*

Yün means something like sympathetic vibration, overtones or resonance, and the compound *ch'i yün* expresses with some element of metaphor the sympathetic resonance as of a musical note between the vital energies of the individual and the vital principles which transfuse external nature. The translation "spirit resonance," proposed by the Chinese scholar Osvald Sirén, is now generally adopted. But it must be prized free of the inevitable associations with cant mysticism, theosophy, or table-turning which the words in English too easily suggest. In Chinese aesthetics the term held certain quite precise and well understood implications, *not* necessarily tied in with an animistic view of nature (although such a view was in fact integral to Chinese thinking), and also some qualities readily appreciated by Chinese connoisseurs though impossible to express in analytical language. Chang Kêng in the eighteenth century wrote: *"Ch'i yün* may be expressed by ink, by brushwork, by an idea, or by absence of idea. . . . It is something beyond the feeling of the brush and the effect of the ink, because it is the moving power of Heaven, which is suddenly disclosed. But only those who are quiet can understand it."

Wu Chên (1280–1354), one of the four great Yüan masters, said: "When I begin painting I am in a state of unconsciousness; I suddenly forget that I am holding a brush in my hand." And in the *Record of Famous Painters* (847) Chang Yen-yüan wrote more fully:

> *Now if one revolves one's thoughts and wields one's brush consciously thinking of oneself as painting, then the more one tries the less success one will have in painting. But if one revolves one's thoughts and wields*

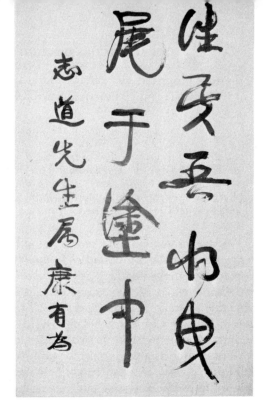

Calligraphy by K'ang Yu-wei, 1858–1927.
Courtesy of the
Trustees of the British Museum, London.

one's brush without being conscious of painting, then as a result one will
have success in painting. When the hand does not stiffen, the mind does
not freeze up, the painting becomes what it becomes without one's
realising how it becomes so.

The demand is for complete concentration upon the object with
elimination of all distractions until the painter becomes, as it were,
identified with his object. Only when the conception is fully formed
in the mind does the painter begin to give expression to it. Of the
painter Ku K'ai-chih, Chang Yen-yüan said:

In the works of Ku K'ai-chih the strokes are firm and tense and connect

Bamboo Shoots *by Wu Chên of Chekiang, 1280–1354.*
Courtesy of the Trustees of the British Museum, London.

with one another uninterruptedly; they circle back upon themselves in
sudden rushes. His tone and style are evanescent and variable, his
atmosphere and interest lightning and sudden. His conception was kept
whole in his mind before he used the brush so that when the painting
was all finished the conception was embodied in it, and therefore it was
all divine breath (shên ch'i) .

Besides identification with his subject the painter must have such
absolute mastery over the technique of the brush that during the
activity of painting he can give complete expression to the *ch'i*
without distracting awareness of the physical processes of painting.
Only if this was achieved could the painting completely embody the

concept so that "even in one brushstroke one can see the *ch'i*."
When this is achieved, the spectator is also transported:

Concentrating one's mind and taking one's thoughts afar, one has subtle insight into Nature. Object and self alike forgotten, one departs from form and rejects discrimination. One's body can really be made to be like dried wood: one's mind can really be made to be like dead ashes. Is not this to have attained the subtle principle? It is what may be called the tao of painting.

This Chinese ideal of concentration and spontaneous execution has sometimes been quoted as a parallel for modern techniques of unconscious painting used by the Surrealists or the spontaneous and undirected work of some Abstract Expressionists. It is, however, almost completely the opposite. The Chinese painter worked spontaneously only after an elaborate preparation consisting of meditation on an idea or concentration on an object, a discipline which required training and cultivation, and he had available a perfected technique of expression. The result to which he aspired was not an expression of his own subconscious imagery but the embodiment of a concept which he had painstakingly achieved by deliberate concentration and the enhancement of his mental energies into harmony with the world outside. Nor did the Chinese aesthetic ideal provide for the painter to be led and guided by the material medium in the course of his work. Feeling for material was embodied in the acquired technique and nowhere else has the Chinese sensibility for materials (ink, jade, etc.) been equaled. But the awareness of the possibilities of the medium was there at hand when the artist began his work and could be drawn on and used without distraction or hesitation. The modern idea that an artist may or should be guided by the accidental qualities of his materials during the working out of his conception and the execution of the work of art was foreign to the main Chinese tradition. Typical of the Chinese attitude is the advice given by the painter Kuo Hsi (1020–90) in his *Essay on Landscape Painting (Lin Ch'üan Kao Chih)*, one of the most famous works in the literature of Chinese painting:

If you wish to record these wonders of creation, you must first be filled with enthusiasm for their beauty, then you must give yourself over to a

Self-Portrait *by Hokusai,*
1760–1849. Courtesy
of the Musée Guimet, Paris.

The Poet Lin P'u
Wandering in the Moonlight
by Tu Chin,
active ca. *1465–1487.*
Courtesy of
The Cleveland Museum of Art,
John L. Severance Fund.

Flute Player Seated on
a Water Buffalo
by Kuo Hsü, ca. *1456.*
Nanking Museum.

detailed confrontation with them and sate yourself with them completely. So you must wander about in them and sate your eye with them; after you have arranged the impressions in your breast you will paint all this with complete ease and fluency, without your eye being aware of the painting-silk and your hand of the brush and ink, and everything will be your own individual image of them.

One of the important results of *ch'i yün* was the quality of spontaneity or naturalness *(tzu jan)*, which was highly prized not only in Chinese art but also in life. As a quality of brushwork and execution it was included among the Six Essentials of Painting derived from an early eleventh-century work attributed to the critic and art historian Liu Tao-ch'un. With regard to representational matter (though the two concepts were little distinct in Chinese critical writing) it ranked with *chên* (truth) as the highest attainment. It includes the idea of effortlessness in execution and the idea of naturalness in the sense that the action of painting would seem to take place of its own accord like a natural process. It was thought to result from the enlightenment which ensues when a painter by concentration saturates himself with the forces of nature—"feeding upon mists and clouds"—until he secures the unity of identification. The high value which was traditionally set on this quality may be gathered from the following lines from the *Tao Tê Ching* of Lao-tzu:

> The ways of men are conditioned by those of earth;
> The ways of earth are conditioned by those of heaven;
> The ways of heaven by those of Tao;
> And the ways of Tao by naturalness (tzu-jan).

The quality *sheng tung*, which Hsieh Ho associates with *ch'i yün*, is usually translated "life movement" or "life rhythm." While a Chinese critic or connoisseur could point to this quality without hesitation, it is very difficult to indicate in words to readers brought up in the Western naturalistic tradition. To a European the words would in all likelihood call up the idea of a representation of a human or animal body, suggesting the characteristic attitudes and as far as possible creating in the beholder visual illusion of movement or life. A Chinese critic would more naturally illustrate the quality from an ink painting of bamboos, trees, or mountains. The idea of visual illusion is absent from the Chinese concept of "life movement"—there is no attempt to create an illusion that the object is in movement or just about to move or that it is in repose just after movement. The quality of *sheng tung* arises when the individual brush-movements and the rhythm of their combination and relations in the painting reproduce and as it were repeat the characteristic movements of growth in the object, the growth rhythms by which, for example, a bamboo differs from a lotus or a willow from a beech tree, the flight of the swallow from the movements of the quail. So far from being identified with optical illusion or photographic accuracy, excessive concern for verisimilitude is often reproved as being destructive of "life movement" and *ch'i*.

Second Canon. Ku fa yung pi. Bone structure, a technique of the brush.

Ku fa was a phrase derived from the pseudoscience of anthroscopy, the art of reading a man's character and disposition from his bones and skeletal conformation. When transferred into the language of art criticism the phrase retained something of its original meaning and could be applied to the strokes which set up the basic formal structure of a composition. George Rowley, for example, in his *Principles of Chinese Painting* (1959) quotes a saying by Hua Lin: "Although these few strokes may be entirely covered up, the painting must have their strength to stand up; otherwise, even scarecrows would have the forms of men." A tradition of painting which was originated by Huang Ch'üang (d. 965) and which was employed chiefly in flower painting modeled the forms by graded washes of color without a skeleton of brushline contours: this was called *mu-ku-t'u*, boneless painting. The concept of a firm underdrawing setting up however roughly the basic structure of a picture is familiar to Western artists. But in China the term never implied a naturalistic reproduction of anatomical structure. This was not the aim. In the painting of mountains *ku fa* arose from the interplay between rhythms of silhouette with the *ts'un*, or wrinkles, the characteristic brushstrokes which indicated the geological and crystalline structure of the mountains. Primarily in art criticism *ku fa*

Rabbit with Figs. *Wall painting from Herculaneum,
second century* A.D. *Museo Nazionale, Naples.*

meant firm and vigorous brushstrokes, a calligraphic technique, a
method of using the brush, and not a rough draft, or abozzo, which
reproduced visually the anatomical structure of the object depicted.
Hence the landscape painters and painters of flowers and plants
were often said not to paint (*hua*) but to *write* (*hsieh*) their subjects. The great popularity of the bamboo as a subject for painting
was due very largely to the fact that the firm and springy bamboo
stem with the infinite modification of its sections was held to
embody most perfectly the qualities of firmness and strength which √
were most admired in the basic techniques of calligraphy. These
properties were associated with the human qualities of steadfastness,
straightness, firmness, and unalterable demeanor which were the
chief Confucian virtues.

Third Canon. Ying wu hsiang hsing. Reflecting the object, which
means depicting (drawing) its forms.

It has sometimes been said that Chinese art depicts the spirit and

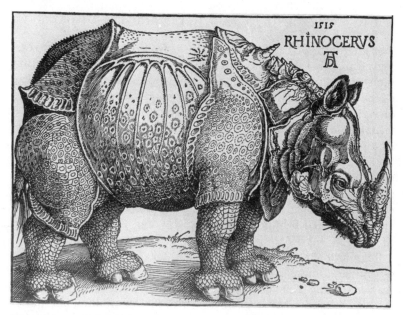

The Rhinoceros *by Albrecht Dürer, 1515. Wood engraving. Courtesy of the Courtauld Institute of Art: Witt Library, London.*

Western art the appearance of things. Rowley quotes Ch'eng Heng-lo as saying: "Western painting is painting of the eye; Chinese painting is painting of the idea." It may be possible to bring these vague generalizations to rather more precision by a consideration of the third, apparently naturalistic, canon of Hsieh Ho.

When the Canons of Hsieh Ho were repeated by Chang Yen-yüan in his *Record of Famous Painters* (A.D. 847) he used the term *hsieh* (write) instead of *hsiang* (depict). Mai-mai Sze in his edition of the *Mustard Seed Garden Manual of Painting (The Tao of Painting*, 1956) sees a significant difference, explaining that the Third Canon was concerned with drawing in the sense of establishing the mass, shape, and particular essence of each object in a picture rather than formal resemblance. Even the expression *hsiang* meant something very different from photographic verisimilitude, as is shown by a quotation given by Acker (p. xxvi): "But the subtle virtue of Chang (Seng-yu) and Wu (Tao-hsüang) is that after just one or two strokes the image is already reflected in them."

The literature of Chinese art criticism from the start and increasingly through the centuries was filled with warnings repudiating the sort of "truth to nature" which was assumed by some ancient Greek and Renaissance critics to be the supreme goal of art, the sort of verisimilitude which aspires to produce a replica which will be mistaken for the object. In his essay *The Sublime Beauty of Forests and Waterfalls* the Sung painter Kuo Hsi (*ca.* 1020–75) wrote: "When the artist paints mountains as they really are the result will resemble a map. Such mistakes arise from lack of the ability to select things." Admiration for photographic realism was regarded as an error of the vulgar and of the Philistine, who is unable to appreciate the spiritual beauty of the brushwork and the resonance of the life force.

The following statements may be taken as representing the central and most typical Chinese attitude toward photographic realism. Chang Yen-yüan said: "What can be seen with the eye is color and shape; what can be heard with the ear is sound and noise. But, alas, the people of this generation think that form and color and sound and noise are means by which they can come to understand the essence of Tao. This is not so." Wang Li, an amateur painter and poet prominent in the Yüan period, said:

> *Although painting is representation of form, it is dominated by idea. If the idea is insufficiently brought out, it may be said that the picture has no form either. But as the idea is in the form, it cannot be expressed if the form is neglected. When the form is grasped, the idea will fill it completely; but when the form is lost, how can there be either form or idea?*

When Chinese writers speak of realistic representation they refer more prominently than Western writers on art to what are nowadays called *physiognomic* properties (such qualities as solitude, menace, gaiety) of visible objects rather than to their scientifically measurable shapes and colors.

Deploring even in the ninth century the "messy and meaningless" modern painting, Chang Yen-yüan explains the Canon as follows:

> *The painters of Antiquity were sometimes able to transmit likeness of form while at the same time giving importance to bone-energy. They*

Puma head from Tiahuanaco,
A.D. *500–700.*
Author's collection.

Painted cotton cloth
from Chancay,
Central Andes,
ca. *200 B.C.*
Kemper Collection.

The Frying Pan
by William Scott, 1946.
Courtesy of The Arts
Council of Great Britain.

sought to extend their painting beyond mere formal likeness. This is something very difficult to discuss with vulgar people. But in modern paintings, even if by chance they achieve formal resemblance, a spirit-resonance does not arise. If they had but used spirit-resonance in their pursuit of painting, then formal resemblance would have been immanent in their work. . . . . Now the representation of things necessarily consists in formal resemblance, but this likeness to form requires to be supplemented with bone-energy. But bone-energy and formal resemblance, while both have their origin in the conception formed by the painter, must finally depend on the use of the brush. That is why those who are skilled in painting generally excel in calligraphy as well.

The Chinese were concerned with what are now called the "physiognomic properties" of things or rather with the class of physiognomic properties which are most indicative of the individual and the type—the featheriness of trees, the spikiness of reeds, the characteristic placing and posture of vegetation in landscape, the textures and conformation of rock formations, the hairiness of animals, lightness of birds and butterflies; with expressive poise or gesture, the attitude of deprecation, the dignity of an eagle or an emperor—all those qualities of things for which no exact words exist and which are for that reason sometimes loosely said to express the "spirit" or "essence" of the thing. These attributes of external things Chinese painting sought to suggest rather than "imitate." But except insofar as it conveys physiognomic qualities Chinese painting was relatively uninterested in external appearances and deprecated the reproduction of appearances as an end in itself. The Chinese had a highly developed sensibility for the sensuous effects of the work of art—line, stroke, tonal values, balance of void and object, etc.—but an inherent antipathy for the imitation in art of the sensuous appeal of external things except insofar as sensuous qualities were related to physiognomic properties. Rowley has said very well that: "To the Chinese, sensuous beauty resided neither in richness of effect nor in physical appeal, but in elegance, refinement and discrimination. The appeal to the senses was ever tempered by the activity of the mind." Dutch still life which sought to reproduce illusionistically in pigment the textures of fur or lace, the sheen of metal or glass, the tactile smoothness of silk or velvet, is at the opposite pole from the Chinese desire to suggest "aesthetic" qualities behind these surface appearances. Still further removed is the Impressionist style, which attempts to put realistically onto canvas the play of light and color, dissolving the object in the optical impression.

The two principles which Chinese criticism associated with the representation of form were *li* and *shih*. *Li* signified the universal principles as exemplified in particular things, the directing idea or basic notion. But these were rather *operative* principles, manifestations of the life and working of the Tao, than generalized appearances of shape and they were indicated primarily by the active rhythm of execution, brushstroke, and manipulation of ink-flow rather than the search for typical generic forms. They were closely related to general physiognomic qualities, the characteristic swaying motion of foliage, the poise of a lighting bird, etc. By absorption with the object the painter must bring himself into union with the life force as characteristically manifested in the object. "To express an idea or represent an object properly the artist must first turn it over and over again in his mind, until it unites with the soul." In Confucianist philosophy the *li* was sometimes spoken of as the form-giving principle which unites with the amorphous life spirit of the *ch'i* for the emergence of an ordered universe of things.

Shih (pictorial reality) is that awareness of immediate *presence* which in Western art also sometimes strikes the observer with the impact of a blow. It does not depend on photographic truth to reality or on fullness of detail. It is as strongly evident in the dream shapes of Tanguy and the fantasies of the Douanier Rousseau as in the angels of Giotto. In Chinese art it is tied more closely than in Western art to vitality of technique and vividness in the depiction of physiognomic qualities. It is not bound up with the collocation of objects in an illusionistic three-dimensional picture space. Indeed the Chinese artist did not in the main think of his picture as an arrangement of forms within a defined and bounded area on which he created illusorily a deeper or shallower space terminated by a background. The paradigm of the Chinese painting was the scroll, which was opened gradually and "read" consecutively in time by the observer, not seen in a piece. Hence the mutual relation of objects in space was always a less important consideration than the tension between object (*shih*) and void (*hsü*). In Chinese painting the void is an element of prime importance, a positive source of tension, and not to be confused with the "spaces between objects" about which Western art criticism speaks.

As Chang Yen-yüan made it clear, *shih* or representational reality was not possible of achievement without *ch'i* and structural strength *(ku fa)*. It was connected in the Chinese mind with physiognomic properties as expressed in posture and also with the problems of structure involved in the fashioning of ideographs. The same aesthetic principles of composition were involved in calligraphic composition and in the obtaining of pictorial "presence" in the painting of objects.

The impression of universality and the sense of "presence" are qualities of all great painting, Western as well as Chinese, and have certainly not been unnoticed in Western writing on art. But in Chinese criticism they were commonplaces and accepted criteria, while in the academic doctrines of the West and the precepts of the Grand Manner they remained at the most peripheral.

Fourth Canon. Sui lei fu ts'ai. Correspondence to type, which has to do with the laying on of colors.

This is a principle of appropriateness or good taste. In Chinese art color symbolism was more important than its representational functions. Color attached to the object and was rarely a compositional element in the structure of the picture as a whole. This canon must be understood in the light of the saying that he who has ink has all five colors. The sensuous beauty of pigment color as an end in itself was little exploited by the Chinese and color played a relatively small part in their theory of art generally. The Chinese aesthetic of color was determined by techniques of monochromatic ink washes for the representation of mood and atmosphere. It was intimately connected with an elaborate aesthetic of ink painting too recondite to be pursued here in detail. All this is implicit in the Fourth Canon. But a rough, though jejune, rendering might run as follows: the mood and atmosphere of a picture are to be achieved by an appropriate technique of ink wash. In using this rendering it should be remembered that for the Chinese connoisseur the emotional impact of a picture depended more on the brush and ink technique than on the formal representation of the subject matter.

Fifth Canon. Ching ting wei chih. Organization and planning, which involves placing and arrangement.

Chinese theory had nothing to do with mathematical systems of proportion either for individual figures or for the composition as a whole within the boundaries of its frame. Composition in the European sense was not discussed except perhaps incidentally as for example in connection with the style known as "asymmetrical balance," where a small figural group in one corner of the picture gives the weight necessary to provide countertension for an immensity of void. Mai-mai Sze explains this canon as follows:

> *The Fifth Canon refers to something more than what we now understand by composition and design: in accord with the premise of Chinese painting that* ch'i *came first and created form, the idea that the elements of a picture should be placed in their proper and natural relationships was rooted in the concept of* Tao *and its total harmony, by which each object and aspect has its proper place in relation to others and to the Centre, which is also the Whole.*

The quality of *ching* in the sense of "seasonal aspect" was also included in the Six Essentials of Painting by the great tenth-century master of landscape Ching Hao. Applied primarily to landscape but also to other genres of painting, the principle of *ching* meant that the picture itself must convey the emotional mood objectively appropriate to the subject and that all the parts must combine to fit in with the mood. The function of *ching* was to "fashion according to the seasons and to study the mysteries to create truth." Chang Yen-yüan had said that seasonal aspect involved understanding the rhythm and mutations of nature, requiring observation, knowledge, meditation, and an intuitive understanding of *ch'i.* In the *Mustard Seed Garden Manual of Painting* it is said: "In one's heart one must be thoroughly acquainted with the *ch'i* of the four seasons—and not only in the heart, for that knowledge must flow to the fingertips to guide the creation of the work."

In Chinese theory the organization of a painting had little to do with scientific proportion but was rather a matter of the equilibrium of tensions, the balancing of contrasts, grouping in such a way that the character of the group balanced and was balanced by the individuality of the units (groups were seldom of more than five units) . It was as much psychological as mathematical. Design aimed at simplicity and economy rather than complexity and emphasis was on the expressive character of technique and its power to suggest the physiognomic properties of the subjects depicted. A classical example of design may be seen in the *Six Persimmons* of Mu Ch'i, a Ch'an monk who painted in the first half of the thirteenth century.

It should not be assumed that Chinese painting entirely lacked proportion and symmetry in the Western sense. Though very different problems were set by the scroll painting intended to be "read" in consecutive sections, it is probable that the systems of proportion traditional in the West could be made to fit much Chinese art as well—or as ill—as they fit much Western art. But mathematical and scientific principles of proportion were not in themselves of interest to Chinese art theory. The principles of composition which Chinese theory recognized were always closely related to the theme.

Sixth Canon. Chuan mo i Hsieh. Transmitting models, which involves reproducing and copying.

The high importance which Chinese art education put upon copying the old masters has often been misunderstood by art historians. In order to see it in the true perspective one must remember that for the Chinese, artist and connoisseur, the most important feature of painting was the brush-and-ink technique, which was for them expressive of the personality and character of the artist and which, more than the subject or composition of the picture, embodied the results of the artist's absorption in his theme, his identification with the life principle. This was a thing that could not be copied by ruler or tracing paper, measurement or accuracy of eye. Its essence lay in spontaneity, and a man who could reproduce another artist's technique with sufficient mastery to satisfy the connoisseur had necessarily to that extent assimilated his artistic personality. The purpose of copying was "to follow and transmit to posterity the methods and principles developed and tested by the masters, and so to sustain the *tao* of painting," both to train oneself in the right path and, as it was said, help to "pull the great cart of tradition." Hence Mai-mai Sze translated the Canon: "In copying, seek to pass on the essence of the master's brush and methods."

In the European tradition the values now placed on originality and on self-expression date only from the Romantic movement which had its roots in the eighteenth century. Despite its reverence for tradition China has been the only highly organized civilization which from an early date recognized and valued both originality and the expression of personality in art. Even the early writer Hsieh Ho says of the artist Liu Shao-tsu: "He excelled in copying but did not study the thought of those whom he copied. . . . His contemporaries in speaking of him called him 'the copyist.' But 'to transmit without originating' is not what painting puts first." Chang Yen-yüan says of the same artist that "it would have been better had he combined the excellences of all the scrolls which he copied by making sketches based upon them but with original ideas of his own." Within the paths hallowed by tradition Chinese painting set a high store by the expression of personality. The painting was infused with the objective spirit of the universal life force, the ordering principle of the Tao; but the concretization of the Tao in each individual was the highest expression of his personality. Roger Goepper, probably rightly, connects this respect for originality and expression with the amateur status of the Chinese artist:

> *This evolution of Chinese painting in the direction of the expression of a personality is intimately linked with the genesis of the conception of an artist who does not feel his activity to be a profession, who has largely freed himself from the shackles of nonartistic demands and whose task is no longer presented to him by society at large for a specific purpose. Art has become a matter for the individual, above all for the creator.*

CRITICAL STANDARDS

In introducing his six canons Hsieh Ho remarked that few artists had been equally at home with all of them and that from ancient times artists had for the most part excelled in one or the other. The utilization of the canons for the grading and classification of artists also throws light on Chinese estimation of artistic merit. Although terminology varied, the traditional bases of appraisal were fairly constant. In making actual assessments of individual artists it was generally assumed that objective criteria applied and that these were not merely a matter of individual taste. Thus in criticizing certain classifications of Hsieh Ho the author of the *Hsü Hua P'in* remarked: "This was simply because his own emotional attitude toward the various painters was uneven and had nothing to do with the merits or defects of the paintings themselves." The traditional classification was partly based on standards established for calligraphy and a convenient statement will be found in the *Mustard Seed Garden Manual,* which Lu Ch'ai (pseudonym of Wang Kai, the general editor) paraphrased from a compilation made by the critic Hsia Wen-yen in the middle of the fourteenth century.

1. The lowest level, called *nêng* or competent, is that of the accomplished painter who has mastered the rules of style and by hard work and practice has acquired the ability to render the visible forms of things.

Chang Yen-yüan says:

> Now as to the transmission of patterns, or reproduction and copying, these should be the painter's least worries. And yet modern painters rather tend to excel in the mere reproduction of shapes. Though they do achieve formal likeness [verisimilitude] yet they are without spirit-resonance, and while providing their work with all the colours complete, yet they fail in their brush technique: how can such be called painting?

2. When brushwork is of a high order, colors appropriate, and expression clear and harmonious, the painter may be placed in the *miao* (marvelous) class. Sometimes, however, this second class is assigned to the masters of aesthetic self-expression, typically the educated literary man who is also an amateur artist. A fine example of this class is the great Yüan master Ni Tsan (1301–74), often called Ni Yün-lin, recluse of the clouds and forests, who said of his painting:

> In my bamboos I am really only setting forth the untrammelled feelings in my breast; how then could anyone ascertain whether the painting shows a formal likeness or not. . . . What I call painting is really nothing else than the purposeless setting down of unforced brush strokes. I do not strive for formal likeness but pursue it exclusively for my own enjoyment.

3. The third and highest class is the painter whose work has the life-movement resulting from spirit-resonance, called the "principle of Heaven." Hsia Wen-yen said of this:

> When it is operating through the painter, the effect in his picture is beyond definition and the painter may be said to belong in the shên (divine) class. At this level the thought (ssu) was said to be at one with the spirit; the painter "penetrated with his thoughts the nature of everything in heaven and earth and thus the things flow out of his brush in accordance with the truth of the subject."

4. Some critics put above the highest class a fourth category which defies definition. The classification was first introduced in the T'ang Ch'ao Ming Hua Lu (T'ang Dynasty Collection of Famous Painters) compiled by Chu Ching-yüan about A.D. 1000 and its distinguishing features were supreme effortlessness (tzu jan) and the quality of spontaneity denoted by the phoneme i. The painters in the i class were said to "grasp the self-existent, which cannot be imitated, and to give the unexpected." The conception of the i approximates most closely in Chinese thought to the idea of genius which arose in the West during the Romantic period. Yet it differed significantly from that conception. The quality was thought to belong most typically, if not exclusively, to mystics and recluses who by meditation had achieved union with the Tao and it was manifested (in the words of Rowley) in "forms which are so simplified that they become intangible or so obliterated that they suggest emptiness which is nonspatial."

Summary. While this represents but the bare bones of an enormously complicated apparatus of criticism, it will be sufficient to illustrate the contrast between the attitudes of thought from which Chinese and Western aesthetic presuppositions derive. The naturalistic attitude, which we have taken as typical of the European aesthetic tradition over the greater part of its course, is the outlook of the man who regards a work of art primarily as a replica of some part of reality (actual or ideal, observed or imagined) other than itself and who, using the work of art as a mirror, directs his aesthetic responses on the reality which it reflects. In this sense Chinese art theory is fundamentally non-naturalistic. The idea of a work of art as a replica or reflection of some part of reality outside itself was relatively unimportant and was for the most part kept subordinate to other, more basic considerations. Attention is concentrated on the artwork as a reality in its own right, which by its technical and structural rhythms bodies forth and makes manifest the unifying cosmic principle of the Tao, particularly as that principle infuses the objects represented. The artwork, especially in its technical rather than its representational aspects, may be regarded as expressing the personality of the artist insofar as that has been brought into unison with the Tao. To this extent Chinese attitudes anticipated the aesthetic of "self-expression" which in Europe came to the fore during the Romantic Age. But whereas in European thought self-expression was often regarded as something worthwhile for its own sake, in Chinese (as also in Indian) aesthetics self-expression was considered to be justified only if the artist had by severe self-discipline and rigorous cultivation brought his empirical personality into harmony with a cosmic Reality so that by expressing himself he was in fact expressing the spirit of a higher, more ultimate Being. (See pp. 87–96.) By Chinese critics and connoisseurs art was thought of primarily and typically as an activity of a ritualistic nature by which the cultured personality is manifested and leaves its mark on the history of civilized society. At the same time it was a manifestation and an embodiment of the cosmic spirit of the Tao.

V. Medieval and Renaissance Aesthetics

The naturalistic attitude in art appears as an aspect of the scientific attitude to nature which emerged at the high point of Greek civilization. It is a habit of mind which treats nature as something external to and set apart from man, something to be studied and observed with scientific objectivity, mastered and harnessed to man's uses, reacted to emotionally or in art to be mirrored, flattered, or improved. In Chinese thought nature and man were not in opposition. Man was assumed to be an integral part of a more stupendous nature: the same life processes and rhythms transfused man and nature. The ideal was to bring about unification of the individual with the cosmic principle, not to master, reproduce or scientifically observe.

During the Middle Ages in the West the naturalistic outlook inherited from classical antiquity was tempered by theological doctrine which regarded both nature and man as the creation of a supreme Deity. The nature of Deity was manifested in His creation and external nature came to be regarded as a *symbol* to man of the Divine Nature. On a less philosophical plane works of art in the Byzantine era took on the character of *theophanies,* manifestations of a transcendent Deity, or of *icons,* objects through which man's devotion could be channeled to the supreme God. In Western Europe Christian art assumed a more directly didactic character or was given a decorative function to glorify the Church on earth. In both these manifestations a religious conception of art was imposed upon but did not entirely change the naturalistic attitude which preceded.

Furthermore, just as in classical antiquity, despite the fine efflorescence of artistic creation, works of art were not valued by aesthetic criteria or appraised for their power to evoke aesthetic enjoyment, but for other secondary purposes they served; so during the Middle Ages there was lacking any overt aesthetic standard, and works of art were discussed in relation to the uses which they could be made to serve. From the point of view of modern aesthetics the values set upon them were instrumental and not intrinsic.

THE THEOLOGICAL CHARACTER OF MEDIEVAL AESTHETICS

"Conscious aesthetic values," wrote Mr. Frank P. Chambers in *The History of Taste* (1932), "would seem to be as wanting in the so-called Dark Ages or Middle Ages of Western Europe as at the height of the Greek era." And in almost the same words André Malraux wrote: "The Middle Ages had no more idea of the concept we express by the word 'art' than had the Greeks or Egyptians, who had no word to express it." To medieval thinking the concept of beauty implied no special connection with what we call the fine arts. Indeed music alone of the fine arts was ranked among the "liberal arts" and poetry was a pendant to logic. Even with music it was the mathematical theory of the musical scales which was held in respect rather than composition and performance. "The performance of plainsong," says Frank Lloyd Harrison (*British Journal of Aesthetics,* vol. 3, no. 2), "was one of the elements in a cycle of ritual acts, the rehearsing of which had no overt aesthetic connotations in the modern sense. It was not aimed, as much church music since the Reformation has been aimed, at arousing devotional or mystical feelings in a congregation. The presence or absence of listeners was quite irrelevant to its function as part of a liturgical ceremony."

In the Middle Ages aesthetics became a branch of theology and lost any incipient link with connoisseurship which it had acquired during the Roman Empire. To the medieval mind the visible world was a symbol of the divine and had neither meaning nor importance except as a symbol. Created things had reality only as manifestations of the divine Nature and as leading to an apprehension of that Nature. The work of art, like all created things, was thought of as an image or symbol, that is a theophany. It achieved its purpose as revelation of the Divine Nature not by naturalistic representation of the persceptible world but by evidencing in its own structure that concinnity or mathematically and intellectually apprehensible consonance among dissimilar parts in which the beauty of the whole universe was thought to reside. Beauty was not conceived as a value independent of other values but rather as the radiance of truth (*splendor veritatis*) shining through the symbol, which was also the splendor of ontological perfection, that quality of things which reflects their origin in God and enables us through them to attain direct insight into the perfection of the Divine Nature. Thus it was a quality ultimately apprehensible to reason rather than the senses. Maximus the Confessor typically defined "symbolic vision" as ability to apprehend through the objects of sense perception the invisible reality of the intelligible that lay behind them. Indeed the dominant motive of religious life and philosophy throughout the Middle Ages was a desire to ascend from the sensory world of shadows and images to direct contemplation of divine perfection, to behold the sacred reality of ultimate truth with the bodily eyes.

This attitude was directly opposed to the naturalism of antiquity and to the classical delight in sensuous, physical beauty, which is apparent in their art and literature though it is taken for granted in the theory. Here and there in the writings of the early Church Fathers we may find incidental evidence of appreciation for the beauties of nature as keen as anything in pagan literature. But this feeling came to be held suspect and all allurement of delight in the sensuous enjoyment of the world of natural things came to be condemned both on moralistic and on theological grounds. The passages in St. Augustine's *Confessions* where he repudiates his youthful addiction to natural beauty and to the sensuous allure of music hung like a pall over medieval thought. True beauty, it was assumed, transcends the sensuous sphere, belongs only to God, and is apprehended either through intellectual or, more perfectly, through mystical intuition. It is manifested in mathematical harmony, proportion, and "concinnity" not by sensual charm. The enjoyment of sensuous beauty and the delight in natural things for their own sake was discouraged. This attitude is aptly summed up in the words of Scotus Erigena: "It is not that creation is bad nor yet the knowledge of it; but the perverse impulse which leads the reasonable mind to abandon the contemplation of its author and turn with lustful and illicit appetite to the love of sensible matter." From similar motives St. Bernard tried to make himself insensible to natural beauty for Christ's sake. In 1335 the poet Petrarch, ahead of his time, felt aesthetic delight in the grandeur of Mount Ventoux, but realizing his fault took out a copy of the *Confessions* and suppressed his feelings of pleasure: ". . . angry with myself for not ceasing to admire things of the earth, instead of remembering that the human soul is beyond comparison the subject of admiration. Once again I descended the mountain, I gazed back, and the lofty summit seemed to me scarcely a cubit high compared with the sublime dignity of man."

The immense gulf between this, a striking if reluctant statement of medieval orthodoxy, and the Chinese attitude to nature hardly needs emphasizing. Like the Chinese, medieval aesthetic was opposed to naturalism. But unlike the Chinese it was an appendage of a theological system which was external and alien to aesthetic considerations. While for the Chinese the art object was both a result and an expression of achieved unity between man and nature, in medieval thought it was a theophany, a revelation or manifestation of a God above nature and intellectually apprehensible, so that the aesthetic way of contact with works of art was subordinated always to the religious. To the end of his life St. Augustine remained firm in the belief that "number" can lead the

The "Good Shepherd" mosaic, fifth century A.D.
*Mausoleo di Galla Placidia, Ravenna. The Mansell Collection
of Photographs. Photo: Anderson.*

mind from the sensuous perception of material things to apprehension of the invisible truth in God. Otto von Simson has well remarked in *The Gothic Cathedral* (1956): "In admiration of its architectural perfection religious emotions overshadowed the observer's aesthetic reaction. It was no different with those who built the cathedrals." The cathedral was regarded both as a model of the cosmos in that it was designed to reproduce in its plan and proportions the mathematical structure of the created universe, and as an image of the Celestial City, of the perfection of the world to come. It was a commonplace that the mathematics of musical theory embodied a universal cosmic principle of harmony. The *Musica Enchiriadis* (A.D. 860) found the deeper and divine reasons underlying musical harmonies in the eternal laws of the cosmos. In the Introduction to his *Speculum Musicae* Jacobus of Liège wrote:

"Music (i.e., musical theory), understood in a general sense, applies objectively to all things, to God and created things, incorporeal and corporeal, to both the theoretical and the practical sciences." Abelard suggested that the proportions of the Temple at Jerusalem were those of the musical consonances and that this symphonic perfection made it an image of heaven. Scotus Erigena held that by the laws of harmony and proportion all contrarieties and dissonances among the individual entities within the universe are reconciled and in this musical law he saw the source of all beauty. "For no beauty is effected unless from the congruence of similars and dissimilars, contraries and opposites" (De divisione naturae, V, 36).

To the medieval mind the sensuous qualities of the visible world were suspect: an allure, but a screen between rational man and divine reality. The true apprehensible reality lay in the concinnity, in formal harmonies. This mathematical concinnity or beauty, it was thought, the artist could genuinely create by embodying such proportions in the art object without aiming at an accurate or illusory image of visible things.

Therefore if we conceive of aesthetics as a branch of philosophy specially connected with the theory of fine art or indeed even if we conceive it as an autonomous theory of beauty, we cannot properly speak of medieval aesthetics. During the medieval period aesthetics was a branch of theologically orientated philosophy which had no essential connection either with fine art or with the physical beauties of nature.

DIDACTIC FUNCTION AND THE MORAL CRITERION

On a rather different plane ecclesiastical art in the Middle Ages was frankly didactic in character. Held in suspicion at first as the relics and depositories of paganism, the arts were gradually accepted on sufferance as the Church came to realize their usefulness for educating a rude and illiterate populace in the rudiments of Christian morality and doctrine. This was particularly the case in the West, but in the East also the didactic motive was by no means absent. In an article on "Byzantine art as a religious and didactic art" (British Journal of Aesthetics, vol. 7, no. 2) Professor P. A. Michelis began: "Byzantine art, especially Byzantine painting, was not only a religious but also a *didactic* art. Its object was by its icons to teach the Christian Orthodox religion even to the illiterate. In the words of Basil the Great: 'What the verbal account presents to the ear the silent picture reveals by imitation.'" The icon was called by Gregory of Nyssa a "language-bearing book," serving to instruct even the unlettered purely through contemplation of the painting. In *The Social Theory of Art* Arnold Hauser (1951) said:

> In the opinion of the Middle Ages art would be superfluous if everyone could read and follow an abstract chain of reasoning; art was originally looked upon just as a concession to the ignorant masses who are so easily influenced by the impressions of the senses. It was certainly not allowed to be a "mere pleasure of the eye," as St. Nilus put it. Its didactic

Spanish Romanesque mural depicting David's victory over Goliath, probably twelfth century A.D. *Museum of Catalan Art, Barcelona.*

Miniature from the Nero Codex depicting the Flight into Egypt (top) and the Massacre of the Innocents (bottom), twelfth century A.D. *Courtesy of the Trustees of the British Museum, London.*

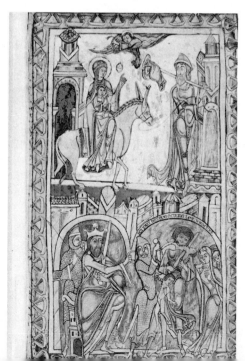

character is the most typical feature of Christian art, as compared with that of the ancients.

This didactic conception of the function of painting may be illustrated from the poetic account written in the early years of the fifth century by Paulinus, Bishop of Nola, who grew concerned at the dancing and merrymaking with which his flock whiled away the hours of vigil during the festival of the patron saint of his church and who in the hope of educating them to a better frame of mind conceived the idea of covering the walls of the church with sacred pictures, both edifying and attractive, in the hope that "the forms and colors might seize upon the astonished minds of the country folk." For, he explains,

> *while the whole multitude in turn point out the pictures one to another, or go over them by themselves, they are less quick than before to think of feasting, and feed with their eyes instead of their lips. In this way, while in wonder at the paintings they forget their hunger, a better habit lays gradual hold on them, and as they read the sacred histories they learn from pious examples how honourable are holy deeds and how satisfying to thirst is sobriety. (Paulinus Nolanus, Poema de S. Fel. natal., ix, 541 ff.)*

A thousand years later Vasari puts into the mouth of the Florentine painter Buonamico Cristofano, called Buffamalco, the words: "we think of nothing but painting saints, both men and women, on walls and pictures . . . we thereby render men better and more devout to the great despite of the demons." In literary theory too it was a commonplace that, in the Horatian phrase, the function of poetry is to instruct and to improve through pleasuring. The doctrine was not always held in so crude a form as when Aeneas Silvius Piccolomini wrote in his treatise *De Liberorum Educatione* (1450) that all other matter of the poets should be neglected save only what they write in praise of virtue and in condemnation of vice. Bernardino Daniello indeed voiced a point of view which lasted more than a millennium when he remarked that: "Poetry can teach more pleasantly than the philosopher by concealing useful lessons in fictions and fables as physicians cover pills with sweet coatings." In similar vein Boccaccio found poetry's justification that "it lures

Fra Luca Pacioli Explains a
Theorem to a Young Man.
Formerly attributed to Jacopo de' Barbari.
Museo Nazionale, Naples.
The Mansell Collection of
Photographs. Photo: Anderson.

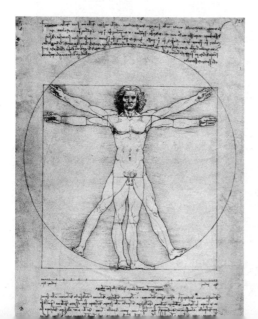

The Proportions of the
Human Figure *by*
Leonardo da Vinci after
Vitruvius, ca. *1492.*
Pen-and-ink drawing.
Academia, Venice.
The Mansell Collection
of Photographs.
Photo: Alinari.

Illustration from the MS of
La Divina Proporcion
by Luca Pacioli,
1509. Courtesy of the
Trustees of the
British Museum, London.

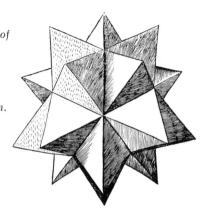

Comedy from
The First Book
of Architecture
by Sebastiano Serlio,
Venice, 1545. Woodcut.
Courtesy of
the Trustees of
the British Museum,
London.

Dr M, Sebaſtien Serlio

away noble souls from those foundering under moral disease," and in his *Apologie for Poetrie* two centuries later Sir Philip Sidney describes it as "virtue-breeding delightfulness." Tasso, somewhat impatient at the moralistic bent, makes his confession: "I have spent most of my efforts in attempting to please, as it seems to me more necessary and also more difficult to attain; for we have found by experience that many poets may instruct and benefit us very much, but certainly give us very little delight."

This didactic conception of art may be compared and contrasted with the moral criterion which was predominant in antiquity. Plato

The Ancient of Days *from* Europe *by William Blake, 1794. Engraving. Courtesy of the Trustees of the British Museum, London.*

admitted some modes of music because of their strengthening and stimulating effects on the character and condemned others because they led to overindulgence in emotionalism. In general he condemned drama because in his opinion it encouraged indulgence of the sympathetic emotions. The Greeks were an emotionally labile people and in all their social philosophy they were obsessed by the need to hold in check a tendency to emotionalism, subordinating it to reasoned self-interest in a social context and putting forward as the moral ideal temperance and moderation. Aristotle took the opposite line from Plato and in his doctrine of *catharsis* held that the arts provide an innocuous outlet for pent-up emotions which are denied their full natural outlet in the conditions of social life. But although their conclusions were contrary, the criterion was the same. The arts were assessed in terms of their effects in ameliorating or debasing the character of the individual as a social unit and for their supposed effects on the social organism itself.

ST. THOMAS AQUINAS

The metaphysical and rationalistic character of medieval aesthetics is exemplified in its treatment by St. Thomas Aquinas (1225–74). He wrote little specifically on the theory of beauty (what he had to say is virtually comprised in three passages from the *Summa Theologica*), but what he wrote was of central significance. He discusses beauty as an aspect of the good—"beauty and goodness in a thing are identical fundamentally"—namely that aspect which consists in a thing's adaptedness for sensory cognition. He defined goodness as desirability—"everything is good insofar as it is desirable"—and a thing is desirable insofar only as it is perfect of its sort. Following previous philosophers he divided goodness into the fitting, the useful, and the pleasant. Beauty belongs to the last aspect of goodness, being that which is pleasant to cognition, in its mere contemplation and awareness. In medieval thought cognition was thought of as a kind of assimilation, as if in knowing something one identified with its form, with that which makes it essentially what it is; and as order and rationality make a thing apprehensible to reason, so due proportion renders the objects of sense apprehensible to sensory cognition. Beauty, says St. Thomas, is

Le Chahut *by*
Georges Seurat, 1890.
Courtesy of the
Rijksmuseum
Kröller-Müller,
Otterlo, Holland.

distinguished from other aspects of goodness in that it relates to cognition.

> *For beautiful things are those which please when seen* (pulchra enim dicuntur quae visa placent). *Hence beauty consists in due proportion; for the senses delight in things duly proportioned, as in what is after their own kind because even sense is a sort of reason just as is every cognitive faculty. Now, since knowledge is by assimilation, and similarity relates to form, beauty properly belongs to the nature of a formal cause.* (Summa, *Q. 5, Art. 4.*)

Though their terminology is different, there is an affinity with Kant's doctrine that beauty consists in the suitability of a thing for human cognition, its adaptedness to the cognitive faculties, and that we recognize it by the special pleasure taken in the free and harmonious play of the cognitive faculties which a beautiful object makes possible.

The beautiful [says St. Thomas again] *is the same as the good, and they differ in aspect only. For since good is what all seek, the notion of good is that which calms desire; while the notion of the beautiful is that which calms the desire by being seen or known. Consequently, those senses chiefly regard the beautiful which are the most cognitive, viz. sight and hearing, as ministering to reason; for we speak of beautiful sights and beautiful sounds. But in reference to the objects of the other senses we do not use the expression "beautiful" for we do not speak of beautiful tastes and beautiful odours. Thus it is obvious that beauty adds to goodness a relation to the cognitive faculty; so that "good means that which simply pleases the appetite, while the beautiful is something pleasant in the mere apprehension of it"* (id cuius ipsa apprehensio placet). (Summa, *Part I–II. Q. 27, Art. 1.*)

The third passage which has been held significant runs as follows:

Beauty includes three conditions: integrity or perfection (integritas sive perfectio) *since things which are imperfect are by that very fact ugly; due proportion or harmony* (debita proportio sive consonantia) *; and lastly brightness or clarity* (claritas), *whence things are called beautiful which have a bright colour.* (Summa, *Q. 39, Art. 8.*)

The precise meaning of these conditions has been often discussed, the most widely known of the many discussions being that in James Joyce's *A Portrait of the Artist as a Young Man.* It would carry us too far from our main theme to enter into a detailed exposition of Thomistic interpretation. The following, however, may be noted.

The idea that beauty consists in perfection has had a long history and is particularly associated with the eighteenth-century philosopher Thomas Reid. In modern times it has been held—by Charles Lalo and others, as has already been mentioned (p. 48)—that one sense at least of the word "beauty" is that in which a thing is said to be beautiful if it is a perfect example of its kind. This concept of beauty was repudiated by Kant on the ground that it presupposes a doctrine of natural kinds and requires a concept of the "type" against which a thing is judged intellectually to be more or less a perfect exemplar. If it has an aesthetic bearing at all, such a theory has meaning for the idea of *intellectual* beauty. It is opposed to the more characteristic modern aesthetic trends which regard beauty as the quality in an object which enables it to arouse and sustain nontheoretical contemplation in an attitude of direct awareness. The phrase "due proportion or harmony" is usually interpreted in medieval thought as a requirement that a thing be adapted to the purpose for which that thing is supposed to exist or conformable to the type to which it belongs. Unless it is understood as an internal proportion among its constituent parts which renders a thing adapted to aesthetic contemplation, this requirement cuts across most systems of post-Kantian aesthetics. "Clarity" is a word which has very wide variations of meaning in medieval writing. It often means the quality of absolute convincingness which a thing, however abstruse, may have for the reason once it has been apprehended. It may mean simply that a thing is clearly seen for what it is by reason of precise shape or, as St. Thomas suggests, bright color. In a more profound sense it may on occasion approximate to the quality of "perspicuity" which the modern philosopher J. N. Findlay has argued is a fundamental aesthetic category (see pp. 260–261).

PRINCIPLES OF RENAISSANCE AESTHETICS

During the Renaissance important advances were made in the practice and techniques of the visual arts leading in the direction of greater naturalism and there was a particularly close linkage between the nascent interest in empirical science and the study of the arts. The discovery of scientific perspective and the elaboration of mathematical theories of proportion were outstanding achievements of the period. But between 1400 and 1600 there was no contribution of importance to philosophical aesthetics or the theory of literature. The revival of interest in classical antiquity was reflected in artistic theory, and the general tone of the period was set by the eclectic Platonism of Marsilio Ficino (1433–99), founder of the new Academy in 1462. The main principles which dominated the Renaissance outlook in aesthetics for some two centuries may be summarized as follows:

1. The arts of painting and sculpture are a thing of mind and intelligence—*cosa mentale*—a branch of learning and not merely or primarily a matter of craftsmanship. This conception was closely

linked with the new social status claimed for the artist as a scholar and gentleman instead of an artisan.

2. Art and poetry "imitate nature" and to this end the empirical sciences provide useful guidance.

3. The plastic arts, like literature, also pursue a moral purpose of social amelioration, aspiring to the ideal.

4. Beauty, which is also the goal of the arts, is an objective property of things, consisting in order, harmony, proportion, and propriety (*concinnitas* and *decorum*). This concinnity could, at any rate in part, be expressed mathematically.

5. Poetry and the visual arts achieved perfection and a definitive form in classical antiquity, since when the secret has been lost and the arts have declined.

6. The arts are subject to rules of perfection which are rationally apprehensible and can be precisely formulated and taught. These rules are inherent in the works of classical antiquity and can be learned by study of these works and of nature.

Formalized and reduced to system these principles provided the basis for the classicism which was taught in the Academies, for the ideal of the Grand Manner and for the intellectualism of the seventeenth-century Enlightenment. About the turn of the century, however, in and about the year 1600, there was a strange if short-lived emergence of conflicting and anticlassical ideas which to some extent foreshadowed the outlook of the later Romantic Age. It is worthwhile briefly to signalize this episode, which rarely finds a place in the standard histories.

Francesco Patrizi (1529–97), an Italian philosopher and theorist, wrote a treatise on poetry in ten parts of which the first two were published in 1586 and the rest remained in manuscript until discovered quite recently in the Biblioteca Palatina of Parma. While during the Renaissance the idea of poetic inspiration was typically subordinated to the natural capacities of the artist with reason at their head (as for example in the *Poetica d'Aristotele vulgarizzata* of Lodovico Castelvetro, 1576), Patrizi held that the *furor poeticus* is the source of all genuine achievement in the arts. Contrary to the classical doctrine of imitation (*mimesis*) he held that the artist is first and foremost a creator (*facitor*), not copying nature but giving expression to his own creative imagination. His view that poetry is a transformation of nature (*finzione*) foreshadowed the Romantic theory of fiction. He held that the one essential quality of fine art is the marvelous (*maraviglia*) : the poet is one who creates the marvelous in his verse (*il facitore del mirabile in verso*) .

In somewhat similar vein the Polish Jesuit poet and theorist Kazimierz Maciej Sarbiewski (1595–1640) maintained that creativity in the sense of imaginative fiction is the essence of poetry (though not of painting or sculpture). The poet, like God, constructs (*quomodo condit*) and creates his new work (*de novo creat*) and every poem is as it were a world of its own (*quoddam mundus*) .

Giordano Bruno (1548–1600), again, in *The Heroic Enthusiasts,* which he dedicated to Sir Philip Sidney, retains many of the typical medieval-Renaissance ideas of an absolute Beauty which contrasts with the beauties of the senses but which can be approached by their help as it were by stepping stones. He conceives the ideal beauty in terms of harmony and consonance intellectually apprehended. But at the same time he exalts the artist as a superior man, a hero who transcends the rules and whose work is interesting because he stamps it with the mark of his own superior personality—coming very close in all this to the Romantic conception of the artist-genius. "Poetry," he wrote, "is not born of rules unless by an accident. But rules are derived from poetry and therefore there are as many correct rules as there are kinds and species of true poets." There is a curiously close parallel with the statement of Francis Bacon in his essay *On Beauty*:

> *There is no excellent beauty which has not some strangeness in the proportion. A man cannot tell whether Apelles or Albert Dürer were the more trifler; whereof the one would make a personage by geometrical proportions; the other by taking the best parts of divers faces to make one excellent. Such personages, I think, would please nobody but the painter that made them. Not but I think a painter may make a better face than ever was; but he must do it by a kind of felicity, as a musician that maketh an excellent air in music, and not by rule.* [Some of this foreshadows what Kant wrote about the works of genius.]

Amidst the many diverse and sometimes conflicting aesthetic principles which were professed during the Renaissance, the new humanistic outlook, the revival of classicism, and the later reign of academic rule and regulation, the one theory which proved most persistent and which predominated into the seventeenth century was that which regarded a work of art, whether poetry or visual art, as a reflection or mirror of reality, but a reality idealized and brought more into accordance with men's desires than the actual world in which we live and move. This is the theory of aesthetic idealism, the form of naturalism which maintains that it is the function and the excellence of art to mirror a reality such as men would have it be rather than reality as they know it to be in experience. Perhaps the most concise and exact formulation of this doctrine of idealistic naturalism in relation to the arts is to be found in Francis Bacon's account of poetry in his great work *Of the Proficiency and Advancement of Learning* (1605). He defines poetry as "feigned history" and writes of it as follows:

> *The use of this feigned history hath been to give some shadow of satisfaction to the mind of man in those points wherein the nature of things doth deny it, the world being in proportion inferior to the soul; by reason whereof there is, agreeable to the spirit of man, a more ample greatness, a more exact goodness, and a more subtle variety, than can be found in the nature of things. Therefore, because the acts of events of true history have not that magnitude which satisfieth the mind of man, poesy feigneth acts and events greater and more heroical; because true history propoundeth the successes and issues of actions not so agreeable to the merits of virtue and vice, therefore poesy feigns them more just in retribution, and more according to revealed providence: because true history representeth actions and events more ordinary, and less interchanged; therefore poesy endueth them with more rareness, and more unexpected and alternative variations: so as it appeareth that poesy serveth and conferreth to magnanimity, morality and to delectation. And therefore it was ever thought to have some participation of divineness, because it doth raise and erect the mind, by submitting the shows of things to the desires of the mind; whereas reason doth buckle and bow the mind unto the nature of things.*

It is significant that Bacon classifies poetry (and the arts) as a branch of learning or knowledge. Of the three divisions of knowledge History belongs to Memory, Philosophy (under which he includes theology and science) to the Reason, and Poetry to Imagination. While memory is confined within the bounds of fact and actuality, imagination is not so restricted but "being not tied to the laws of matter, may at pleasure join that which nature hath severed, and sever that which nature hath joined, and so make unlawful matches and divorces of things." It was the function of the arts in Bacon's view to present a simulacrum of reality, but they avail themselves of the power of imagination to present a simulacrum of a reality modified to suit human ideals of what is right and proper, brought more closely into accordance with human desires and generally smartened up and titivated to be more interesting and exiting than the humdrum reality of actual life. Of the many writers who shared this view of the function of art not all found the same justification for the arts. The most highflown spoke of the artist as one who partakes of the functions of deity, creating a world better than the world we know. Others assimilated this idealizing function to the moral purpose of art and thought that by picturing an idealized world the artist would induce the generality of men to pursue the good and the ideal: what the philosopher taught by argument and precept the artist commended by picturing an imaginary ideal world. Others again, like Bacon, regarded poetry and the arts as a refreshing but not entirely serious indulgence.

VI. Eighteenth-Century British Aesthetics

It is often said that modern aesthetics began with the eighteenth century, and more specifically with the English eighteenth-century philosophers and essayists who wrote on the theory and enjoyment of the arts. There is ground for this opinion. It was then that the aesthetic impulse in human nature, which had, we believe, throughout history guided the creation and enjoyment of art objects, emerged to consciousness and men began to be aware of and to deliberate about that special mode of contact with the environment which we now call "aesthetic." Gradually in the course of the century the concept of "fine art" came to the fore, without which there can be no independent aesthetics of art and beauty. For the first time it became possible to apply to the appreciation of the arts "autonomous" aesthetic criteria in something resembling the modern sense. New problems engaged the interest of philosophers, old problems were discussed in a new light, and new questions were asked. The tone of discussion took on a "modern" feel. Nevertheless in two quite important aspects eighteenth-century writers on aesthetics and art theory failed to anticipate the modern outlook, and in consequence of this failure much of their writing may strike the casual reader as outmoded. Because of this it is easy to overlook the revolutionary character of the new ideas which did emerge and in particular the significant switch of attention to a new set of problems which are still valid today.

We shall first mention two major respects in which eighteenth-century writing was out of line with present-day attitudes and we shall then go more fully into the nature of the revolution which took place and the manner in which the new awareness prepared the way for subsequent developments in aesthetics.

In the first place the modern assumption that the cultivation of the arts and the appreciation of beauty are "self-rewarding" activities susceptible of and needing no justification outside themselves was still foreign to eighteenth-century thought. In the eighteenth century, on the contrary, as had been the case throughout European history from classical antiquity, it was taken for granted that appreciation is an indulgence which needs to be justified in its results. Most writers sought to justify the arts as a source of innocent pleasure, a harmless means of preserving the mind from vacuity, or as a beneficial relaxation favoring cultivation of the higher intellectual and moral impulses. The beauties of nature particularly, but also the beauties of art, were often extolled for their influence in leading to a reverential apprehension of Divine Providence and for inclining the mind to ponder on manifestations of Divine purpose in the universe. The tone was set by Addison when he wrote that the Pleasures of the Imagination

do not require such a Bent of Thought as is necessary to our more serious Employments, nor, at the same time, suffer the Mind to sink into that Negligence and Remissness, which are apt to accompany our more sensual Delights, but, like a gentle exercise of the faculties, awaken them from Sloth and Idleness, without putting them upon any Labour or Difficulty. (Spectator, No. 416, 1712.)

His tribute to the art of horticulture (at that time regarded as one of the "fine arts") was typical of much that was to follow:

> *I look upon the Pleasure which we take in a Garden as one of the most innocent Delights in human Life. . . . It is naturally apt to fill the Mind with Calmness and Tranquillity, and to lay all its turbulent Passions at rest. It gives us a great Insight into the Contrivance and Wisdom of Providence, and suggests innumerable Subjects for Meditation.* (Spectator, No. 477.)

So Hugh Blair, in his *Lectures on Rhetoric and Belles Lettres* (1783), says: "The pleasures of taste refresh the mind after the toils of the intellect, and the labours of abstract study; and they gradually raise it above the attachments of sense, and prepare it for the enjoyment of virtue." So too in his very influential *Elements of Criticism* (1762) Lord Kames emphasized the moral effects of appreciation in fostering the social and sympathetic affections, while criticism strengthens the reasoning powers and thus prepares us for the more arduous labors of science. Archibald Alison at the end of the century sums up this attitude when he says of the emotions of taste: "From the earliest period of Society, to its last stage of improvement, they afford an innocent and elegant amusement to private life, at the same time that they increase the Splendour of National Character; and in the Progress of Nations, as well as of individuals, while they attract attention from the pleasures they bestow, they serve to exalt the human mind from corporeal to intellectual pursuits" (*Essays on the Nature and Principles of Taste,* 1790). The conception of the enjoyment of beauty as a harmless indulgence, a healthy relaxation or a useful ancillary to more important and exacting activities has something in common with the Plato of the *Laws* and even more in common with the views expressed by Aristotle in the *Politics*, but is opposed to the assumption, which colors most modern writing on the arts, that the appreciation of beauty and its cultivation in the arts has an intrinsic value of its own germane to the development of a fully rounded personality.

The second important respect in which eighteenth-century attitudes differed from those which prevail today is in the primacy which they gave to natural over artistic beauty and the common assumption that the beauty of a work of art is derived from the beauty of that which it depicts. Burke made this assumption explicit. "Painting," he said, "when we have allowed for the pleasures of imitation, can only affect simply as the images it presents . . . because the images in painting are exactly similar to those in nature." Even Kant, who is rightly regarded as the founder of modern aesthetics, endorsed the preference for natural beauty and in discussing the beauties of art never wholly won free from the trammels of traditional naturalism. "The superiority which natural beauty has over that of art," he says, "even when it is excelled by the latter in point of form, in yet being alone able to awaken an immediate interest, accords with the refined and well-grounded habits of thought of all men who have cultivated their moral feeling. If a man with taste enough to judge of works of fine art with the greatest correctness and refinement readily quits the room in which he meets with those beauties that minister to vanity or, at least, social joys, and betakes himself to the beautiful in nature, so that he may find there as it were a feast for his soul in a train of thought which he can never completely evolve, we will then regard this his choice even with veneration, and give him credit for a beautiful soul, to which no connoisseur or art collector can lay claim on the score of the interest which his objects have for him" (*Critique of Judgment,* p. 48). Kant distinguished between "free beauty" (*pulchritudo vaga*) on the one hand, which belongs to natural objects such as flowers and shells where we have no preformed concept of functional type and to nonrepresentational art such as nonvocal music and arabesque; and on the other hand "dependent beauty" (*pulchritudo adhaerens*), where beauty implies recognition of a thing's perfection in relation to a preformed idea of the type or purpose. Only judgments about beauty of the former type were regarded by him as genuine or pure aesthetic judgments. Despite Kant's theory of "aesthetical ideas," we miss in his writings and in other writings of the age any clear understanding of what has now become a commonplace, the fact namely that works of art, even though they are figurative and representational, may nevertheless exist as objects with a beauty of their own, to be enjoyed for what they are as natural objects are enjoyed without any necessary idea of purpose or type, and that the beauty we appreciate in representational art is not necessarily at all a reflection of some natural beauty inhering in the objects represented.

In these two respects eighteenth-century thought fell short of modern ideas. In most other respects it was both revolutionary and fertile for the future.

THE DISINTERESTED ATTITUDE

Historically the notion of "disinterestedness" came into prominence in opposition to the "intelligent egoism" of Thomas Hobbes, who had argued that all the precepts of morality and religion can be reduced at bottom to enlightened self-interest. Against this view Lord Shaftesbury (1671–1713), together with Cudworth and the Cambridge Platonists, maintained that virtue and goodness must of necessity be "disinterested." They must be pursued for their own sake and not from motives of self-interest. Actions done from fear of consequences or in the hope of reward—that is "interested" actions—however enlightened the self-interest may be, have no moral value. In the religious sphere the concept of "disinterested" love of God—that is love of God for Himself and not from hopes of heaven or fear of hell—arose out of a controversy between the Jansenists and the Jesuits. In a letter to the Scottish savant Burnet, written in 1697, Leibniz defined disinterested love as "finding one's pleasure in the happiness of another." When Burke in his *Enquiry* defined beauty as "that quality . . . in bodies by which they cause love," he used a very similar conception of love, distinguishing it from "desire or lust, which is an energy of the mind that hurries us on to the possession of certain objects" and describing it as the satisfaction which "arises to the mind on the contemplation of anything beautiful." This was the sense in which "disinterestedness" became a guiding concept in eighteenth-century aesthetics. It has become a commonplace of aesthetics today that appreciation of beauty requires a "disinterested" attitude of attention, a state of mind in which we are absorbed in the object presented, in becoming fully and completely aware of the object itself without being deflected by concern for its practical and utilitarian implications. But in the eighteenth century the idea was a new one. The word "disinterested" did not, of course, imply lack of interest in the object of attention but the absence of any "self-interest," any considerations of advantage or utility, and indeed any interest at all other than the direct contemplation of the object and satisfaction achieved from our awareness of it.

Shaftesbury contrasted the "disinterested attention" which is essential to what we now call the "aesthetic attitude" with any desire to use or possess or otherwise manipulate the object of attention. Our interest, if it is an aesthetic interest, "terminates" in the object and we are wholly engrossed in perceiving, contemplating, and perfecting our awareness of the object upon which our attention is directed. Shaftesbury proposed as a paradigm of this attitude our enjoyment of mathematics, where our perception does not relate to any "private interest of the creature, nor has for its object any self-good or advantage." As he says: "The admiration, joy, or love turns wholly upon what is exterior and foreign to ourselves." Hutcheson went further and eloquently distinguished aesthetic awareness from the analytical and discursive understanding which belongs to scientific observation and theoretical reasoning. When we contemplate something aesthetically, whether it is a natural scene or a beautiful statue, we direct perception upon qualities—those qualities now termed "aesthetic properties"—which are not susceptible of measurement or analysis, which belong to the object as a unified whole and cannot be built up out of the elements into which it is analyzed for scientific purposes. In this contrast between scientific and aesthetic perception Hutcheson anticipated the German philosopher Baumgarten, who originated the term "aesthetics." This aspect of eighteenth-century thought was summed up by Archibald Alison, who excluded from the field of the aesthetic "the useful, the agreeable, the fitting, or the convenient in objects."

In similar fashion aesthetic pleasure regarded as a satisfaction in the mere apprehension of the object of aesthetic attention was distinguished from what Addison called the "grosser" pleasures of the senses and from the satisfaction of desire. Hutcheson stated that aesthetic enjoyment is not connected with allaying any "uneasiness of appetite" but is inherent in the act of apprehension itself when exercised upon an appropriate object. Shaftesbury maintained that aesthetic pleasure has nothing to do with "interested regard" but

"can be no other than what results from the love of truth, proportion, order and symmetry in the things without." Here in embryo
we may see the notion of "disinterested pleasure," which was a key
concept in the aesthetics of Kant. From Kant the idea of disinterested pleasure as distinctive of aesthetic experience remained central with Schiller and the German Idealists until it was reformu-
lated and popularized in this country by Vernon Lee in *The
Beautiful* (1913), a book which had considerable popularity in the
early decades of this century.

Among Shaftesbury's followers we see also the first hints of an
interest in the psychological or phenomenological examination of
aesthetic experience. Casual but often penetrating remarks about
the state of mind appropriate to aesthetic appreciation bear witness
to an interest in the subjective, psychological approach heralding
the enormous importance which this has assumed in contemporary
aesthetics. As an example we may refer to Hume, who in his essay
Of the Standard of Taste said of the feelings by which we respond
to beauty:

> *Those finer emotions of the mind are of a very tender and delicate
> nature, and require the concurrence of many favourable circumstances
> to make them play with facility and exactness, according to their general
> and established principles.The least exterior hindrance to such small
> springs, or the least internal disorder, disturbs their motion, and con-
> founds the operations of the whole machine. When we would make an
> experiment of this nature, and would try the force of any beauty or
> deformity, we must choose with care a proper time and place, and bring
> the fancy to a suitable situation and disposition. A perfect serenity of
> mind, a recollection of thought, a due attention to the subject; if any of
> these circumstances be wanting, our experiment will be fallacious and
> we shall be unable to judge of the catholic and universal beauty.*

Hume also thought that in order to achieve the "natural" and
appropriate response we must slough off the "prejudices" of our age
and time, discard the particular influences of our education, temperament and the society in which we live, and react to the artwork
as a "man in general."

This power of dissociation at which Hume hints has been the
most remarkable feature in the emancipation of artistic apprecia-

tion during the last hundred years, as the revolution in aesthetic consciousness which had its roots in the eighteenth century has come to fruition. Partly this emancipation has been helped by the opening up of a vastly heterogeneous and hitherto inaccessible artistic heritage from widely separated ages and cultures. Not until the art products of the world were displayed in isolation from the living cultures which gave them birth could people begin to see them with mature aesthetic awareness as works of art divorced from the social or religious purposes for which they were made, stripped of the extra-aesthetic values which they once carried. When the art objects of the past have ceased to be cult objects or social symbols and have become for us products of "fine art," we no longer know or greatly care what functions they were fashioned to serve, whether utilitarian, social, or magicoreligious. If we were dependent on this, they would be little more for us now than objects of historical interest, for the extra-aesthetic values of which they were once the vehicles have disappeared with the flight of time. But we have found other ways of appreciating them and we respond emotionally not to the lost values but to the vehicles, to which we attribute the new values of art. It is because we are—perhaps for the first time on an extensive scale—able to abstract from the historical and changing values which works of art have been designed to communicate and confirm, that we are able to appreciate them as works of art. Previously the power to appreciate art in other traditions from one's own was restricted to the actual dissemination of ideas and technology: beyond this everything foreign seemed barbarous and grotesque. The art of each group was tied within the ideologies and institutions and technologies of the group. Appreciation was cramped within the boundaries of the familiar. No long time ago "gothic" was synonymous with "barbarous"; and Hegel and after him Friedrich Theodor Vischer, whose *Aesthetik der Wissenschaft des Schönen* (1847–57) in six large volumes set the coping stone to German Romantic aesthetics, thought that "mummylike" was an apt description of the "ascetic and ossified" forms of Byzantine painting. It is in our own age first that Hume's notion of transcending the limitations of time and place have acquired genuine significance in aesthetics. There are those who maintain that our awareness and therefore our appreciation of any human artifact is necessarily stunted and warped if we do not know the iconographical significance it had and the functions which it served for the people and in the society for which it was made. With this we need not disagree. But when the functions and significance of artifacts recovered from past ages are no more known, or when the values of which they were once bearers can no longer be accepted by us even imaginatively as values, the objects are not necessarily rubbish but may still exert an aesthetic appeal upon us. And the aesthetic value we ascribe to many such "denuded" art objects may be far higher than that which we find in other artifacts whose original significance and functions are known to us.

We return then to the idea of "disinterested" attention and "disinterested" pleasure, which from Shaftesbury until our own time has remained a key notion of all systems which recognize a special mode of experience called "aesthetic."

In an article tracing the origins of the concept of aesthetic disinterestedness to eighteenth-century British thought (*The Journal of Aesthetics and Art Criticism,* vol. 20, no. 2) Professor Jerome Stolnitz writes: "When Shaftesbury formulated the concept of 'disinterestedness,' he took the first and crucial step toward setting off the aesthetic as a distinctive mode of experience. That there is such a mode of experience was a radically new idea in Western thought." What happened was something more than just a new theory or a new twist to theoretical habits. It was more akin to the discovery of a new dimension of self-consciousness: the latent "aesthetic impulse" which from Paleolithic times had been operative though unrecognized in the arts and crafts of human manufacture first emerged to awareness so as to become a self-conscious motive. The concept of disinterestedness in theory of art had its analogue in the notion of "fine art," which first came to prominence at the same time. In the past, as has been said, works of art were made for a purpose; and like all other artifacts they were valued, for the excellence of their workmanship and for their efficiency in serving the purpose for which they were intended—as vehicles or promoters of social values, for their moral influence, their didactic uses, and so on. The concept of the "fine arts" was based on the idea of a class of artifacts constructed solely or primarily for the purpose of being contemplated aesthetically. It was very different from the medieval concept of the "liberal arts," which was based on a contrast between intellectual and manual occupations. It was indeed closer to the Greek notion of "pleasure-giving" arts, though the notion of a special kind of "disinterested" pleasure arising from aesthetic contemplation gave a very different color to the concept. Until the idea of a special aesthetic attitude of disinterested attention had been achieved it was not possible for works of art to be deliberately made or appraised in relation to their suitability for aesthetic enjoyment or for a class of "fine arts" to be recognized whose value rests not on any extraneous usefulness but on "autonomous" artistic standards.

The full implications of these ideas were not realized in the eighteenth century. They were sidetracked by different concerns which predominated in the Age of Romanticism. But they lie at the root of the most powerful and general assumption of contemporary aesthetics and practical art criticism, the assumption that works of art are to be valued and appraised at least in part by "autonomous" aesthetic standards and that these standards are related to their suitability to become objects of a special attitude of disinterested attention.

Most people would now accept almost as a matter of course the following account of the "aesthetic attitude" given by Professor Valentine and used by him for the purposes of experimental aesthetics: "We may say roughly that an aesthetic attitude, in the wider sense of the term, is being adopted wherever an object is apprehended or judged without reference to its utility or value or moral rightness; or when it is merely being contemplated" (*The Experimental Psychology of Beauty*, 1962, p. 5). In different words the metaphysical philosopher Paul Weiss expressed something very similar when he said in *The World of Art* (1961): "An aesthetic experience is all surface, and here and now. Its content is sheer quality, the immediate, the intuited, and felt aspect of things. . . . We fasten on an aesthetic object when, by a mere shift of attitude, we hold something away from nature and outside the web of conventional needs." The Polish sociological writer on aesthetics, Stanislaw Ossowski, has emphasized the "here and now" quality of aesthetic experience in his book *U Podstaw Estetyki* (third edition, 1958, pp. 271 ff). The greater part of our active life, he says, is lived in such a way that present experience is subordinated to the future and the past. And this happens not only when we envisage some far-reaching aims, when we are planning ahead or exercising forethought. Our most ordinary and everyday perceptions are attended to primarily for their practical significance, and in the very act of perception we interpret them for their implications of what is to come. As we go about our quotidian occasions, whenever we are expectant, whenever we are anxious or apprehensive, hopeful, confident or exultant, whenever we experience something as suspicious, dangerous, or innocuous in all these and the like situations we are shaping the present experience in the light of its implications for the future. Similarly when we are surprised, disappointed, filled with regret, and self-congratulation, soothed with the comfortable feeling of familiarity and recognition or disturbed by a sense of the unfamiliar, we are experiencing the present in the context and coloring of a selected past. All these attitudes and emotions are foreign to aesthetic contemplation (although they may of course enter into the *content of a work of art* toward which we take up the aesthetic attitude of attention).

Shaftesbury's concept of "disinterested attention," or something very close to it, often appears in modern aesthetic theory under the name "aesthetic distance," a concept which was first formulated by Edward Bullough (see his " 'Physical distance' as a factor in art and an aesthetic principle," *The British Journal of Psychology*, vol. 5, no. 2, pp. 87–118; reprinted in the collected *Lectures and Essays* edited by Elizabeth Wilkinson, 1957). Bullough illustrates his idea of "distance" by our experience of a fog at sea. For most people this is one of acute unpleasantness but it can become a source of intense delight if one succeeds for the moment in disregarding the implications of danger or practical inconvenience and fixes one's attention upon the immediately presented features:

The veil surrounding you with an opaqueness as of transparent silk, blurring the outline of things and distorting their shapes into weird grotesqueness . . . the carrying power of the air, producing the impression as if you could touch some far-off siren by merely putting out your hand and letting it lose itself behind the white wall . . . the curious smoothness of the water, hypocritically denying as it were any suggestion of danger; and, above all, the strange solitude and remoteness from the world, as it can be found only on the highest mountain-tops; and the experience may acquire, by its uncanny mingling of repose and terror, a flavour of such concentrated poignancy and delight as to contrast sharply with the blind and distempered anxiety of its other aspects.

When we take up an aesthetic attitude toward something we put it as it were "out of gear with our practical, actual self, allowing it to stand outside the context of our personal needs and ends." This is the eighteenth-century attitude of disinterested attention. It is a special posture of attention which comes more naturally to some people than to others and which is susceptible of cultivation. Though often described as "objective," it is not therefore devoid of emotion and feeling. Indeed in some people aesthetic commerce with the arts is highly charged with feeling. But in making aesthetic contact with things we become alert to their emotional qualities, not by direct response[1] but as something to be observed, savored, and delicately tasted. We are not unaware of the dangers attendant on a fog at sea, and the contrast between its apparent placidity and its real potentialities of danger or annoyance lends an added piquancy to our apprehension of the immediate presented qualities on which we concentrate in the aesthetic state. But insofar as we are experiencing actual alarm or annoyance, or are intent on the proper precautions in the situation, we are responding practically and not aesthetically to the phenomenon. We may appreciate works of art as vehicles for nonaesthetic values—moral, social, religious, intellectual, and others; and the experience will be the richer for it. But if we respond directly to those other values (so the doctrine of disinterestedness or psychical distance maintains), we are not appreciating the object aesthetically as a work of art. A person who is roused to patriotic enthusiasm by a political harangue or to religious fervor by a revivalist sermon is not at the same time appreciating these as works of art. In artistic contacts, so long as they remain in the aesthetic sphere, there must necessarily be restraint from full commitment to the urgencies and values of ordinary life.

This conception of aesthetic experience, though not the experi-

---

[1] If we dance and sing and clap our hands when the band plays a jolly tune in the park, this response could at best be regarded as very imperfectly an aesthetic one.

ence itself, had its roots in eighteenth-century thought and was matured in the twentieth century. In one form or another it has permeated most of the manifold theories of art which have been current in this century.

The gradual substitution of feeling instead of reason as the fundamental criterion in our commerce with the fine arts had its roots far back in the later years of the seventeenth century when critics came bit by bit to believe that literature and art are not to be judged by reference to classical canons of correctness but rather by the direct appeal they exert on men of cultivated and refined sensibility—on "men of delicate taste" to use Hume's term. In France as early as 1687 Bouhours in *La Manière de bien penser dans les ouvrages de l'esprit* had elevated *la délicatesse* into an aesthetic principle in opposition to Boileau's *justesse*. The popularity of Longinus' treatise *On the Sublime* was in keeping with a growing tendency to emphasize the importance of emotion and sentiment in appreciation. Such terms as "sentiment," "emotion," "feeling," "imagination," "sensibility," became the new catchwords in a tendency to assert the ultimacy of individual response against the authority of reason and rule. Concurrently with this the concept of "taste" acquired a new prominence. In England during the last decade of the seventeenth century the word "taste"—new in this context—was made current by John Dryden and Sir William Temple, later to be popularized by Shaftesbury and Addison on the analogy of *gusto* and the French *goût*. The coalescing of these two tendencies led to a doctrine of aesthetic apprehension which, although later overshadowed by Romantic emotionalism, has perhaps more relevance for modern art theory than the "expression" doctrines which emerged from Romanticism.

It was assumed in the first place that when we have taken up the attitude of disinterested attention which is the hallmark of aesthetic awareness, our apprehension of beauty—or the contrary quality of "deformity"—is a direct and immediate intuition after the manner of sensation. Indeed it was often referred to as an "inner sense." Thus Shaftesbury says that beauty "is immediately perceived by a plain internal sensation." Addison preferred to speak of the "imagination" but regarded awareness of beauty as a kind of inner vision. Hutcheson, whose name is chiefly associated with the "inner sense" doctrine, was willing to use Addison's term "imagination" or the term "taste." The same writers nevertheless regarded this intuition, this "inner sense" by which we perceive beauty, as a mode of feeling—pleasure or satisfaction experienced in the mere apprehension of the object or of its formal properties. Even writers who did not specifically maintain an "inner sense" doctrine spoke of feeling as a mode of directly apprehending beauty. Hume is typical. He speaks of the "sentiment of beauty or deformity," of "feeling," "sentiment," "taste," the "finer emotions," as "internal organs" whereby we "perceive" beauty. And he elaborately compares aesthetic taste with gustatory taste. The notion of feeling as a mode of cognition operative most strikingly in the aesthetic field, introduced in the eighteenth century, is also one of the most important aspects of modern aesthetic theory insofar as it has cut loose from the heritage of Romanticism. It would be a gross mistake to confuse this idea of aesthetic feeling as a mode of cognition, analogous to an "inner sense," with the Romantic idea of feeling as a pathological effect induced in us by works of art.

In the Introduction to his *Essays* Archibald Alison defined taste as "that faculty of the Human Mind, by which we perceive and enjoy whatever is Beautiful or Sublime in the works of Nature or Art." He then goes on: "The perception of these qualities is attended with an Emotion of Pleasure, very distinguishable from every other pleasure of our Nature, and which is accordingly distinguished by the name of the Emotion of Taste." This is a surprisingly close anticipation of Clive Bell's doctrine of a unique category of aesthetic pleasure which had considerable influence in the 1920s and 1930s.[2] Bell wrote:

[2] There is this difference, typical of the difference between the centuries, that Alison thought primarily of natural beauties, which he assumed would be enjoyed by all sensitive persons; Bell, however, was concerned primarily with the beauties of art, which he attributed to "significant form," and said (in "The Metaphysical Hypothesis") that *only creative artists* are ordinarily capable of perceiving this in nature.

The starting point for all systems of aesthetics must be the personal experience of a peculiar emotion. The objects which provoke this emotion we call works of art. All sensitive people agree that there is a peculiar emotion provoked by works of art. . . . This emotion is called the aesthetic emotion; and if we can discover some quality common and peculiar to all the objects that provoke it, we shall have solved what I take to be the central problem of aesthetics.

This program of aesthetics was anticipated by Alison, who stated that "the two great objects of attention and inquiry, which seem to include all that is either necessary or perhaps possible for us to discover on the subject of Taste" are (1) "to investigate the nature of those Qualities that produce the emotions of Taste; and (2) to investigate the Nature of that Faculty, by which these Emotions are received."

Though the "inner sense" theory was too crude for contemporary philosophical taste, some writers in the eighteenth century were undoubtedly groping toward an idea of aesthetic experience which has closer affinities to current thinking than had the emotionalist theories of the Romantics. It is the idea that we become aware of beauty by a direct, quasi-perceptual intuition manifested in or somehow bound up with a special feeling of satisfaction. In much aesthetic writing today it is assumed that our apprehension of beauty is neither a matter of reasoning and argument from causes nor is it reducible to emotional response. It is regarded as a cognitive mode of experience, a direct insight attendant on clear and complete awareness of an appropriate object, yet at the same time it is emotionally colored in a way that makes it impossible to fit into a crudely categorized scheme of mental responses. That our apprehension of beauty is a matter of feeling and that it is a form of direct intuition akin to sense perception were parallel lines of thought which ran through most of the aesthetic writings of the eighteenth century.

THE STANDARD OF TASTE

Shaftesbury's idea that our apprehension of beauty is a form of direct awareness achieved through the pleasure we experience in disinterested contemplation of an appropriate object had affinities also with the medieval doctrine that the beautiful is that of which the mere apprehension is pleasant (*id cuius ipsa apprehensio placet*). But the conceptual background of the two theories was very different. For medieval philosophers thought of all cognition as a sort of identification with the object or recognition of an identity between the cognizing mind and the object cognized. All cognition was assumed to be intellectual and the world was regarded as knowable because and insofar as it was rational. Cognition by the senses was, they thought, possible because the senses "partake of the character of reason" or because sensory cognition "is analogous to reason," and it was possible insofar as the objects of sense perception display order and rationality (see p. 183). Part, but only part, of what was meant by this can be explained in modern terminology by saying that medieval thinkers recognized the conceptual character of perception. In the present context the important point is that the medieval alignment of our apprehension of beauty with the rational element in cognition guaranteed it a universality which was lost when it came to be linked more closely with feeling. Reason is presumed to be universal and the same in all men. The light of reason shines more brightly in some men than in others, but insofar as men are rational they do not differ. Feeling, however, was a different matter and variations of feeling and inclination from one man to another were seen to demand a more subjective view. The psychological and empiricist tradition, strongly inaugurated by Hobbes, effectively compelled recognition of the actual diversities of taste and quite early in the century it was accepted as a truism that men's sense of beauty is influenced by such factors as history and nationality and by the accidents of culture and temperament. In France similar views were put forward by Dubos in his *Reflexions sur la poésie et la peinture* (1719) and were supported by Diderot and Voltaire.

Furthermore, as we were thought to become aware of beauty by a kind of emotionally conditioned "inner sense" on the analogy of perception, Locke's distinction between "primary" and "secondary" qualities of things made its way into the aesthetic field. It was believed that the beauty we perceive is not a quality which the object possesses in its own right but is a function of the emotional response and apt to vary with the different emotional makeup of different observers. In his *Inquiry into the Original of Our Ideas of Beauty and Virtue* (1720) Francis Hutcheson says that by beauty "is not understood any quality supposed to be in the object, which would of itself be beautiful, without relation to any mind which perceives it." He adds: "Were there no mind with a sense of beauty to contemplate objects, I see not how they could be called beautiful." So too Addison, no robust original thinker but also a faithful mirror of his age, wrote in *The Spectator,* No. 413:

> *There is not perhaps any real beauty or deformity more in one piece of matter than another, because we might have been so made that whatever now appears loathsome to us might have shown itself agreeable; but we might find by experience that there are several modifications of matter which the mind, without any previous consideration, pronounces at first sight beautiful or deformed.*

In an essay entitled *The Sceptic* (1741) Hume maintained that the qualities in virtue of which we call things beautiful or deformed (in the vocabulary of the time "deformed" was the opposite of "beautiful") are not "really in the objects" but "depend upon the particular fabric or structure of the mind. . . . Vary the structure of the mind or inward organs [Hume's expression for the "inner sense"], the sentiment no longer follows though the form remains the same."

So it was that as aesthetic judgment was tied to feeling and emotion rather than reason, and as the empirical differences in emotional disposition among men were recognized, a new set of problems arose which until this time had not assumed major theoretical importance. It had to be asked whether beauty is in the last resort a matter of individual likes and dislikes, of individual emotional response, or whether there is an objective and valid standard of good and bad taste against which individual likings can be assessed. If there is correct and incorrect judgment about the beauty of things, what is the criterion of right and wrong judgment? Despite the powerful subjective trends it remained an article of faith with most eighteenth-century writers (including Hume) that there is "a rectitude of judgment in the arts," there is good and bad taste, and that good taste can and should be cultivated. The sturdy common sense of the age refused to lose sight of the fact that appreciation of beauty implicitly claims to be something more than the vagary of private emotion and that aesthetic judgments, as Kant later made clear, contain an implicit claim to validity. In his essay *Of the Standard of Taste* Hume repudiated the "species of philosophy" which, drawing a sharp line between the true claims of theoretical judgments on the one hand and the verdicts of "sentiment" on the other, maintained that "all sentiment [i.e., emotionally dictated responses] is right because sentiment has a reference to nothing beyond itself, and is always real wherever a man is conscious of it." Against this aesthetic relativism he says, "there is certainly a species of common sense, which opposes it, or at least serves to modify and restrain it." Like most writers of his time Hume believed it was natural and reasonable to seek a *standard of taste,* "a rule by which the various sentiments of men may be reconciled; at least a decision afforded confirming one sentiment and condemning another." Similarly in the essay "On Taste" added to the second edition of his *Enquiry* (1759) Edmund Burke, that most articulate mouthpiece of other men's ideas, stated that the purpose of his investigation was

> to find whether there are any principles, on which the imagination is affected, so common to all, so grounded and certain, as to supply the means of reasoning satisfactorily about them. And such principles of taste I fancy there are [he declares], however paradoxical they may seem to those who on a superficial view imagine that there is so great a diversity of tastes, both in kind and degree, that nothing can be more indeterminate.

Burke also affirmed his belief in the perfectibility of taste. "It is known," he says, "that the taste (whatever it is) is improved exactly as we improve our judgment, by extending our knowledge, by a steady attention to the object, and by frequent exercise." Lord Kames in the dedication of his *Elements of Criticism* to George III, says that its aim is "to form a standard of taste by unfolding those principles that ought to govern the taste of every individual" and to establish practical rules for the arts by exhibiting "their fundamental principles drawn from human nature, the true source of criticism."

The belief on the one hand in the subjectivity of beauty, a consequence of relating it to feeling and emotional response, and on the other hand in the possibility of rules and standards of right and wrong in aesthetic judgment, in good taste and bad taste, raises two problems. The first is a logical one: In what sense can emotional response be correct or incorrect? The second is an empirical problem: If there is a right and wrong in aesthetic response, how can we differentiate and find a standard?

The logical problem was seldom explicitly discussed by English eighteenth-century writers but became central to the argument of Kant's *Critique of Judgment*. It is clear, however, that Hume and probably other writers of his time dealt with it—by assuming that there is a "natural" or "appropriate" emotional response to any object and that in the absence of disturbing circumstances this natural response will occur in an ideal critic or beholder. Hume speaks of "beauties which are naturally fitted to excite agreeable sentiments," forms or qualities which "from the original structure of the internal fabric are calculated to please, and others to displease," objects which "by the structure of the mind" are "naturally calculated to give pleasure." While he seems to hold that beauty and ugliness are not properties of objects out of relation to human beings, he nevertheless said that "there are certain qualities in objects which are fitted by nature to produce those particular feelings." He thus assumed that beyond the empirical variety of emotional responses, there is a "natural" or "appropriate" response to any object arising from the constitution of the human mind as such and he takes this "natural" response as a norm.

Although he believed that such a norm of human nature exists, affording a standard for correct taste, he nevertheless recognized that on account of the many factors leading to deviation from it the norm is very rarely exemplified in any particular individual. "Thus," he says, "although the principles of taste be universal, and nearly if not entirely the same in all men; yet few are qualified to give judgment on any work of art, or establish their own sentiment as the standard of beauty." He suggested a fairly comprehensive list of the causes for deviation from the "natural" response or norm. In this one essay he mentions defective endowment; lack of experience; abnormality of the "organs of internal sensation"; wrong mood;

distracting circumstances; and finally prejudice, by which he means an inability to transcend the parochiality of one's society and training. He also seems to assume that general lack of sound sense will be a potent factor impeding the correct appreciation of works of art. He nevertheless believed that with due care the norm—"the relation which nature has placed between the form and the sentiment"—can be discovered empirically by looking for "what has been universally found to please in all countries and in all ages." This was the view of most eighteenth-century writers up to Alison. They hoped that by studying what things had pleased people universally and always, instead of passing fashions favored by the few, they would discover principles of feeling inherent in human nature as such and that these principles could properly be regarded as norms of correct aesthetic judgment.

It was also thought that by a similar empirical method it might be possible to arrive at general principles of beauty in the arts and by studying the "natural" response of feeling and emotion in matters of taste to lay down laws.

In the Preface to the first edition of the *Enquiry* (1757) Burke stated that he had found the ideas of beauty and sublimity "indiscriminately applied to things greatly differing" and set himself to remedy the confusion by "a diligent examination of the passions in our own breasts" and "a careful survey of the properties of things which we find by experience to influence those passions." He believed that if this could be done, "the rules deducible from such an inquiry might be applied to the imitative arts, and to whatever else they concerned, without much difficulty." Addison found the source of those pleasures we derive from the exercise of taste in the three qualities "greatness," "novelty," and "beauty." (The last in the narrower sense of the word then current, in which it contrasts with other aesthetic qualities such as sublimity, grace, etc. Addison's "greatness" was close to what others called "sublimity.") This classification was adopted by Akenside, Joseph Warton, and even by the "commonsense" philosopher Thomas Reid (1710–96). Hutcheson claimed a single objective principle of beauty in the "compound ratio of uniformity and variety." The artist Hogarth, in his *Analysis of Beauty* (1772), tried to find a general principle of beauty in his "precise serpentine line"—a line such as would be formed by a string running in a single sweep around the surface of a cone from base to apex. This line, Hogarth thought, is composed of two contrasting curves moving in opposite directions and unites in itself the maximum of variety. Hogarth originated the phrase: "The art of composing well is the art of varying well." Lord Kames proposed to go about his task by investigating "such attributes, relations and circumstances, as in the fine arts are chiefly employed to raise agreeable emotions," and thus empirically to "ascend gradually to principles from facts and experiments" so as to reach a standard of taste. Alison proposed to investigate the "origin of the beauty and sublimity of the qualities of matter" as "signs or expressions of qualities capable of producing emotions."

It was the conflict between this belief in a universal standard of taste and the recognition that feeling and emotion are integral to aesthetic appreciation which set the stage for the logical system of Kant, the first systematic philosophy of aesthetics and the first systematic exposition of the logical problems involved. It is becoming apparent only in our own day that many of these problems arise from the fact that most of the great systems of philosophy and the categories of thought which they utilize were evolved and elaborated before the "revolution of self-consciousness" whereby the aesthetic impulse and aesthetic experience were recognized as independent and autonomous modes of experience.

VII. Kant's *Critique of Judgment*

Kant's *Critique of Judgment* (1790), from the same year as Alison's *Essays*, is one of the most remarkable books in the history of philosophy. Hegel said that in it "Kant spoke the first rational word on aesthetics." E. F. Carritt, on the other hand, was not alone in thinking that "there are few original ideas in Kant's aesthetic." Both judgments may well be right. In working out his system of philosophical aesthetics Kant relied heavily on the ideas and critical doctrines of others, including those prevalent among the eighteenth-century English aestheticians. He gave philosophical expression to some of the leading notions of the Romantic Movement—the concepts of originality and genius, for example, and the phenomenology of the aesthetic experience. It is owing to the reformulation of ideas which were less systematically discussed by the English aestheticians that his work stands at the source of very much that has mainly preoccupied aesthetics today. Kant's own contribution lay chiefly in his ability to give a logically articulated form to the attitudes which were prevalent and to mold them into a coherent system. In doing this he displayed singular acuity in pinpointing the questions whose importance has persisted into the twentieth century.

Kant's feat was the more astonishing since he had little firsthand experience in the appreciation of the arts and showed little talent for it. His life was passed in a backwater of East Prussia in or near the town of Königsberg. He seems to have been impervious to most forms of beauty, emotionally jejune and sensuously obtuse. He had no taste for music and apart from some literary works the supreme artistic achievements of the world were a closed book to him. In poetry he draws his examples from the indifferent verse of Frederick the Great and the *Moral Poems* (1755) of Withof. Kant himself was not stylistically gifted as for example were Plato, Hobbes, and Hume. That the *Critique of Judgment* is still the most important single work in modern aesthetics is a tribute to the vigor of the thought contained in it: it has more sound sense—as well as some nonsense—than anything written on the subject since Plato. Most astonishing of all is the grasp of the essential phenomenology of the aesthetic experience shown by a person whose own aesthetic experience was limited. In the collected volume *Immanuel Kant, 1724–1804*, Kuno Francke has said: "That he should have arrived at his ideas without any aesthetic experience of his own, in surroundings barren of artistic influences, unaided by any sort of psychological experimentation, solely through abstract reasoning, is indeed a striking proof of his speculative genius." It would be more correct to find Kant's genius in the intuitive grasp of the importance and logical bearing of ideas current in his day than to present him as an originator of speculative ideas in aesthetics. He was, nevertheless, the most powerful mind to have written on aesthetics in modern times.

Kant presents his system of philosophical aesthetics in the context of his general metaphysical system, which he had worked out in the *Critique of Pure Reason* (1781) and the *Critique of Practical Reason* (1786). He brought the theory of beauty, that is the theory of the aesthetic judgment, within the ambit of a general theory of "teleological judgment" by which he believed that he had bridged the "immeasurable gulf" excavated in his previous works between the sensible world of appearances and the supersensible world of ultimate realities to which as moral beings we belong; between the concept of Nature, which is the realm of law and science, and the concept of Freedom, which is the realm of self-imposed rational principles or "ends." In the teleological judgment, under which he subsumes the aesthetic judgment, he believed that he had found the link between the spheres of natural science and morality. His exposition of aesthetic judgment often becomes more tortuous than it need have been because of his constant desire to give it this teleological and metaphysical slant.

This metaphysical scheme exercised a long and, as it now seems, a pernicious influence on the subsequent development of German aesthetic Idealism. Availing themselves of the general idea that the enjoyment of beauty provides a speculative link between scientific knowledge and our intimations of a supersensuous region of ultimate Reality, and interpreting this idea in accordance with the exalted but poorly defined metaphysical yearnings of Romanticism, the Idealists elevated beauty to the supernatural plane. In our commerce with beautiful things, they believed, the unknowable Absolute, which transcends the phenomenal world of appearances and cannot be grasped by theoretical reason, is rendered concrete and is sensuously apprehended. In the history of art the Cosmic Spirit is progressively incarnated. In art the infinite enters into the finite, the transcendental and the inexpressible lie open to the grasp of the senses. Both philosophers and artists, said Schelling, penetrate to the essence of the universe and break through the barriers between the actual and the Ideal; but the artist alone presents the Absolute concretely, visibly to perception. Art is an analogue of the creative power of Nature, it is "the Spirit of Nature which speaks to us only through symbols." But the symbol, added Solger, "is the existence of the Idea itself. It really is what it signifies. It is the Idea in its immediate reality." "Art," said Frederick Schlegel, "is a visible appearance of God's Kingdom on earth." These half-poetical, half-metaphysical astronautics culminated in the grandiose imaginings of Hegel, who pictured the gradual process by which the Cosmic Spirit, the Absolute, incarnates itself in sensuous being through the history of man's artistic achievement until in his own day art had transcended itself, the spiritual need which gave rise to it had been fulfilled and—as Kant himself had hinted—art must give place to religion, which in its turn would fulfill itself and make way for the philosophy of Idealism.

The present temper of philosophy is to fight shy of such meta-physical redundancies and in the following exposition we shall attempt to present Kant's aesthetics without the more speculative features which were seized upon by Idealism but today have little relevance.

In the opening sections of the "Critique of Aesthetic Judgment," the First Part of the *Critique of Judgment,* Kant takes over Shaftesbury's revolutionary discrimination of a specifically "aesthetic" attitude to the world and casts it into a logical mold. Where the English successors to Shaftesbury were interested in the psychological description of the "aesthetic attitude" and the psychological differences between it and the attitudes of attention we adopt in practical life, Kant concerned himself with the grounds of judgment, differentiating the logical basis of aesthetic judgments from that of the judgments we make about the other kinds of pleasure things give us, and from that of judgments about utility and judgments about goodness (both moral goodness and intrinsic perfection). He also differentiated the aesthetic experience, as a mode of direct awareness, from all forms of conceptual thinking. He made it clearer than it had ever been made before that a thing cannot be *proved* to be beautiful on the ground that it belongs to a certain class of things or has certain definable characteristics. Kant's treatment was by and large what we should nowadays call "phenomenological" instead of psychological. He made explicit and precise what had been implicit or partially glimpsed in the writings of his predecessors. Up to this time in the history of Western thought works of art and natural beauty had always been appraised for the pleasure they give, for their moral influence or their educative or ameliorative effects, for their practical utility of one sort or another or intellectually because they embodied certain approved principles or conformed with certain rules. By rejecting all these grounds of judgment and showing that aesthetic judgments are differently based and form a class on their own Kant was breaking new ground and laid the basis for aesthetics as a distinct branch of philosophy.

Kant begins by defining "Judgments of Taste" as judgments which are about the feelings of the observer for perceived objects and not about any characteristics perceived in the object.

To apprehend a regular and appropriate building with one's cognitive faculties, be the mode of representation clear or confused, is quite a different thing from being conscious of this representation with an accompanying sensation of delight. Here the representation is referred wholly to the Subject, and what is more to its feeling of life—under the name of the feeling of pleasure or displeasure—and this forms the basis of a quite separate faculty of discriminating and estimating, that contributes nothing to knowledge.

Kant has here in mind the theory of Alexander Gottlieb Baumgarten (1714–62), originator of the term "aesthetics," that judgments of beauty fell within the province of an "inferior cognition" which is mediated by the senses and which supplements the "clear and distinct" cognition mediated by the intellect. Kant is denying that our apprehension of beauty is cognition at all. Beauty judgments are of a different class from cognitive judgments and do not merely differ in degree of clarity. They refer not to our cognition of an object but to our feelings of satisfaction or dissatisfaction in the perception of the object. They are therefore subjective judgments by definition. They are defined as the class of judgments which refer to our satisfaction or dissatisfaction in the perception of things.

From this premise he derives his repudiation of the intellectualism which had prevailed in art criticism and teaching from the Renaissance through seventeenth-century Neoclassicism and academicism. It is "absolutely impossible," he claims, to find "principles of taste" of the form "any object which possesses such and such properties is beautiful." It is impossible to find theoretical rules for the construction of beautiful objects. This is impossible because when I judge an object to come under a certain general principle or to conform with such and such a rule I am making an intellectual judgment not a judgment about my feeling for it: and from such an intellectual judgment I cannot "draw the inference that it is beautiful." "For I must feel the pleasure immediately in the representation of the object (i.e., in my perception of it), and I cannot be talked into it by grounds of proof." Critics, he says, "are not able to look to the force of demonstrations" for the determining ground of their judgment, "but only to the reflection of the Subject upon his own state of pleasure or displeasure, to the exclusion of precepts and rules."

Kant agrees that there may be empirical generalizations of the sort which had played so large a part in the aspirations of English writers about the kind of things which most men at most times have in fact found beautiful. We can say "all roses are beautiful" as a summation of the empirical fact that we and all other people have always taken pleasure in the sight of roses. But such empirical generalizations are no more than empirical. We cannot derive from them norms or standards of taste. From the fact that all men have found the sight of roses beautiful we cannot infer that all men *ought* to judge roses to be beautiful or that a man is wrong who does not so judge.

Here Kant revealed a logical error which had been implicit in much of the thinking of English writers when they expected by the discovery of empirical uniformities among the actual fluctuations of men's taste to reach objective norms or standards of correct taste. He was emphatic that the only ground of aesthetic judgment is the immediate pleasure taken in awareness of the object. "Hence," he said, "there is no empirical ground of *proof* that can coerce any one's judgment of taste." And for this reason Kant was not himself greatly interested in the sort of empirical or sociological study of taste which had concerned the English writers. He repudiated on principle all such objective principles or standards of taste, holding that the only and ultimate ground of the aesthetic judgment is the direct aesthetic experience of a person in contact with the beautiful object. "There can be no objective rule of taste," he says, "by which what is beautiful may be defined by means of concepts. For every judgment from that source is aesthetic, i.e., its determining ground is the feeling of the Subject, and not any concept of an Object." Again: "It is only throwing away labor to look for a principle of taste that affords a universal criterion of the beautiful by definite concepts."

On similar grounds Kant repudiated the view which had been held by certain philosophers (notably by Thomas Reid) that a thing is held to be beautiful because it is perfect in its kind. The notion of perfection, Kant maintained, involves a prior concept of the sort of thing it should be, the sort of properties such a thing should have. If we judge a particular thing to be perfect, we are making an intellectual judgment that it conforms to a high degree with this prior concept. We are not making a judgment about our feeling toward it in our awareness of it and therefore our judgment is not an aesthetic judgment. Having made this point, Kant immediately qualified it by distinguished two kinds of beauty (§ 16) : free beauty (*pulchritudo vaga*), which is independent of any concept of perfection or use, and dependent beauty (*pulchritudo adhaerens*), which is ascribed to things which do fall under such a concept. Only judgments relating to the former kind of beauty are regarded as "pure" aesthetic judgments. Pure or independent beauty belongs, he thinks, only to things about which we judge without any concept of perfection or usefulness, such things as certain natural forms and nonrepresentational art (he instances arabesques and wallpaper designs), nonvocal music, etc. The distinction leads him to the conclusion, so incongruous to modern habits of appreciation, that many birds (the parrot, the hummingbird, the bird of paradise) and a number of crustacea can be judged as "independent" or "pure" beauties because they please us without any idea of a type of perfection to which they conform (he calls this idea "internal purposiveness"), whereas the beauty of a man or a horse or a building is merely "dependent" because it presupposes a concept of the sort of thing it ought to be or the use it ought to serve. Hogarth had already made this distinction in terms of two *meanings* of the assertion "this is beautiful": it may imply perfection of its kind or suitability for its purpose, or it may refer to the delight we take in the shape and appearance. In common with most people of his time Kant failed to see that even where we have a concept of a perfect type or an idea of use we may still take aesthetic delight in the appearance of a thing out of relation to this concept; we may appraise a representational painting for what it is in itself and not for the accuracy or significance with which it depicts the objects portrayed and the "perfection" of those objects in their kind.

Kant expresses this differentiation of aesthetic from theoretical judgments succinctly by his definition: "The beautiful is that which pleases apart from a concept." His attitude toward what we should now call "intellectual beauty" was, however, a curious one. We do take intellectual delight in the recognition that something (whatever its appearance) is perfectly and economically suited to its function or in the recognition that it is a perfect example of its kind (for example De Quincey's instance of a "beautiful ulcer") or in the apprehension (apart from appearance) of the intricate and successful interadaptation of parts in an organism. The pleasure we take in these things is obviously akin to our delight in an elegant, correct, and economic mathematical proof or a chess problem. The term "intellectual beauty" is now thought to be appropriate in such cases. Kant recognizes the intellectual pleasure we take in an elegant mathematical proof, for example. But he is unwilling to use the term "intellectual beauty" because to do so would be to deny to the delight of the intellect its superiority over that of the senses ("Analytic of Teleological Judgment," § 1). Kant had not completely emancipated himself from the values of the rationalistic philosophy in which he was trained. Nor does he grasp that we may make aesthetic judgments about utility objects and about those things where we possess a concept of type. The difference lies, as Shaftesbury saw better than Kant, in the attitude of mind rather than the class of objects.

In order to differentiate beauty judgments from moral judgments, utility judgments, and judgments based on the pleasure of the senses Kant makes use of Shaftesbury's concept of disinterested pleasure. Kant assumed that aesthetic judgments must be entirely free of interest. "Every one must agree that a judgment about beauty in which the least interest mingles is very partial and is not a pure judgment of taste." At the end of The First Moment of his "Analytic of the Beautiful" he defines the beautiful as follows: "*Taste* is the faculty of judging an object or a mode of representation by a satisfaction or dissatisfaction entirely *apart from interest*. The object of such satisfaction is called *beautiful*." Like Hutcheson, Burke, and the rest Kant assumes that "interest" implies or involves *desire*. He defines it as a concern for the *existence* of a thing. He then argues that sensory pleasure, as well as pleasure in a useful or morally desirable object but in contrast with the disinterested satisfaction which is our criterion for attributing beauty to a thing, is concerned with the existence of the object which is the source of pleasure. Utility judgments are treated as a subdivision of judgments about the "good." When we call a thing useful we mean that it is *good for something*, it pleases as a means to something else. The good-in-itself is something which by its mere concept is commended by reason as a thing whose existence is to be willed. "But to will something and to have a satisfaction in its existence, i.e., to take interest in it, are identical." Hence, Kant maintains, judgments of beauty are differentiated by their character of disinterestedness from judgments resting on sensory pleasure, utility, or goodness.

The English aestheticians had tried to characterize the disinterested attitude of attention by contrasting it with "interest" in a thing in the sense of active or latent desire to possess, use, or manipulate that thing. A similar position was taken up by Kant's German predecessor Mendelssohn, who said: "It appears to be a particular mark of the beautiful that it is contemplated with quiet satisfaction, that it pleases, even though it be not in our possession and even though we be never so far removed from the desire to put it to use." Kant went further than his predecessors and gave a metaphysical twist to the doctrine when he excluded from the aesthetic attitude not merely considerations of advantage and disadvantage, desire for possession and use, but any concern for the *existence* of a thing. To reach a pure aesthetic experience, he says, "one must not be in the least prepossessed in favor of the real existence of the thing, but must preserve complete indifference in this respect in order to play the part of judge in matters of taste." In one sense this is true but nugatory. If we see a beautiful castle, from the aesthetic point of view we are indifferent whether the castle exists or is a hallucination so long as the beautiful appearance persists. But the same could be said of practical interest: so long as all the consequences for pleasurable sensation remain, we do not mind whether the things occasioning them really exist (whatever that means) or not. On the other hand we do have an interest in the *existence* of beautiful things apart from our possession of them. The point was well put by Leibniz in the *Lettre à Nicoise* (1698) :

> He who finds pleasure in the contemplation of a beautiful picture and would suffer pain if he saw it spoiled, even though it belongs to another man, loves it so to speak with a disinterested love; but this is not the case with him who thinks merely of making money by selling or getting applause by showing it, without caring whether it is spoiled or not when it no longer belongs to him.

This position of Kant rendered more acute a difficulty which he inherited from the English school, the difficulty namely of discriminating the disinterested pleasure of aesthetic appreciation from the "interested" pleasures of the senses on the ground that the latter are connected with desire. Kant says: "The delight which we connect with the representation of the real existence of an object is called interest. Such a delight, therefore, always involves a reference to the faculty of desire. . . ." Shaftesbury, Hutcheson, Burke, and the rest had connected sensory pleasure with desire. It is a view which goes back as far as Plato and was commonly held in the Middle Ages. Yet it has proved impossible to substantiate. It leads Kant to the extraordinarily difficult position of claiming that for this reason the pleasure we take in the sight of a rose is aesthetic because disinterested and free from desire but the pleasure we take in the smell of the rose is sensuous and not aesthetic.[1] It seems as certain as anything can be that the pleasure we take in the taste of a good wine, a scent, or the touch of jade is not due to the satisfaction of an antecedent desire. We can indeed experience a general desire for refined sensory pleasures; but we can also experience an antecedent desire for the experience of beauty and some people suffer discomfort when starved of beauty. Kant indeed specifically states only that a judgment about the pleasantness of anything to sensation expresses an *interest* (i.e., is not disinterested) because "by sensation the object excites a desire for objects of that kind; consequently the satisfaction presupposes not the mere judgment about it, but the relation of its existence to my state so far as this is affected by such an Object." But Shaftesbury had already observed that although the aesthetic pleasure I take in anything is itself disinterested, my experience of aesthetic pleasure in a thing may arouse in me the desire for similar aesthetic experiences in contact with that thing or others which affect me similarly.

The important point is—and it is a very important one—that the concept of "disinterestedness" cannot, as the English "inner sense" school assumed, of itself mark out a particular class of objects or experiences as relevant for aesthetic experience. We can take up an attitude of disinterested attention to any experience at all—to an odor or a taste as well as a sound or sight. We can even with an effort attend objectively to the sensory quality of toothache and partially forget its unpleasantness. Even when satisfying hunger we

1 The aesthetic character of visual and auditory experience, but not of olfactory or gustatory sensation, is based on the capacity of the former for formal organization not on a different sort of relation to antecedent desire.

can take a grip of ourselves and attend disinterestedly to the quality of the taste of what we are eating. For this reason Kant's distinction of sensory pleasures from aesthetic pleasures has been discarded by some modern philosophers. For example in an essay "What Makes a Situation Aesthetic?" J. O. Urmson takes sensory pleasure in general as the paradigm of aesthetic experience and says specifically: "If I value the rose aesthetically the most obviously relevant grounds will be the way it smells; the same grounds may be a basis for aesthetic dislike." He makes the general statement: "If we examine, then, some very simple cases of aesthetic evaluation it seems to me that the grounds given are frequently the way the object appraised looks (shape and color), the way it sounds, smells, tastes or feels." This seems to go too far. We must distinguish the view that the "disinterested" posture of attention is a necessary part of the aesthetic attitude from the assumption that it is all that is needed for aesthetic awareness.

Those who have accepted satisfaction or pleasure as the ground of aesthetic judgment have seldom been content with a generalized hedonism but have sought some principle of relevance by which to discriminate those pleasures which are an aesthetic criterion from others which are not. This is particularly true of writers who have been interested in theory of art rather than natural beauty. As Professor Ruth Saw has said, "the ultimate test of what is to be regarded as a work of art must be commonsense agreement with the sort of things which critics and aestheticians have taken to be worthy of attention" ("What Is a Work of Art?" *Philosophy,* vol. xxxvi, no. 136, 1961). Works of art are by common agreement restricted to the senses of sight and hearing; but the ground for such restriction cannot be found either in the principle of "pleasure" or in "disinterested attention."

Dugald Stewart, whose *Philosophical Essays* were published in 1810, was content to rely on the accidents of linguistic usage in order to distinguish some categories of pleasure which he admitted to be aesthetic from others which are not, and he has been followed in this by most later writers:

> The word Beauty . . . *always, indeed, denotes something which gives. not merely* pleasure *to the mind, but a certain* refined *species of pleasure, remote from the grosser indulgences which are common to us with*

the brutes; but it is not applicable universally in every case where such refined pleasures are received, being confined to those exclusively which form the proper objects of Intellectual Taste. We speak of beautiful colours, beautiful pieces of music; we speak also of the beauty of virtue; of the beauty of poetical composition; of the beauty of style in prose; of the beauty of a mathematical theorem; of the beauty of a philosophical discovery. On the other hand, we do not speak of beautiful tastes, or of beautiful smells; nor do we apply this epithet to the agreeable softness, or smoothness, or warmth of tangible objects, considered solely in relation to our sense of feeling. Still less would it be consistent with the common usage of language to speak of the beauty of high birth, of the beauty of a large fortune, or of the beauty of extensive renown.

William James (*Principles of Psychology,* vol. 11, p. 468) thought that "aesthetic emotion, *pure and simple,* the pleasure given us by certain lines and masses, and combinations of colors and sounds, is an absolutely sensational experience, an optical or auricular feeling that is primary, and not due to the repercussion backward of other sensations elsewhere consecutively aroused." He maintained that aesthetic feelings, together with moral and intellectual feelings, are "genuinely *cerebral* forms of pleasure and displeasure" and that they "borrow nothing from any reverberations surging up from the parts below the brain."[2] The French philosopher Guyau maintained that sensations of taste, touch, and smell may be aesthetic (*Les Problèmes de l'esthétique contemporaine,* 1884). In modern times Ossowski regards the pleasures of sight and sound and smell as aesthetic but rejects taste and touch. Professor Valentine, representing the usual assumptions made in experimental aesthetics, says that the color of a patternless wallpaper and the sound of a bell may properly be called beautiful but the taste of toffee may not, although it may give keen pleasure (Introduction to *The Experimental Psychology of Beauty,* 1962).

These limitations imposed by psychologists and theoreticians have remained quite arbitrary, being justifiable neither by degree or intensity of pleasure nor by the principle of disinterested attention. Common sense meanwhile has fairly consistently restricted the field of artistic beauty to visual and auditory sensation together with certain nonsensory intellectual constructs such as works of literature. A possible ground for this discrimination would be that

[2] By this term he apparently meant physiological impulses and desires generally.

some qualities of visual sensations (spatial extension, hue, shade) and of auditory sensations (duration, volume, pitch, but not timbre) constitute a continuum capable of being organized into complex constructs which display emergent "field" properties, whereas tastes, smells, and tactile sensations do not form a continuum and cannot be so organized. Kant does not explicitly make this distinction. But it would fit in with his claim that aesthetic objects are adapted to the faculties of apprehension since only such complex constructs with interacting field qualities are able to evoke, sustain, and satisfy prolonged and intense contemplation.

Kant is very downright in his exclusion of any element of sensory pleasure (which he calls "charm") or emotional appeal from aesthetic experience. "That taste is still barbaric," he says, "which needs an added element of *charm* and *emotion* in order that there may be satisfaction, and still more so if it adopts these as the measure of its approval." He will allow only that they have a use in luring attention to the object if a man's taste is still rude and immature. The pure aesthetic judgment takes no account of them. This leads him to deny aesthetic value to beautiful tone in music and beauties of color in painting: these are but sensuous charm and not germane to beauty.

> In painting, sculpture, and in fact in all the formative arts, in architecture and horticulture so far as they are fine arts, the design is what is essential. Here it is not what gratifies in sensation but merely what pleases by its form, that is the fundamental prerequisite of taste. The colours which give brilliancy to the sketch are part of the charm. They may, no doubt, in their own way, enliven the object for sensation but make it really worth looking at they cannot. . . . The charm of colours or the agreeable tones of instruments may be added: but the design in the former and the composition in the latter constitute the proper object of the pure judgement of taste. To say that the purity alike of colours and tones, or their variety and contrast, seem to contribute to beauty is by no means to imply that, because in themselves agreeable, they therefore yield an addition to the delight in the form and one on a par with it. The real meaning rather is that they make this form more clearly, definitely and completely intuitable and besides stimulate the representation by their charm, as they excite and sustain attention directed to the object itself.

In common with most writers of his day Kant regarded color as a mere accessory and enlivening adjunct to painting and had not understood that color may itself be an element in the visual material which is organized into pictorial form. Still less had he understood that musical form may (as in the music of such composers as Boulez and Martinů) consist of or include the organization of timbres. He nevertheless touches on what is still an unresolved problem in appreciation and criticism. We evaluate a musical composition as something in itself, apart from this or that performance of it. A member of the audience at a concert who harps too insistently on the beauties of vocal or instrumental "tone" may not have apprehended the music. Nonetheless a considerable part of the training which musical performers undergo is devoted to the production of good sound and few people would go so far as to claim that the pleasure we take in beautiful tone, instrumental or vocal, is wholly irrelevant to our aesthetic experience of a performance. Certain modern schools of painting, notably Cubism, have deliberately eschewed the sensuous appeal of fine color, pigment texture, and calligraphic line. Yet where these are used they do seem to be integral to the total aesthetic experience, and the sharp segregation which Kant voices does not seem to correspond to the general experience of those most versed in appreciation of the arts.

Kant's attempt to exclude our apprehension of the good entirely from the aesthetic sphere, on the ground that it is coupled with interest, purpose, and desire, has also been called into question. His argument is that alike when we recognize something as good instrumentally (i.e., useful) and good intrinsically (good of itself) reason impels us to concern ourselves with bringing it into existence or maintaining it in existence. In contrast with Kant, however, when we recognize something to be good in itself (e.g., knowledge for its own sake, religious experience, the development to capacity of a man's talents and personality, the cultivation of aesthetic experience) philosophers from Shaftesbury to Charles Peirce have seen this as an act of insight leading to a judgment of intrinsic value closely akin to an aesthetic judgment. The reasonableness of our interest in the existence of what we recognize to be intrinsically good is perhaps not essentially different from the reasonableness of our interest in bringing about or maintaining the existence of things which we have judged to be beautiful. In Kant's presentation there is a confusion, also found in most modern writing on aesthetics, between the attempt to discriminate aesthetic experience from other modes of experience by means of salient characteristics and the axiological judgment that cultivation and enjoyment of aesthetic experience is one among the things which we judge to possess ultimate intrinsic value.

As has been said, Kant begins his discussion by affirming the subjectivity of aesthetic judgments: they do not refer to any properties of the object by which they can be verified as true or false, but to the feeling response of the subject in apprehending the object. In the Second Moment, while accepting the subjectivity of aesthetic judgments, he opposes the relativistic doctrine usually supposed to flow from the subjective position, the doctrine namely that the beauty of things depends on individual likes and dislikes, varies from person to person, so that when we say of something that it is beautiful our statement would not be complete unless we say *for whom* it is beautiful. On the contrary he maintains that every judgment about the beauty of a thing contains an implicit claim to universal validity and demands the assent of all men. This claim to universal validity has nothing to do with empirical uniformity of taste: it "is not that everyone *will* fall in with our judgment, but rather that everyone *ought* to agree with it." We differ in our individual likes and dislikes (though there are some empirical uniformities of taste), in our desires and aversions, in the things which give us sensory pleasure, and we accept such differences with equanimity. "To one a violet color is soft and lovely, to another it is faded and dead. One man likes the tone of wind instruments, another that of strings. To quarrel over such points with the idea of condemning another's judgment as incorrect when it differs from our own . . . would be folly." But judgments of beauty carry with them a claim to be correct and in making such a judgment we implicitly allege that if the judgment is correct, anyone who does not accept it is mistaken. It is as though we were asserting the existence of a certain property in the object although we are not in fact asserting this.

> It would be ridiculous [Kant says] *if anyone who plumed himself on his taste were to think of justifying himself by saying: "This object . . . is beautiful* for me." *For if it merely pleases* him, *he must not call it* beautiful. . . . *He judges not merely for himself but for all men, and*

then speaks of beauty as if it were a property of things. . . . It is not as if he counted on others agreeing in his judgment of liking owing to his having found them in agreement on a number of occasions, but he demands *this agreement of them. He blames them if they judge differently, and denies them taste.*

Kant's argument is phenomenological. He points to certain features in our concept of beauty, integral to the language we use, and invites us to see that they belong to the essence of the concept. Aesthetic judgments are *singular*. They assert beauty of this or that particular object as unique and not as a member of a class. They do not take the form of generalizations that any work of art or any natural object which has this and that qualities, or this and that combination of qualities, will be beautiful. They cannot be proved or supported by logical inference or verified by weight of empirical evidence. They are expressions of a direct and immediate intuition. Nevertheless they do not affirm private and individual reactions but carry an implicit claim to be correct or incorrect equally for all men. Most but not all modern philosophers have regarded this phenomenological analysis as both acute and substantially correct.

"In all judgments by which we describe anything as beautiful we tolerate no one else being of a different opinion, and in taking up this position we do not rest our judgment upon concepts but only on our feeling. We therefore base them on feeling not as a private feeling but as a common sense." In order to find an issue from the apparent anomaly of a subjective judgment which nonetheless claims to be correct or incorrect universally for everyone, Kant has recourse again to the principle of disinterestedness. He argues that all feelings which are allied to interest and desire are private and individual, varying from man to man. But disinterested pleasure, where there is no element of desire or private inclination, may be ascribed to a "common sense." By "common sense" or, as he also calls it, "public sense" (*sensus communis*) Kant means an "inner sense" not mediated through external sense organs alone but through feeling. He believed that such a common sense is a necessary assumption of the communicability of ordinary knowledge by perception of a common world; consequently we need not be surprised that in the aesthetic sphere "the universal communicability of a feeling presupposes a common sense." He thought that men appreciate beautiful things only as social beings and that communicability of the feeling which is our criterion of beauty, as a criterion of the nonsubjectivity of our judgment, is also a necessary presupposition of our ability to appreciate beauty. In reaching a verdict of the common sense a man must "detach himself from the subjective personal conditions of his judgment" and judge from the universal standpoint. Kant sums up this difficult idea as follows: "The judgment of taste, therefore, depends on our presupposing the existence of a common sense. (But this is not to be taken to mean some external sense, but the effect arising from the free play of our powers of cognition.) Only under the presupposition, I repeat, of such a common sense, are we able to lay down a judgment of taste." Elsewhere he says: "We might even define taste as a faculty of estimating what makes our feeling in a given representation *universally communicable* without the mediation of a concept." This idea of a common sense is analogous to Hume's notion of a universal and natural disposition of sentiment common to human nature as such. For Kant's argument the important feature is that this common sense of disinterested feeling by which we judge of beauty does not vary from man to man like sensuous pleasure or desire but is in principle uniform and unvariable. At the end of the Fourth Moment he therefore defines the beautiful as "that which without any concept is cognized as the object of *necessary* satisfaction."

Kant shared with Shaftesbury and the "inner sense" school the notion that our appreciation of beauty is a kind of immediate intuition analogous in this respect to sense perception, and that it nevertheless depends on a feeling of satisfaction. His claim that it depends on a "common sense" not variable from person to person was not so outrageous as it might at first seem to those who have studied the maelstrom of conflicting and evanescent aesthetic judgments, the clashing and fluctuating manifestations of taste revealed by the history of art and its criticism. Kant was not speaking about empirical judgments but about the logical nature of aesthetic judgment as such. We assume that reason and sense perception too are common faculties and that their pronouncements have rightness or wrongness independent of individual desire or inclination, and we continue to assume this despite the patent facts that people are differently endowed and that they always have been and probably always will be at loggerheads about many matters of reason and the sense properties of the external world. Kant is not asserting any empirical uniformity among aesthetic judgments but that what he calls the "faculty of aesthetic judgment" is the same in all men in the same sort of sense as in his day it was held that reason is the same in all men everywhere.

Kant's position becomes more comprehensible perhaps in the light of his treatment of teleology. This is not the place to go at length into this very difficult aspect of his transcendental philosophy. In brief, he holds that the fact and possibility of our knowledge of nature, or at least of organic nature, impels us to consider nature as adapted to our powers of understanding (which he calls its "subjective purposiveness"). "We have," he says, "on transcendental principles good ground to assume a subjective purposiveness in nature, in its particular laws, in reference to its comprehensibility by human judgment." Things may be adapted to our powers of cognition either in the form of theoretical understanding, ratiocination, scientific system-building, or in the form of immediate apprehension through sense perception or intellectual intuition. When we are aware that something is particularly well adapted to our powers of perceptive awareness, apart from any reasoning *about* it or any intellectual analysis, we enjoy an aesthetic experience and call that thing beautiful.

Kant nowhere expounds this view very lucidly but he returns again and again to it, always asserting that what we call beauty in an object is the quality of adaptedness to human mentality which renders it able to expand and further our powers of direct nonconceptual cognition. One might suggest a distant analogy with the medieval *candor* or Professor Findlay's fundamental aesthetic property of "perspicuousness." In the first section of the "Critique of Teleological Judgment" he says that many products of nature "as if they were devised quite specially for our Judgment," are of a form conformable to it; "through their manifoldness and unity they serve at once to strengthen and to sustain the mental powers that come into play." To them therefore we give the name of *beautiful* forms. In the Introduction (§ VIII) he says that an object may be represented as having *subjective* purposiveness on the ground that its form *in apprehension* is in harmony with the cognitive faculties. This, the adaptedness of things to human apprehension, we call natural beauty in contrast with objective purposiveness or teleological organization. "The former of these we judge by Taste (aesthetically, by the medium of the feeling of pleasure), the latter by Understanding and Reason (logically, according to concepts)." The "harmony" of an object with our cognitive faculties, its adaptedness to be apprehended directly and not by analytical or classifying reason, is a matter for aesthetic judgment to decide, guided by the pleasure which we experience in the apprehension of such well adapted objects. "For the judgment of taste consists precisely in a thing being called beautiful solely in respect of that quality in which it adapts itself to our mode of taking it in." ("Analytic of the Sublime," § 32.)

Kant has excluded from the aesthetic sphere both "internal purposiveness" (the quality of being a perfect example of a type) and "external purposiveness" (fitness for a purpose, utility). He introduces the idea of "purposiveness without purpose" in his assertion that beauty is the adaptedness of a thing to our cognitive faculties. The aesthetic judgment is not a judgment *about* such adaptedness but expresses the special "disinterested" pleasure we experience when we concentrate our attention on apprehending an object which is so adapted.

He discusses the logical standing of aesthetic pleasure in one of the obscurer sections (§ 9), but one which he himself says is "the key to the Critique of taste" and "worthy of all attention." With typical Germanic heaviness he heads this section: "Investigation of the question whether in the judgment of taste the feeling of pleasure precedes or follows the judging of the object." Despite this odd way of putting the matter (he is undoubtedly concerned with logical precedence rather than temporal sequence), the section does seem to be central to Kant's aesthetic doctrine. He appears to intend somewhat as follows. When we have contact with any object in aesthetic experience (i.e., when we have taken up toward it the disinterested aesthetic posture of attention) and judge it to be beautiful, we are not judging about the pleasure we experience in its contemplation although that pleasure is our criterion for judging it to be beautiful. If the judgment were about the experienced pleasure, the claim to universal communicability of the experience (or universal validity for the judgment) would be "self-contra-dictory"; for pleasure has "no more than private validity" and "nothing is capable of being universally communicated but cogni-tion and representation so far as it belongs to cognition." The pleasure we experience is pleasure "in the harmony of the cognitive faculties." The effect of which we become conscious in favorable aesthetic experience is a "mutual subjective harmony of our cogni-tive powers," the more lively play of these powers (which Kant calls "imagination" and "understanding") when stimulated to free play and "animated by mutual agreement." The beautiful object, the source of this pleasure, is the object which is adapted to our cogni-tive powers, which allows them free and unrestricted play and stimulates them to the full. Adaptedness to such powers does not vary from individual to individual and so, logically, the aesthetic judgment correctly claims universal validity although it is subjec-tive in that it is based on the adaptedness of an object of attention to *human* faculties and although the criterion by which we judge is the private individual pleasure we experience in the full stimula-tion and sustaining of our cognitive faculties.

One of the most recondite parts of the *Critique* is Kant's theory of the "free and unimpeded interplay of imagination and understand-ing" which, he held, is characteristic of aesthetic activity. It seems likely that this part of his theory was fairly closely linked with his notions of *genius* and the character of *vitality* which he held to be an essential of great art, though he does not succeed in making clear what he means. Perhaps he comes closest to clarification in section 49 and Remark 1 to section 57, where he defines Ideas as "repre-sentations referred to an object according to a certain principle (subjective or objective), insofar as they can still never become a cognition of it." He distinguishes two classes of Ideas, rational and aesthetic. *Rational* ideas or concepts (which he also calls "intellec-tual ideas") are referred to transcendental concepts, to which experience can never be fully adequate (examples given are: in-visible beings, the kingdom of the blessed, hell, eternity, creation, etc.). They "strain after something lying out beyond the confines of experience." By the free use of imagination the poet and the artist try to "body them forth," to find a concrete expression more adequate and complete than experienced nature can achieve. *Aesthetic* ideas are "representations of imagination" which "induce much thought, yet without the possibility of any definite thought whatever, i.e., concept, being adequate to it, and which language consequently can never get on level terms with or render completely intelligible." Kant may here be echoing a view popular in his time and most fully expressed by Archibald Alison, namely that a thing of beauty (particularly where natural beauty is concerned) is one which sets in train a chain of thought and imagination under the impulse of an emotional sense of mysterious importance and quasi-revelatory significance which can never be fully encapsulated in matter-of-fact concepts. There is always a feeling of something just out of grasp, a sense of something still to be apprehended, a revelation, and a light just beyond the reach. This way of regarding aesthetic activity lay perhaps at the heart of the Romantic conception of our commerce with art and beauty. It is one which, although out of favor today, we cannot afford prematurely to dismiss.

Summary. Appreciation, Kant holds, is direct but nonconceptual apprehension. We hold an object in attention, become more and more fully aware of it, but without analyzing or classifying it theoretically, without thinking *about* it. We contemplate it in the attitude of *disinterested* attention. When we so contemplate a beautiful thing, the powers of perception are activated and stimulated to a more than usually intense and harmonious activity; the object is such as to allow them full scope and to satisfy and sustain them. The signal that this is happening is the pleasure we feel in this full and unimpeded exercise of our faculties. Then Kant goes on to say that since our faculties of apprehending or perceiving objects do not in principle vary from person to person (although of course empirically we are all differently endowed), our judgments about the stimuli which satisfy and allow full play to these faculties (i.e., about things of beauty) are judgments about the adaptedness of objects to human cognition as such and therefore do not depend on individual variations and differences but claim to be generally valid for all men as such. This theory is the most important anticipation of modern aesthetic outlook in any philosopher before the twentieth century.

VIII. The Aesthetics of Romanticism

The word "Romantic" established itself in the language of literary and art criticism during the course of the eighteenth century. It was taken from the "Romances" of the Middle Ages—the cycles of story and legend which existed in most of the vernacular medieval "Romance" languages—and at first the word carried a suggestion of something fanciful and strange, or even *outré*, after the pattern of medieval chivalry in more or less deliberate contrast with the till then preponderant classical tradition deriving from ancient Greek and Roman models. By the later decades of the eighteenth century "Romantic" had become pretty generally recognized as a portmanteau term covering a complex of new tendencies in general opposition to the principles of Classicism which from late Renaissance times were the settled doctrine of the Academies. The so-called Romantic Movement extended for roughly a hundred years.

In the visual arts Romanticism was not part of the main stream after about 1850 and by the end of the nineteenth century it had begun to acquire a pejorative sense. In present usage the term "Romantic" is not necessarily tied to this historical movement but is applicable to art objects or movements of any age or period which display certain characteristics. The descriptive content of the term clarified itself very gradually and even today it is easier to detect than to define; the term indicates perhaps an attitude rather than a set of demonstrable characteristics. Though constituting one of the major contrasts in critical classifications, both the classical and the Romantic are modes of "Ideal" art. Both embrace concepts of nobility, grandeur, and superiority and involve an artistic reorganization of the everyday environment with repudiation of the usual and commonplace. Perhaps the core of difference may best be expressed by saying that while the ideal of Classicism is presented as a possible one and one according to which man and society can be molded by orderly stages toward an improved condition, the Romantic artist pits himself against a basically hostile environment and envisages the unattainable, an ideal beyond the possibilities of human adaptability. Whereas Classicism belongs to naturalistic art as described previously in this book, it is less clear that Romanticism falls wholly within the ambit of naturalism.

We shall here be concerned not so much to elucidate the implications of "Romantic" as a descriptive term of criticism or to trace the history of the Romantic Movement, but rather with a cluster of ideas which took on new significance in the course of that movement and so revolutionized the theory of art. The key ideas were those which are indicated by the words: genius, creative imagination, originality, expression, communication, symbolism, emotion, and sentiment. None of these ideas was new. But whereas before they had been peripheral, the central importance now assigned to them in conjunction with one another constituted a new attitude toward art with new concepts of its functions and new standards of assessment. Although Romantic art is no longer in vogue and the more articulate ideas of the Romantic Movement are under a cloud, many of the assumptions which took root at this time survive in current art theory and flourish with unsuspected vigor in the current language of criticism. Whenever in contemporary criticism an artist or an artwork is commended for expressiveness, originality, imagination, the effects of ideas which blossomed at the Romantic era are operative. Yet it must be emphasized that incompatible as many of the assumptions implicit in Romanticism were with the naturalistic outlook, their prevalence did not automatically eliminate the characteristic assumptions of naturalism. In the field of practical aesthetics people have always been tolerant of a high degree of inconsistency among prevalent beliefs, and mental habits associated with naturalism persisted alongside the new theories of Romanticism. Thus Ruskin, who was in many ways typical of moralistic Romanticism, wrote to his father as follows when he first saw daguerreotypes in Venice in 1845:

> *Daguerreotypes taken by this vivid sunlight are glorious things . . . every chip of stone and stain is there . . . it is a noble invention . . . anyone who has worked and blundered and stammered as I have done for four days and then sees the thing he has been trying to do so long in vain done perfectly and faultlessly in half a minute won't abuse it afterwards.*

Among the most influential of the attitudes in the light of which new trends in art theory associated with the so-called Romantic Movement fall into place and achieve some measure of coherence were: the elevation of the artist; the exaltation of originality; the new value set on experience as such with a special emphasis on the affective and emotional aspects of experience; and the new importance attached to fiction and invention.

The old theory of inspiration according to which the poet or artist was regarded as a "seer," a man "possessed" by a power outside himself and acting through his art as a channel for a divine message not his own, underwent a metamorphosis at this time. To the Romantic age the artist was no longer a man inspired by the god, but was himself elevated to the status of hero or almost a god. The notion of genius as exceptional intellectual and spiritual endowment (not merely exceptional talent or skill in a particular direction) though not restricted to the arts, came to be associated more particularly with the artist. Genius from the time of the Romantic Movement has come to be connected especially with artistic activity; and although it may be achieved only by a few most fortunate practitioners of the arts, it is considered the natural condition to which all artists aspire. Sometimes the artist-genius was thought of as having exceptional insight into ultimate Reality or as himself being in some special sense an embodiment or manifestation of the Absolute Spirit revered by German Idealistic philosophers; but even so the artist was thought to enjoy this special relation to Reality in virtue of his superior natural endowments. Furthermore the notion of genius was very closely linked with that of originality. Genius in Romantic theory manifests itself not by following the rules or conforming to tradition with more than average skill and efficiency, but by making its own rules and effecting a breakthrough which will be accepted by subsequent generations of artists as the source of new possibilities or modified rules. A genius was essentially original. One who was without originality could not be a genius, could not even be a good artist. For the fine arts were regarded as essentially the product of genius. All this was expressed by Kant in the sections of the *Critique of Judgment* about genius. He defined genius as the natural endowment or innate mental aptitude which "gives the rule to art." Fine art, he argued, "is only possible as a product of genius," and "originality must be its primary property." Everyone, he says, is agreed "on the point of the complete opposition between genius and the spirit of imitation."

For the first time in history, apart from some early anticipations in Chinese art theory, originality came to be accepted as a necessary quality of great art and of the artist. A similar background of assumption, albeit somewhat more hazy and diffused, is implicit in the twentieth-century use of the word "creative" as a term of approbation in connection with the arts although it is no longer so closely allied with the Romantic conception of genius as involving all-round spiritual superiority.

One consequence of these changes was that beauty gradually ceased to be a communal idea and became an idea molded very largely by a handful of exceptionally endowed individuals. From being an integrated member of society working within a framework of traditional standards of excellence the artist became either a potential genius, and therefore a rebel, or a potential imitator. Social changes in the structure of patronage helped along this change. The artist-genius could not rely on the traditional patron-age of the Church, the Court, or the state but had to find his own market through dealers and collectors in conflict with middle-class taste, while the artist who served established taste was denied the title of artist because he was regarded as a workman operating according to the rules, an imitator, no genius—or as we should now say, "noncreative." Thus were born the subsidiary notions of Bohemianism and Philistinism so important in the second half of the last century.

The most characteristic offspring of these new ideas—or new emphasis on older ideas which from being peripheral had become central—were the Expression and the Communication theories of art. To say that an artist expresses himself by his art, trite as it now seems, would have been incomprehensible or a rather stupid irrele-vance to classical antiquity and the Middle Ages or the Rennais-sance. Such a conception was first given importance by the Chinese ideal of the cultivated amateur artist. In China it was a corollary of the view that an artist must first cultivate and mature his own personality, then by long and arduous training achieve mastery in the techniques of expression. In the West the Romantic exaltation of the artist in conjunction with an emphasis on originality led naturally to theories of this type. By "expressing" his superior nature, embodying his superior endowment in his art, it was held that the artist-genius could enable less fortunate men through the medium of the artwork to make contact with him and benefit from communion with the artist's personality. This is quite different from the idea of expression discussed by Socrates and Leonardo. They meant by "expression" the facial signs or bodily gestures or attitudes by which painted (or sculptured) figures should manifest to the spectator the emotions that the depicted figure is experienc-ing. But in the Romantic conception the artist expresses *his own* feelings or emotional nature or whatever through the artwork as a whole and not by identification with this or that figure depicted in the artwork. It is the artist-genius himself who is being expressed. The real subject of every work of art is the artist. And through the artwork the spectator comes into sympathetic emotional contact with the artist. Unlike naturalistic theories the artwork is not regarded as a mirror through which we see some (actual or ideal) reality beyond it. It is regarded primarily as an instrument by which we come into contact with the creative mind of the artist. If a mirror, it is a mirror which reflects its maker.

Communication theories are closely connected with the Romantic valuation of experience as such and with the assumption that any (or almost any) expansion, enrichment, diversification of experience is a good thing. Theories of this class regard art as a "language of the emotions" and usually draw an analogy between artistic and linguistic communication. But emotional communication through the arts is usually not conceived as simply conveying factual information about the occurrence of real or imaginary emotional situations objectively in the manner in which a newspaper report gives information about events; artistic communication is thought of as inducing some sort of sympathetic sharing of the emotion conveyed so that the observer not only receives information about the occurrence of emotions already familiar to him but through commerce with the arts to some extent achieves emotional experiences he has not known before and could not otherwise know. In theories of this kind it is indeed sometimes (but not always) regarded as an essential of good art that it does communicate shades and colors of feelings not otherwise accessible or enables the observer to experience standard emotions with fresh insight or vividness, thus adding an increment to the sum total of human experience. This is connected with the demand for originality. This is what "creativeness" means within the context of communication theory. Most exponents of communication theories recognize that the induced emotions experienced in contact with works of art are different from the full-bodied emotions of real life and different also from the sympathetic emotion which we may experience by identifying ourselves with this or that personage in a film, drama, or novel. We savor rather than in the fullest sense live through the particular emotions or emotional overtones communicated by artworks. This matter of emotional response to works of art aesthetically enjoyed has been comparatively little studied in Western aesthetic, much more fully elaborated by several schools of Indian aesthetics.

Both expression theories and communication theories of art are *instrumental*. The work of art is not, as in naturalistic theories, regarded as a mirror through which we see a presented section of

"Grotesque Heads"
by Leonardo da Vinci,
1485–90.
Pen-and-ink drawing.
Windsor Castle.
Reproduced by gracious
permission of Her Majesty
Queen Elizabeth II.

"Astonishment,"
drawing from
Têtes d'expression by
Charles Le Brun,
1619–90.
Louvre Museum, Paris.
The Mansell Collection
of Photographs.
Photo: Giraudon.

reality but as an instrument by which we make contact with the personality of the artist or by which the artist communicates with us. Theories of this sort give rise to their own standards and require works of art to be judged by the success with which expression or communication is achieved. These standards are often combined with *moral* criteria and the work of art is also appraised by reference to the quality of the artist's personality which is expressed or the quality of the emotions which are communicated.

Artists are in point of fact not often, indeed rather rarely, men of exceptionally wide experience. Therefore an artist must be able to extend his actual experience by sympathetic imagination, by putting himself into the other man's place or by inventing fictitious situations and reacting to them appropriately as if they were real. The observer must have sufficient flexibility of imagination to follow the lead of the artist and project himself into the situations which the artist has created for his contemplation. Hence in the Romantic period, and more particularly within the ambit of expression and communication theories of art, a very high value was set on imaginative power and on fiction in general. From the Romantic period until today, but not before, even in Longinus, "imagination" or "creative imagination" has come to be almost synonymous with artistic power and it is sufficient to say that an artwork is "imaginative" in order to convey approval of it. Imagination, fictive power, were for the Romantics the means of transcending the limitations of individual experience. An early exponent of this type of theory, Eugène Véron, wrote as follows: "As man is essentially sympathetic and his joy or pain is often caused as much by the good or evil fortunes of others as by his own; as, besides, he possesses in a very high degree the faculty of combining series of fictitious facts, and of representing them in colors even more lively than those of reality: it results that the domain of art is of infinite extent for him." The same writer defined art as "the direct and spontaneous manifestation of human personality" and introduced frankly the moral criterion when appraising it with the remark that "it is from the worth of the artist that that of his work is derived" (*Aesthetics,* 1878; translated into English 1879).

With this introduction we shall give some more detailed account of the ideas which make up this constellation, of their history before

Rocky Landscape
with Figures *by*
Marcellus Laroon, 1743.
Pen-and-ink drawing.
Courtesy of the
Courtauld Institute of Art:
Witt Collection, London.

Romanticism in some cases and of the repercussions from them
which persist in contemporary art theory or critical outlook.

INSPIRATION

The doctrine of Inspiration goes back to very early times. Both
the *Iliad* and the *Odyssey* open with an invocation to the Muse,
"goddess daughter of Zeus," and in *Odyssey*, XXII, 347–348, the
bard Phemius says: "The god has put into my heart all manner of
lays, and methinks I sing to thee as a god." In the introduction to
the *Theogony* the poet Hesiod tells how the Muse had breathed
into him the art of divine music as he tended his flocks on Mount
Helicon. The additional conceit that inspiration derived from a
draught of the holy well Hippocrene or Arethusa seems to have

been an elaboration of the Alexandrine age. But the doctrine of inspiration itself was much more than a literary conceit and was nonetheless seriously held because it was expressed with the characteristic Greek exuberance of mythological imagery. Inspiration was a form of *possession* by some divine force outside the artist—the Greek word was *enthousiasmos,* "enthusiasm" or literally the state of being possessed by a god—and was commonly spoken of as a kind of madness *(mania)* because it was outside the bounds of ordinary reason. It was put into the same class of phenomena as religious frenzy, hysteria, and prophetic utterances of the oracles. Plato again and again speaks of poetry as a form of alienation. "But whosoever without the frenzy of the Muses shall come to the doors of poesy, persuaded that by craftsmanship forsooth he can become a successful poet, will achieve nothing and the poetry of sobriety shall be overshadowed by that of the mad" *(Phaedrus,* 245A). The classical statement of his theory of inspiration is found in the *Ion,* which was translated as follows by the poet Shelley:

For the authors of those great poems which we admire do not attain to excellence through any rules of art, but utter their beautiful melodies of

"Siva and Parvati,"
Indian sculpture
from Ovissa,
twelfth–thirteenth
century A.D. *Courtesy of*
the Trustees of the
British Museum, London.

verse in a state of inspiration and, as it were, possessed *by a spirit not their own. Thus the composers of lyrical poetry create those admired songs of theirs in a state of divine insanity, like the Corybantes, who lose all control over their reason in the enthusiasm of the sacred dance; and during this supernatural possession are excited to the rhythm and harmony which they communicate to men. . . . For a Poet is indeed a thing ethereally light, winged, and sacred, nor can he compose anything worth calling poetry until he becomes inspired and, as it were, mad or whilst reason remains in him. For whilst a man retains any portion of the thing called reason, he is utterly incompetent to produce poetry or to vaticinate. . . . The God seems purposely to have deprived all poets, prophets and soothsayers of every particle of reason and understanding the better to adapt them to their employment as his ministers and interpreters; and that we, their auditors, may acknowledge that those who write so beautifully are possessed, and address us inspired by the God.*

The results of inspiration were on the one hand *charm*—that quality in great poetry which gives delight and takes the mind of the listener captive as if by enchantment (the Greek term was "conjuring the soul")—and on the other hand the wisdom of the prophet or sage, the sort of wisdom which does not come by logic but by intuition. In the *Timaeus* Plato speaks in very similar language about the inspiration of prophets.

And here is a proof that God has given the art of divination not to the wisdom but to the foolishness of man. No man when in his wits attains prophetic truth and inspiration, but when he receives the inspired word either his intelligence is enthralled in sleep or he is demented by some distemper or possession. And he who would understand what he re-members to have been said, whether in a dream or when he was awake, by the prophetic and inspired nature, or would determine by reason the meaning of the apparitions which he has seen . . . must first recover his wits.

The other corollary of inspiration was that poetry and art cannot be wholly reduced to a craft based on a system of rules derived from experience and embodied in craftsman's tradition. To this extent poetry is *not* what the Greeks understood by *techne*—a system of practical rules derived from general principles. Something more was needed, something which is not fully susceptible of rational expla-nation or analysis. The doctrine of "inspiration" or "possession by a god" was in a sense the recognition of this fact: the rationalistic Greek temperament was content to assign to "the divine" whatever was not susceptible of rational explanation or whatever regions of experience they were not interested to subject to rational analysis. The Greeks did not adopt the "romantic" attitude toward inspiration which we have inherited from Shelley, Coleridge, and others of this age. Indeed when Plato was writing as a political philosopher or educational theorist the fact that poetry lay outside reason (was inspired or a form of divine madness) and the fact that it could not be reduced wholly to a craft were his chief reasons for repudiating it.

The two aspects of the classical notion of inspiration which persisted most strongly, even to the extent of becoming literary convention, were the ideas of *alienation* (the artist under inspiration is not "in his right mind") and the idea of a force acting upon the artist from outside him. In Christian literature the idea of inspiration as a divine force from outside was strengthened by such passages in the Old Testament as Ezekiel 11:1–10 and Joel 11:28–30, where the spirit of Jehovah is said to enter into men and speak through them. The most noble and serious invocations to an external power of inspiration in English poetry are to be found in Milton's *Paradise Lost,* where he appeals to the Spirit of divine Wisdom:

> *Thou with Eternal wisdom didst converse,*
> *Wisdom thy sister, and with her didst play*
> *In presence of th' Almightie Father, pleas'd*
> *With thy Celestial Song. Up led by thee*
> *Into the Heav'n of Heav'ns I have presumed,*
> *An Earthlie Guest, and drawn Empyreal Aire,*
> *Thy tempring; with like safety guided down*
> *Return me to my Native Element.*

The sense of control by an external force remained among the Romantics. But whereas Milton looked to inspiration for wisdom and illumination which would enable him to "assert Eternal Providence, And justifie the wayes of God to men," the Romantics increasingly regarded inspiration as a function of the subconscious, nonrational, even automatic parts of the mind. Blake believed that his poems were quite literally dictated to him in a quasi-trance state by heavenly spirits. Coleridge described the automatic and visionary origin of *Kubla Khan*. Wordsworth thought of inspiration as a mystical force or *mana* in external Nature impinging on the poet's unconscious mind. Shelley regarded it as an "invisible influence," not like reasoning, "a power which can be exerted according to the determination of the will," but an involuntary force from within. "The conscious portions of our nature," he says, "are unprophetic either of its approach or its departure." He recognized too that inspiration in the plastic arts is the same sort of unconscious process: "The very mind which directs the hands in formation is incapable of accounting to itself for the origin, the gradations, or the media of the process."

From classical antiquity artistic inspiration was thought of as the invasion of the artist by an outside power, a form of "possession." During the Romantic age this idea gradually changed. The artist was not thought of as the channel through which an external force was manifested. The source of inspiration lay within him, in the unconscious part of his own being. Instead of being the passive instrument or voice of an alien power the artist, through the unconscious and involuntary part of himself, was identified with the Absolute. In modern times inspiration is often attributed to the upwelling of unconscious material without necessarily postulating any contact with cosmic or suprapersonal forces.

The word "unconsciousness" was used in the literature of the Romantics before it entered into formal psychology. It was used by Wordsworth. Carlyle, distinguishing between artificial and natural, or inspired, poetry, said: "The artificial is the conscious, mechanical; the natural is unconscious, dynamic." And he says: "Unconsciousness is the sign of creation; consciousness at best that of manufacture." Indeed, it has been claimed that Freud himself derived his concept of the unconscious from this literary theory of artistic creation as expressed particularly in an essay by a German writer Ludwig Börne, who in 1823 wrote an essay on "The Art of Becoming an Original Writer in Three Days." The idea of inspiration as a mysterious force acting on the artist from without did not disappear. The modern aesthetician Croce, for example, said: "The person of the poet is an Aeolian harp which the wind of the universe causes to vibrate." But the exaltation of the artist, the emphasis which was set on creative imagination and the new concept of genius, tended to give predominance to the source of inspiration in the artist's own unconscious mind. From about 1840 the processes of artistic creation were studied by descriptive psychology without reference to an external source. The main trend of theory ceased to regard the artist as a mere channel of divine inspiration from without and found the source of his creative power in his own unconscious mind. The sense of external control which is so strongly felt by many artists, particularly literary artists, when engaged in creation was aligned with the feeling of compulsion which occurs in other forms of mental dissociation and came to be thought of as a phenomenon attendant on the emergence of unconscious material into the consciousness. The culmination of this tendency may be seen in the theories of the Surrealists, who devised numerous methods of releasing subconscious material and eliminating or sidetracking the control of conscious reason in artistic composition. Contemporary studies of artistic production in terms of unconscious "creativity," the release of material from the unconscious mind or the imposition of an unconsciously controlled form on consciously assembled and elaborated material, have been very numerous.

GENIUS

The concept of *genius* is perhaps the most characteristic of those which emerged in the Romantic age. The word itself appeared in the English language early in the sixteenth century as the equivalent of the Latin *ingenium* in the sense of "native talent." Alongside the doctrine of inspiration the need for native talent, or endowment, had been recognized in antiquity. Pindar, who is today recognized as one of the most lyrical of poets as well as a great craftsman, insisted again and again that craftsmanship is not enough; a poet must also have natural talent (the word he uses is *phua*), which cannot be taught. In an often quoted passage from the *Poetics* Aristotle seems to have preferred the well-endowed poet (he uses the word *euphues,* which was adopted by John Lyly in the title of his prose romance, 1579) to the one who composes in the frenzy of inspiration. "For," he says, "the former kind are adaptable, the latter unbalanced." The context of this remark, however, is the argument that a dramatist should be able to experience in himself a wide variety of emotions because this helps him to visualize scenes most vividly, as if they were "before the eyes," and so to write convincingly.

The question arises whether genius and talent differ in kind or only in degree. A great deal was written about genius in the second half of the eighteenth century. Those writers who followed the empirical tradition of Hobbes regarded genius as exceptional natural endowment or unusual talent rather than something *sui generis* and differing in kind. For John Dennis (1657–1734), whose outlook had affinities with that of Longinus, genius was the capacity for emotion. In *The Advancement and Reformation of Modern Poetry* (1701) he mentions the things which contribute to excellence in poetry, defining genius as follows: "The first is Nature, which is the foundation and basis of all. For Nature is the same thing as Genius, and Genius and Passion are all one. For Passion in a Poem is Genius, and the power of exciting Passion is Genius in a Poet." John Armstrong (1709–79), physician and poet, said that genius "may be said to consist of a perfect polish of soul, which receives and reflects the images that fall upon it, without warping or distortion." In his famous book *Hereditary Genius* (1869) Sir Francis Galton used the term in the sense of "mental abilities" and in a prefatory chapter to the second edition regretted that he had not chosen the title "Hereditary Ability." Others, however, more in keeping with the new Romantic outlook, regarded genius as something distinct. Whereas talent and ability may be either native or acquired, genius was regarded as inborn. Moreover genius was essentially linked with originality. Kant, who restricts genius to the domain of fine art, calls it the "exemplary originality (*meisterhafte Originalität*) of the natural endowments of an individual." Alexander Gerard in *An Essay on Genius* (1774) said that genius "is confounded not only by the vulgar, but even sometimes by judicious writers, with mere capacity. Nothing, however, is more evident than that they are totally distinct. . . . Genius is properly the faculty of invention; by means of which a man is qualified for making new discoveries in science or for producing original works of art." In his book *Philosophie en France* Ravaisson (1813–1900) said: "It is in invention above all that one sees that force and grandeur of spirit to which in our day we give the name 'genius.' All agree that genius consists above all in inventing, creating." Thus a new conception of genius and the new valuation placed upon originality were linked closely together.

At the same time there grew up a fairly well-defined notion of the artistic genius as a psychological type, much in favor among the Romantics, a person with an abnormally strong sense of vocation, one who labors under an obsessive feeling of compulsion which is expressed in an anguished need to realize latent capacities—to "be oneself"—or to discover some transcendental and inexpressible truth which can only be embodied in a chosen art form. Compulsive striving for self-expression, the search for "rightness," harassing doubts and intensive relief resulting from successful achievement have all come to be regarded as standard symptoms of genius. Regarding Picasso as such a genius, Christian Xervos wrote of his manner of artistic creation as follows:

> *The moments of creation with Picasso are dominated by anguish. This anguish Picasso analysed for me recently. His only wish has been desperately to be himself; in fact, he acts according to suggestions which come to him from beyond his own limits. He sees descending upon him a superior order to exigencies, he has a very clear impression that something compels him imperiously to empty his spirit of all that he has only just discovered, even before he has been able to control it, so that he can admit other suggestions. Hence his torturing doubts.*

Subsequent research into the psychology of artistic creation has shown that these stock characteristics of genius may also be manifested by artists of indifferent merit. The value of such compilations as Rosamund Harding's *An Anatomy of Inspiration* (1948), including as it does both great and mediocre talents, is the striking witness it bears to the uniformity displayed by introspective accounts of the artistic process whether by a good or by a bad artist. The phenomena of compulsion, a guiding sense of right, and a feeling of extreme relief on achievement are not restricted to artists who are acknowledged geniuses. They can all be found in the *Journal,* for example, of Benjamin Robert Haydon (1786–1864), the history painter, who thought himself a genius but was not. Indeed the relief afforded by bringing to light what has been repressed, or is buried, in the subconscious mind is common to other spheres than artistic creation. The multiple murderer Christie is reported to have said to a pathologist after his arrest: "I think there is something on my mind but I can't get it—that's what's hurting. It seems to be forming a picture, then, before it gets clear, it all gets jumbled up again. My head starts hurting as the picture is getting clear and that's what stops me getting it clear. I know there is something." On the other hand there have been artists of importance who have displayed none of these psychological birth pangs but appear to have produced their works with the workmanlike placidity of the craftsman. The effect of the Romantic Movement was to give prominence to a particular psychological type among practicing artists and although the Romantic notion of the inspired "genius" has become somewhat passé, the notion of self-expression which was tied up with it still dominates criticism and is assumed by most contemporary writing on the theory of art.

APPENDIX

IMAGINATION

Nowadays what is most commonly, though vaguely, understood outside formal psychology by "imagination" is not necessarily a power to form mental images but a power of the mind to mold experience into something new, to create fictive situations and by sympathetic feeling to put oneself into the other man's place. In this sense classical antiquity had no theory of the imagination. Nor did they see any specially close connection between imaginative powers and artistic production except insofar as mental imagery can be a help when one wishes to obtain or convey to others a vivid impression of a situation.

Plato speaks of imagination chiefly in connection with his theory of knowledge and ranks it lowest of the faculties. In his view the highest form of cognition was that imparted by *Nous* or Reason: the intellectual apprehension of concepts. Next below that came the knowledge imparted by Understanding, whereby we apprehend mathematical truths. The third, which he called belief rather than knowledge and thought to be inherently illusory, was the apprehension of particular things imparted by the senses. Last of all comes "conjecture," a combination of perception and judgment which occurs when I see an indistinct figure, or a memory image, and rightly or wrongly judge it to be something I know (*Theaetetus*, 195d, 264b). He likens imagination to the work of a sort of painter in a man's mind who makes portraits or images of things (*Philebus*, 39b). Plato held that there is no power to imagine or form mental images of the intellectual Ideas which are the objects of true knowledge. The "knowledge" we obtain through sense perception is necessarily inferior and uncertain. Where we rely on mental imagery rather than direct perception a further element of uncertainty and unreliability is introduced. Although in some of his more poetical dialogues (especially *Phaedrus* and *Symposium*) Plato seems somewhat to modify this disparagement, he inaugurated a long tradition of distrust for the imagination which was hardly dissipated until the sturdy empiricism of Hobbes.

Aristotle was more interested than Plato in the psychological analysis of mental processes and he first attempted to define imagination as the "imaging" faculty. He used the word *phantasia* in a new sense which he carefully differentiated from that of Plato, denying that imagination in his sense of the term was either a combination of judgment and perception or judgment by means of perception as Plato had said. He described imagination as a faculty intermediate between perception and thought which revives sense images in the form of afterimages, dream images, and memory from the residual impressions left by primary sensation. It is the basis of all memory, which cannot occur without images of the imagination. Imagination occurs only in sentient beings and only in relation to what is perceived. Without perception there is no imagination and without imagination there is no thought or belief. This Aristotelian view of imagination as a mode of mental activity between perception and thought held the field up to and including Kant and it may therefore be worthwhile to describe it in a little more detail.[1]

---

[1] Aristotle's theory of imagination is contained in *De Anima*, 427b–429a and *De Somniis*, 459.

Imagination, Aristotle held, differs from thought in two ways: (1) It is in our power to form mental images at will just as painters make pictured images at will, but it is not in our power to form opinions at will. (2) When we hold beliefs we are not emotionally indifferent to them (for example if we believe an approaching shape is an angry lion we experience terror), but we are as unaffected by the images of imagination (apart from belief) as are those who look at paintings they know to be unreal. Imagination differs from perception because it is active when there is no sensation, as in dreams or when our eyes are shut. Aristotle also held that all sensations of particular individual things are true but that most imaginings are false. He did not connect imagination specifically with artistic creation and did not recognize the synthetic power of imagination to recombine images into new formations.[2] This function he attributed to Reason and it was not until Campanella (1568–1639) and Hobbes (1588–1679) and later Hume (1711–76) and Tetens (1736–1805) that the synthetic powers of imagination were explored.

In literary theory, at any rate after Aristotle, imagination was conceived as the power of visualization whereby things absent appear "to the inner eye" as if they were present. The Greeks called such visualizations *phantasiai*, the Romans *visiones*. In both the theory of poetry and the theory of oratory vivid visualization was closely connected with the power of language to communicate emotion from speaker to hearer. Longinus, whose treatise *On the Sublime* exercised an important influence during the eighteenth century on those currents which led toward Romanticism, regarded such visualization as one of the elements of sublimity. He says:

> *A most effective way of attaining weight, grandeur and a vivid sense of actuality is afforded by visualisations* (phantasiai). *Some people call this image-making. The term "imagination"* (phantasia) *is used generally for anything whatever in the mind which suggests a thought productive of*

[2] There is some connection of imagination with Aristotle's theory of metaphor, but where he develops this theory in the *Rhetoric* he sets his main emphasis on intellectual recognition of a revealed similarity.

words. But in its now prevailing sense the word applies when inspiration and emotion make you appear actually to see what you describe and bring it before the eyes of your hearers.

Longinus quotes in illustration three lines from the *Orestes* of Euripides (lines 255–257) where in hallucination Orestes sees his mother Clytemnestra setting the Furies upon him and a line from the same dramatist's *Iphigenia in Tauris* (line 291) where a herdsman describes to Iphigenia how he has seen Orestes in a fit of madness hallucinating the pursuing Furies. Longinus' comment is: "Here the poet himself sees the Furies and almost compels his audience to see what he had visualized." A similar formula is applied to emotional transference. He assumes that the poet must experience in himself the emotions he attributes to his characters in order to be able to create illusion and to cause his audience to experience the same emotion in sympathy. Quoting a passage from the lost *Phaëthon* of Euripides where Phaëthon drives the chariot of the Sun, Longinus asks: "Would you not say that the soul of Euripides had mounted the chariot with him and shared the dangers of those winged horses' flight? Unless he had himself indeed been swept along in that celestial race, he could not have visualized it so." In public speaking, Longinus tells us, such vivid pictorial realism can be more effectively convincing than logical argument.

All this was accepted doctrine in antiquity and went back to Aristotle's *Rhetoric,* where in his discussion of wit and metaphor he says that a good metaphor or simile is one which brings the thing "before the eyes" and that those expressions do this which "signify actualities." A similar view was taken by the Roman rhetoricians. Cicero thought of imagination as a power of visualization whereby the poet or orator was able to picture a scene vividly and cause his hearers similarly to see it vividly in their mind's eye *(On Oratorical Partitions,* vi) . Quintilian taught that this power of visualization must be cultivated by the successful orator (see quotation pp. 235–236) . It is the theory of naturalistic illusionism applied in the realm of literature. That which is "imitated" must be presented not only accurately but vividly and to do this the verbal artist must actually picture it to himself in order that by his words he may cause his audience to visualize it for themselves. The "image-making" faculty which made this possible was imagination or *phantasia*.

Among modern writers the same view has been expounded by Ezra Pound, who used to teach (e.g., *A. B. C. of Reading*, 1934) that in order to charge language with meaning to the highest possible degree we have three chief means. *Phanopoea* he described as "using a word to throw a visual image onto the reader's imagination." *Melopoea* is charging a word by the sound or inducing emotional correlations by the sound and rhythm of the speech. And *Logopoea* consists in "inducing both of the effects by stimulating associations (intellectual or emotional) that have remained in the receiver's consciousness in relation to the actual words or groups of words employed." These methods of charging language with meaning were known to the Greeks. In all the treatises on rhetoric which have come down to us—Aristotle, Theophrastus, Dionysius of Halycarnassus, Demetrius, Longinus—they are carefully distinguished and illustrated. *Phanopoea* is what the ancients meant by imagination in the context of literature and the other arts. It is "to make manifest," to bring an absent reality "before the eyes" by the power of mental imagery.

The first and perhaps the only occasion in antiquity where imagination rather than reason is credited with the power not only to revive and recall images of past experience but to build up and construct new inventions or idealizations occurs in a life of the itinerant Pythagorean mystic Apollonius of Tyana written in the third century A.D. by Philostratus. Responding to a sarcastic inquiry whether he supposed that the artists Phidias and Praxiteles "went up to heaven and took a copy of the shapes of the gods," which they reproduced in their sculptures, Philostratus says:

Imagination wrought these works, a wiser and a subtler artist by far than imitation; for imitation can only create as its handiwork what it has seen, but imagination goes on to what it has not seen; taking this as the standard of reality. . . . When you entertain a notion of Zeus you must, I suppose, envisage him along with heaven and the seasons and stars as Phidias in his day endeavoured to do, and if you would fashion an image of Athene you must imagine in your mind armies and cunning and handicrafts and how she leapt out of Zeus himself.

Plotinus also thought that the artist does not copy the visible world but obtains an insight into an ideal reality behind and above the appearances.

> *The arts do not merely copy the visible world but ascend to the principles on which nature is built up; and further many of their creations are original. For they certainly make good the defects of things, as having the source of beauty in themselves. Thus Phidias did not use any visible model for his Zeus, but apprehended him as he would appear if he deigned to show himself to our eyes.*

Plotinus has been thought to have approached most nearly to the modern conception of "creative imagination" as expressed for example by Coleridge. But Plotinus still attributed this power of apprehending an ideal not to the visualizing power of imagination but to intellectual insight or Reason.

During the Middle Ages and into the Renaissance the Platonic prejudice against imagination persisted, fortified perhaps by biblical phrases about "vain imagination" and given authority by St. Augustine. In the psychological scheme of the scholastics imagination was a faculty, operating between sensation and understanding, whose function was to reproduce from the data provided by sensory experience the images of objects and their relations and so to make them available for memory and thought. It was also recognized that imagination cannot only reproduce sensory material as it were photographically, but can dissociate and recombine images at will (see the quotation from Lord Bacon, below). It was this freedom to change and reconstitute imagery, sometimes distinguished from the reproductive power of imagination by the word "fantasy" or "fancy," that remained the source of suspicion and made imagination something of an epistemological scapegoat. According to the most general doctrine reason made use of the images called up by imagination to extract from them general ideas and concepts, which were retained by memory. But since imagination could supply changed and therefore false imagery, by addition, subtraction, and recombination of attributes, its material had to be subject to the judgment and interpretation of reason and imagination held a place inferior to reason. Imagination might get the upper hand of reason during dreams, in fits of madness, when a person suffered hallucinations, or was subjected to the influence of excessive passion; but its proper place was in a hierarchy anchored in the senses but subject to the wisdom and discrimination of reason. This idea of the imagination is well summed up by Burton in the *Anatomy of Melancholy* (Pt. 1, Sec. i, Mem. 2, Subsec. 7) :

> *Phantasy, or imagination, is an inner sense which doth more fully examine the species perceived by common sense, of things present or absent, and keeps them longer, recalling them to mind again, or making new of his own. In time of sleep this faculty is free, and many times conceives strange, stupend, absurd shapes, as in sick men we commonly observe. His organ is the middle cell of the brain; his objects all the species communicated to him by the common sense, by comparison of which he feigns infinite other unto himself. . . . In poets and painters imagination forcibly works, as appears by their several fictions, antics, images. . . . In men it is subject and governed by reason, or at least should be; but in brutes it hath no superior, and is* ratio brutorum, *all the reason they have.*

Bacon similarly defined imagination as an intermediary power on which both thought and action depend (*Advancement of Learning*, Bk. V, Ch. 1) :

> *The imagination, indeed, on both sides, performs the office of agent, or ambassador, and assists alike in the judicial and ministerial capacity. Sense commits all sorts of notions to the imagination, and the reason after judges of them. In like manner reason transmits select and approved notions to the imagination before the decree is executed: for imagination always precedes and excites voluntary motion.*

But although a necessary and useful function for the imagination was admitted, its freedom to distort the data of the senses, its capacity to furnish "false shows and suppositions" confirmed the traditional distrust in which it was held. An extreme example of this suspicion may be seen in the treatise *On Imagination* by Gianfrancesco Pico della Mirandola, where he writes:

> *Nor is it hard to prove that universal errors which occur as much in civil life as in the philosophic and Christian life, take their beginnings from the defect of the imagination. The peace of the State is disturbed by*

*ambition, cruelty, wrath, avarice, and lust. But then the depraved
imagination is the mother and nurse of ambition. . . . Cruelty, wrath
and passion are born and nourished by the imagination of an ostensible
but deceptive good. . . . And what else, if not the deceitful imagination,
brings to the fore the other vices which for want of time I omit to
mention?*

Other writers began to look for a defense of imagination from the
point of view of its aesthetic functions. Apart from the reproductive
power of imagination, traditionally accepted as necessary to knowledge, it began to be held that the reproductive or inventive activity
of the imagination need not necessarily be disordered but could be
healthy and useful. The most important representative of this point
of view in England was George Puttenham, who wrote as follows in
The Arte of English Poesie (1589). The passage is so important
that it is quoted at length:

*For as the evill and vicious disposition of the braine hinders the sounde
judgement and discourse of man with busie and disordered phantasies,
for which cause the Greeks call him* phantastikos, *so is that part, being
well affected, not onely nothing disorderly or confused with any monstrous imaginations or conceits, but very formall, and in his much
multiformitie* uniforme, *that is well proportioned, and so pasing clear,
that by it, as by a glasse or mirrour, are reprsented unto the soule all
manner of bewtifull visions, whereby the inventive parte of the mynde is
so much holpen as without it no man could devise any new or rare
thing. . . . And this phantasie may be resembled to a glasse, as hath
bene sayd, whereof there be many tempers and manner of makinges, as
the* perspectives *doe acknowledge, for some be false glasses and shew
thinges otherwise than they be in deede, and others right as they be in
deede, neither fairer nor fouler, nor greater nor smaller. There be again
of these glasses that shew things exceeding faire and comely; others that
shew figures very monstrous and ill favoured. Even so is the phantasticall
part of man (if it be not disordered) a representer of the best, most
comely, and bewtifull images or appearances of things to the soule and
according to their very truth. If otherwise, then doth it breede Chimeres
and monsters in mans imaginations, and not onely in his imaginations
but also in all his ordinarie actions and life which ensues. Whereof such
persons as be illuminated with the brightest irradiations of knowledge
and of the veritie and due proportion of things, they are called by the
learned men not* phantastici *.but* euphantasioti, *and of this sorte of
phantasie are all good Poets, notable Captaines strategmatique, all
cunning artificers and engineers, all Legislators, Polititiens and Coun-*

*sellors of estate, in whose exercises the inventive part is most employed,
and is to the sound and true judgement of man most needful.*

Shakespeare, who speaks much about imagination and fancy,
accepts the orthodox Renaissance psychology: imagination, under
the sway of a dominant passion, leads to a kind of madness, a
disorientation or alienation from logical reality. When Hotspur is
carried away by anger and excitement his father remarks:

> *Imagination of some great exploit*
> *Drives him beyond the bounds of patience.*
> I HENRY IV, *I.iii.199–200*

Othello is led astray by his false fantasies and imaginings into
believing that his wife has betrayed him. In his fits of madness Lear
hallucinates a world different from the actual world. Yet Shakespeare, while accepting the current psychology, sets a different
valuation on imagination. It is after all Hotspur and not the
sensible Worcester or Northumberland who wins our sympathies. It
is precisely in his fits of alienation that Lear's imagination conveys
the most tremendous insights into the human condition. It is where
reason falls short that imagination, and poetry which is born of
imagination, provide an apprehension or intimation of truths
"More than cool reason ever comprehends." The key passage is
Hippolyta's answer to Theseus in the fifth act of *A Midsummer
Night's Dream:*

> HIPPOLYTA: *'Tis strange, my Theseus, that these lovers speak of.*
> THESEUS: *More strange than true: I never may believe*
> *These antique fables, nor these fairy toys.*
> *Lovers and madmen have such seething brains,*
> *Such shaping fantasies, that apprehend*
> *More than cool reason ever comprehends.*
> *The lunatic, the lover and the poet*
> *Are of imagination all compact:*
> *One sees more devils than vast hell can hold,*
> *That is, the madman: the lover, all as frantic,*
> *Sees Helen's beauty in a brow of Egypt:*
> *The poet's eye, in a fine frenzy rolling,*

> *Doth glance from heaven to earth, from earth to heaven;*
> *And as imagination bodies forth*
> *The form of things unknown, the poet's pen*
> *Turns them to shapes and gives to airy nothing*
> *A local habitation and a name.*
> *Such tricks hath strong imagination,*
> *That, if it would but apprehend some joy,*
> *It comprehends some bringer of that joy;*
> *Or in the night, imagining some fear,*
> *How easy is a bush supposed a bear!*
> HIPPOLYTA:　*But all the story of the night told over,*
> *And all their minds transfigured so together,*
> *More witnesseth than fancy's images,*
> *And grows to something of great constancy;*
> *But, howsoever, strange and admirable.*

Perhaps we may see here a hint of Shakespeare's justification of the poetic imagination in the picture of minds "transfigured so together" and the images of fancy given "great constancy." The dramatist John Marston was still more forthright when in *What You Will* he made Quadratus speak of fantasy as:

> *a function*
> *Even of the bright immortal part of man.*
> *It is the common passe, the sacred dore,*
> *Unto the prive chamber of the soule. . . .*
> *By it we shape a new creation,*
> *Of things as yet unborne, by it wee feede*
> *Our ravenous memory, our intention feast.*

Dislike and suspicion of the imagination certainly continued to accord with the logical, rationalistic temper of the seventeenth and eighteenth centuries. Dr. Johnson expressed that attitude when he wrote: "Imagination, a licentious and vagrant faculty, unsusceptible of limitations, and impatient of restraint, has always endeavoured to baffle the logician, to perplex the confines of distinction, and burst the enclosures of regularity." But the different valuations put upon poetic imagination by Puttenham, Marston, and Shakespeare stood at the source of a trend which culminated in Romanticism.

Lord Bacon, as we have seen, made imagination the special

The Fall of Babylon
by John Martin, 1831.
Courtesy of
the Trustees of the
British Museum, London.

Epouvantée de l'Héritage
by Honoré Daumier,
1871. The Mansell
Collection of Photographs.

faculty which supports poetry and the arts: the faculty by which artists invent an unreal world more in accordance with man's desires and moral sentiments. He did not attribute to it the sort of insight into truths beyond the comprehension of reason which was suggested by Marston and Shakespeare. Hobbes, whose influence was powerful in inaugurating an empirical approach, seems to have attributed a more restricted role to imagination, though he was not consistent in his pronouncements. His view of poetry is summed up in the statement: "Time and education beget experience; experience begets memory; memory begets judgment and fancy; judgment begets the strength and structure, and fancy begets the ornaments, of a poem." Addison's essays on "The Pleasures of the Imagination" had a very powerful influence in eighteenth-century thought, making imagination central to the aesthetic experience and connecting it with the experience of "transportation" or ecstasy which was associated with Longinus' notion of the Sublime (Addison used the word "greatness"). He recognized both the reproductive power of imagination to call up images "when objects are not actually before the eye" and its capacity by "altering and compounding" these images to "fancy to itself things more great, strange or beautiful than the eye ever saw." Thus imagination "has something in it like creation: it bestows a kind of existence." The poet must "humor the imagination" for by it he "seems to get the better of nature: he takes indeed the landscape after her, but gives it more vigorous touches, heightens its beauty, and so enlivens the whole piece that the images which flow from the objects themselves appear weak and faint in comparison with those that come from the impressions."

Imagination had a prominent position in the philosophy of Hume, who held that to think is to have ideas and equated ideas with images. Hume distinguished between free imagination as "fancy," which produces daydreams and idle suppositions, and imagination as a factor necessary to all belief. Belief, in his theory, is to have an enlivened, vivacious, forcible idea accompanied by a special feeling and to produce this vivacity and liveliness of the idea imagination is a necessary factor. Hume also thought that our common beliefs in a stable material world cannot be completely accounted for by present experience (impressions), past experience (memory), and reasoning, but that imagination occupies a central place in a full description of how such beliefs are formed. Imagination furthermore was closely allied to *sympathy,* which was the key concept in his ethical theory.

> *Our affections* [he says] *depend more upon ourselves, and the internal operations of the mind, than any other impressions; for which reason they arise more naturally from the imagination, and from every lively idea we form of them. This is the nature and cause of sympathy; and 'tis after this manner we enter so deep into the opinions and affections of others, whenever we discover them* (A Treatise of Human Nature, *Bk. II, sec. xi*).

In his *Enquiry Concerning the Principles of Morals,* where he discusses at some length the importance of sympathy in enabling us to enter into the feelings of others, he says: "It is the business of poetry to bring every affection near to us by lively imagery and representation, and to make it look like truth and reality: A certain proof that, whenever that reality is found, our minds are disposed to be strongly affected by it." In the same place he notices the irradiation of shared emotion which is communicated by a theatrical performance enjoyed in common with others.

> *A man who enters the theatre, is immediately struck with the view of so great a multitude, participating of one common amusement; and experiences, from their very aspect, a superior sensibility or disposition of being affected by every sentiment which he shares with his fellow-creatures. He observes the actors to be animated by the appearance of a full audience, and raised to a degree of enthusiasm which they cannot command in any solitary or calm moment.*

Hume contributed little specifically to aesthetic doctrine. But his doctrine of sympathy and of the function of imagination as a factor which makes possible sympathetic understanding among men and the sympathetic sharing of experience was an important anticipatory statement of assumptions which underlay Romantic theories of art as the expansion and communication of experience.

The strands and clusters of ideas which contributed most prominently to the Romantic concept of creative imagination were no doubt the following.

1. Imagination is the mind's power to present vividly a scene or a situation and its emotional aura with a strong impact of actuality. This aspect goes back to classical antiquity and the rhetorical

Calavera Huertista
by José Guadalupe Posada,
ca. *1912.*
*Wood engraving. Courtesy
of the Instituto
Nacional de Bellas Artes
y Letras, Mexico City.*

The Cry
*by Edvard Munch,
1895. Woodcut.
Courtesy of the Courtauld
Institute of Art:
Witt Library, London.*

theories of Aristotle and Longinus. The power to communicate such vivid impressions to others by telling words was often assumed to follow automatically from the power to present absent realities vividly to oneself.

2. Imagination by its power to change and recombine the stored impressions of experience is the source of inventiveness and originality. It enables poets and artists not only to idealize the actual world but to present it convincingly as more strange and more interesting than it is. It lies at the root of *fiction*.

3. Imagination may be the source of insights more profound than the logical understanding and not fully comprehensible to abstract reason.

4. Imagination is the ground of sympathetic understanding whereby we can enter into the feelings of other men and communicate our feeling to them. In the fervor of Romantic enthusiasm these notions were fused to a white-hot luminescence and linked with the new idea of artistic genius. It was an intuitive rather than a logical combination of ideas.

In language very similar to that of Bacon, Kant described the ability of imagination to transcend nature not only (as Bacon had held) for entertainment but also to give concrete substance to "rational ideas" beyond the limits of experienced actuality. In section 49 of the *Critique of Judgment* he wrote:

The imagination (as a productive faculty of cognition) is a powerful agent for creating, as it were, a second nature out of the material supplied to it by actual nature. It affords us entertainment where experience proves too commonplace; and we even use it to remodel experience, always following, no doubt, laws that are based on analogy, but still also following principles which have a higher seat in reason (and which are every whit as natural to us as those followed by the understanding in laying hold of empirical nature). By this means we get a sense of our freedom from the law of association (which attaches to the empirical employment of the imagination), with the result that the material can be borrowed by us from nature in accordance with that law, but be worked up by us into something else—namely, what surpasses nature. Such representations of the imagination may be termed ideas. This is partly because they at least strain after something lying out beyond the confines of experience, and so seek to approximate to a presentation of rational concepts (i.e. intellectual ideas), thus giving to these concepts the semblance of an objective reality.

Blake, unique personality though he was, exemplifies the extremes of the Romantic attitude toward imagination. Blake believed that reality is ultimately spiritual and art is "prophetic" insight into spiritual reality. Imagination is the organ by which alone we gain insight into reality and achieve knowledge of it. It is the "first principle" of knowledge, it is "spiritual sensation." In his battle against materialism and empiricism he condemned those who believed that art imitates nature and who "pretend to Poetry that they may destroy Imagination by imitation of Nature's Images drawn from Remembrance." For to the man of imagination "Nature is Imagination" and creative imagination results not in fiction but in the highest truth. In *Jerusalem* he pictured imagination as the Divine Body stalked by Reason:

> *The Spectre is the Reasoning Power in Man, & when separated*
> *From Imagination and closing itself as in steel in a Ratio*
> *Of the Things of the Memory, It thence frames Laws & Moralities*
> *To destroy Imagination, the Divine Body, by Martyrdom & Wars.*

In the "Vision of the Last Judgment" he described it as follows:

> *The Nature of Visionary Fancy, or Imagination, is very little Known, &*
> *the Eternal nature & permanence of its ever Existent Images is con-*
> *sider'd as less permanent than the things of Vegetative & Generative*
> *Nature; yet the Oak dies as well as the Lettuce, but its Eternal Image &*
> *Individuality never dies, but renews by its seed; just . . . so the Imagi-*
> *native Image returns . . . by the seed of Contemplative Thought; the*
> *writings of the Prophets illustrate these conceptions of the Visionary*
> *Fancy by their various sublime & Divine Images as seen in the Worlds of*
> *Vision.*

The imagination of the Romantics was much more than a mental faculty to receive, recall, and manipulate images; but just what else was never clearly defined. The Romantic concept of creative imagination was not a concept of psychology and no clear psychological description of it is available.

Subsequent theories of the creative imagination have been voluminous rather than illuminating. Coleridge, basing himself on the ideas of Kant through the intermediary of Schelling, differentiated imagination from fancy, regarding the latter merely as a mode of memory free from the restrictions of order in time and space by which true memory is confined. In an often quoted passage but one of which interpretations have not always agreed, he differentiates primary and secondary imagination:

> *The primary imagination I hold to be the living power and prime agent of all human perception, and as a repetition in the infinite mind of the eternal act of creation in the infinite I AM. The secondary imagination I consider as an echo of the former, co-existing with the conscious will, yet still as identical with the primary in the kind of its agency, and differing only in degree and in the mode of its operation.*

Whatever this may mean, it seems that Coleridge identified his "secondary imagination" with the creative imagination of the poet and artist and hoped to give a philosophically reputable basis to the idea of the artist as creator by representing his activity as the finite counterpart of God's eternal creativity. Coleridge also tried to make respectable the old doctrine of art as an imitation of nature by a theory that art does not copy *natura naturata* (nature formed) but imitates *natura naturans* (nature creative) in symbolic fashion. Shelley opposed imagination to reason and attributed to it all creative activity in life as well as art. He thought that imagination has direct vision of the Platonic Ideas or Essences of things and like Hume made it the source of that sympathy which makes social relations possible. Ruskin distinguished a *penetrative* activity of imagination by which the artist pierces to the essence of his subject, an *associate* activity whereby in contrast to deliberate composition he unconsciously organizes the detail to enhance the general effect, and a *contemplative* activity by which he presents analogically a subject which has no concrete image. Ruskin was inclined to deny a creative function to art and to imagination, holding that its capacity lay in the intuitive apprehension of truths beyond the scope of reason.

In the twentieth century imagination has played an important role in the aesthetics of Croce and his English follower, Collingwood. In general, however, the creative imagination of the Romantics has become of less and less interest to theories of art, although it has remained a primary catchword of critical and appreciative language.

IX. Theories of Expression and Communication

Expression theories of art tie in closely with theories which regard art as an instrument of emotional communication, a language of the emotions, and the two types of theory will be discussed together. Both classes of theory have usually held that the expression—or communication—of emotion is the central function of art and that works of art are successful insofar as they express—or communicate—emotion. It is possible, however, to hold such a theory while maintaining that expression, or communication, of emotion is one of several functions of works of art. Both classes of theory came to prominence in the West at the time of the Romantic Movement, and since that time have been taken for granted and are accepted with as little question as were didactic theories in classical antiquity and through the Middle Ages.

It is convenient to discuss these theories under three general heads, although in many formulations ideas from each of the three clusters may be combined. These heads are: (1) art as self-expression on the part of the artist; (2) art as the transmission of emotion from the artist to his public; (3) art as the embodiment of emotion in an art object. The word "expression" is commonly used in all three cases. Works of art may be called "expressive" under any of these heads and are valued for their "expressiveness" in any of these senses. The senses are not, of course, usually kept distinct.

ART AS SELF-EXPRESSION

We speak popularly of gnashing the teeth, jumping for joy, frowning, blushing, weeping, etc. as "expressing" emotion. By this is sometimes meant that these modes of behavior are *signs* of emotion insofar as other people can infer from them the feelings by which a person is actuated, the inner subjective nature of his experience.[1] They are also *expressions* in the sense that they afford some relief from emotional tension—the curative value of a "good cry" is widely recognized—and insofar as they are generally spontaneous: a person will ordinarily "give vent" to his emotions by such characteristic behavior unless either he deliberately suppresses the appropriate reaction or has trained himself to suppress certain manifestations of emotion. They are either inborn or conventional, either idiosyncratic or general to a particular culture pattern. For example, widening the eyes is a sign of surprise in the West but the average European reading a Chinese novel would need an explanatory note to tell him that among the Chinese putting out the tongue is a sign of surprise and widening the eyes a sign of anger.

Both particular passing emotions and more permanent emotional dispositions plant their characteristic impress on the conformation and movements of the body, in particular on the configuration of

---

[1] In current philosophy of mind emotional states are partly identified by the characteristic modes of behavior formerly spoken of as their signs or expression. Othello's being jealous or angry is in part a matter of his behavior (or having an impulse to behave) in a certain way. Talk of the "inner nature" of an emotional experience as an inner "object" entirely distinct from the outer "signs" expressing it is now held to be based on a false model of mental phenomena as forming a distinct realm over against physical phenomena.

the features, on bodily habit and posture, and on modes of gesticulation. The outward manifestations of relatively stable emotional propensities, often regarded as qualities of character and temperament, belong on the one hand to the science of physiognomy, foreshadowed by Lord Bacon, and on the other hand to the study of gesture. Charlotte Wolff, for example, in her *Psychology of Gesture* investigated gesture, and in particular manual gesticulation, as "a subconscious expression of personality." Particular emotions also have their characteristic modes of manifestation. They were much studied by artists of the Renaissance and were elaborately classified by Lomazzo in his *Treatise on the Art of Painting* (1584). Le Brun's *Conférences sur l'expression des différents caractères des passions,* published in 1667, remained a standard textbook for two centuries. In *The Anatomy and Philosophy of Expression as Connected with the Fine Arts* (first published in 1806 and later in a third and enlarged edition posthumously in 1844) Sir Charles Bell set himself to ground the study of emotional expression on a firmer basis of scientific anatomy. Charles Darwin, dissatisfied with Bell's assumption that men are born with certain muscles specially designed for the expression of their feelings, assembled material over many years for a comparative study of emotional expression and claimed to show that our ways of expressing feeling and emotion have an evolutionary origin, having once served a biological purpose and afterward become innate when their original function was superseded in the more complicated framework of social life. The *Expression of the Emotions in Man and the Animals,* published in 1872, initiated a long series of modern physiognomic investigations in which the close relation between the study of emotional expression and the fine arts has been severed.

There is an enormous reservoir of popular lore in this matter of emotional expression preserved and embalmed in proverb and story, literature, handbooks, and designs from most of the great cultural traditions of mankind. In ancient India with its passion for classification the analysis of expressive gestures was carried to surprising lengths in the handbooks of etiquette and instructions for dance, drama, and song. The *Sangita Damodarah* of Subhankara, ascribed to the fifteenth century, is a compilation from earlier works on music and dramaturgy. The nine (or as some say, ten) main *sentiments* (*ragas*) are described and subdivided at length with the appropriate gestures and expressions for each—the fifty *bhavas* (enduring, fleeting, and ennobling), the fourteen *havas* (gestures of damsels to attract young men and make them succumb to the flame of love), and the well-nigh innumerable *anubhavas*. The expressive postures of the limbs in the dance (*angaharas*) were similarly analyzed and categorized: fourteen varieties of movements of the head, seventy-one different postures of the hand, and so on. These appear not to have been purely conventional, as for example were many of the gestures of the Japanese Noh drama, but a formalization of naturally expressive movements. Western literature and painting is replete with a host of stock emotional expressions: weeping, sighing, frowning, sneering, smiling, laughing, and the rest. But popular and literary lore also recognizes the large element of ambiguity in spontaneous emotional expression. Regarded as a means of communication it is hit-and-miss and clumsy. There is seldom a single unambiguous physical manifestation of a particular subjective emotion. Laughter, it is said, is close to tears and there may be genuine doubt whether a person is weeping or amused. Ovid, describing the terror of the Sabine Women, wrote:

> *Nam Timor unus erat, facies non una timoris,*
> *Pars laniat crines, pars sine mente sedet.*
> *Altera moesta silet, frustra vocat altera matrem,*
> *Haec queritur, stupet haec, haec fugit, illa manet.*

> (*For their Fear was one, but the manifestation of fear was manifold. Some tore their hair, some sat bereft of wit. One was silent in her grief, another called vainly on her mother. One lamented, one sat stunned, one sought to flee, another stayed rooted to the spot.*)

Still more difficult is it to infer the subjective feeling or behavior-impulse unambiguously from outward expressions. We need not go all the way with such modern psychologists as Carney Landis or Samuel Fernberger, who in opposition to Darwin have claimed that it is impossible ever to diagnose emotion from facial expression and bodily gesture alone unless one is given also a clue from the situation and context. Darwin himself admitted that the varieties of expression are not adequate to discriminate the varieties of emotion known to popular wisdom and enshrined in common knowledge.

Dislike, he says, easily rises into hatred; but such feelings, if experienced in moderate degree, "are not clearly expressed by any movement of the body or features, excepting perhaps by a certain gravity of behavior, or by some ill temper." Anger and indignation "differ from rage only in degree, and there is no marked distinction in their characteristic signs." Scorn and disdain "can hardly be distinguished from contempt, excepting that they imply a rather more angry frame of mind. Nor can they clearly be distinguished from feelings . . . of sneering and defiance." Extreme contempt "hardly differs from disgust."

On the other hand outward manifestation is often more precise than verbal description. In the ordinary affairs of life, traveling in a train or watching a crowd, we may often see a quirk of the lips, a twitch of the eyebrows, a gesture of the hand, which seem exactly and precisely indicative of a mood we have no words to describe. The expression portrayed by a great artist may impress us as both precise and profound, whether of character or of passing emotion, yet pages of prosaic, scientific reporting may still be wide of the mark. As Sartre has emphasized, and Darwin would not have denied, we are continually aware introspectively of subtle qualitative differences in the feeling-tone of emotions even where we cannot point either to a characteristic inclination in behavior or to a corresponding mode of expression. Those who hold an expressive theory of art often claim that it is the qualitative character of felt emotion which is expressed by works of art, and either by them only or at any rate much more adequately by them than by any other means of communication.

A very simple form of expression theory was once popular in language theory distinguishing the evocative language of poetry from the factual communications of scientific prose. A classical statement of the theory was given by Rudolf Carnap in *Philosophy and Logical Syntax:*

> *Many linguistic utterances are analogous to laughter in that they have only an expressive function, no representative function. Examples of this are cries like "Oh, Oh," or, on a higher level, lyrical verses. The aim of a lyrical poem in which occur the words "sunshine" and "clouds" is not to inform us of certain meteorological facts, but to express certain feelings of the poet and to excite similar feelings in us.*

The distinction between "referential" or scientific-informative language and the "suasory and emotive" use of language was developed at length by I. A. Richards in *The Meaning of Meaning* (with C. K. Ogden) and *Principles of Literary Criticism.* To the same class belongs the theory which traces the origin of music to instinctive or reflex vocalizations or modifications of the human voice under the stress of emotion. The theory was argued by Herbert Spencer among others in an essay on *The Origin and Function of Music* (1857). In the plastic arts a rather similar view underlies statements by artists such as Van Gogh about the emotional expressiveness of color or line.

In fact, however, the analogy between the natural expression of emotions and emotional expression in works of art is not very close. The mode of expression in art is not instinctive, stereotyped, or ready to hand. It has to be sought in each case and the search is often complicated and arduous. It is to some extent original in each new instance. Works of art are not, typically, made in the white heat of emotion, and the idea that the artist in some way puts into them an emotion he is experiencing at the time he is making them is not nowadays seriously considered. It is plausible only for exceptional instances, such perhaps as the extempore performance of "Blues" music. More often a work of art germinates, perhaps for a long time, in the artist's mind and needs a cool and collected head for the execution. It was to guard against a too crude theory of emotional expression that Wordsworth used the phrase "emotion recollected in tranquillity."

Nor is it plausible to suppose that the artist only embodies in the artwork emotions or emotional situations which he has experienced in his own person. There are male painters who have expressed in paint the emotions of maternal love and, as Lalo remarked, Malraux, d'Annunzio, and Saint-Exupéry are not the only or necessarily the best poets of aviation. An artist may express the emotions of a slave without himself having been in the situation of a slave. This ability to transcend the limitations of personal experience is precisely the power claimed for the poetic or artistic imagination.

Nowadays therefore the expression theory often assumes the modified form of a claim that the artist is able with some degree of vividness and concreteness to express in his chosen medium the inner feel, the subjective experienced quality, of emotional situations actual, recollected, or imagined, which cannot be conveyed by ordinary language. This is what is generally meant by calling art a "language of the emotions." This form of expression theory is often combined with a naturalistic conception of art in the claim that works of art do indeed "imitate" natural situations, real, imagined, or ideal, but do not "imitate" them objectively; they "imitate" them as colored by the particular emotional attitude which the artist has toward them—un coin de la nature vu à travers un tempérament (Zo Za). Thus the work of art is conceived *both* as a mirror through which we look at a segment of reflected reality and *also* as a mirror of the artist's emotional attitude toward it. That this is now regarded not as an unfortunate failing of artists to achieve objectivity but as a specific value of art is one of the inheritances of the Romantic Movement with its glorification of the artist and of experience.

A corollary of the modern claim that good artworks achieve superior precision in the expression of emotions is the view that the "content" of a work of art—its message or what it is saying—is so intimately linked to the form that it could be expressed in no other way. This is the antithesis of the older doctrine, voiced for example by Horace in his *Ars Poetica* (ll. 309–311), that the poet must express sound doctrine in attractive language. Modern critics usually take for granted that in poetry the meaning cannot be adequately stated apart from the actual words of the poem in which it is embodied—a poem cannot be adequately paraphrased. The ancients held the opposite and the opposite is implied in such statements as Pope's "what oft was felt but ne'er so well expressed." The modern view involves the consequence that poetic truth is ineffable in the sense that it cannot be formulated fully in discursive language; it can only be apprehended intuitively by contemplating just that set of words which constitutes the poem. Similar claims are made *a fortiori* for the other arts. Schopenhauer was one of the first to maintain such a view of art. In *The World as Will and Idea* (Bk. III, ch. xxxiv) he said:

We are only perfectly satisfied by the impression of a work of art when it leaves something which, with all our thinking about it, we cannot

bring down to the distinctness of a conception. . . . Therefore it is an
undertaking as unworthy as it is absurd if . . . one seeks to reduce a
poem of Shakespeare's or Goethe's to the abstract truth which it was its
aim to communicate.

The claim that such precision and this particular kind of uniqueness are specific characteristics of works of art, indeed that they go
hand in hand and are criteria for the excellence of any work of art,
derives from the new outlook on art and the artist which came to
the fore with the Romantics and which still reigns almost unchal-
lenged in contemporary criticism.

A special twist was given to this theory by the Neo-idealist
aesthetics of Croce, who was followed by R. G. Collingwood in
England and more recently by Professor J. M. Cameron in his
Inaugural Lecture *Poetry and Dialectic.* According to this view the
feeling-emotion (actual, recollected, or imagined) does not first
emerge in the experience of the artist and then find expression in a
work of art. The feeling attains concreteness in expression and is
apprehended by the artist only in and through the process of
expressing it. It is by the expression of his feeling in art forms, this
theory maintains, that an artist comes to terms with it, gives it
contour and shape, actualizes it for apprehension. It is by being
clarified through the formative impulse of art that the formless and
elusive feeling tone and mood which accompany all our perceptions
and our other commerce with the world outside us acquire in the
case of the artist both structure and precision. The obsessive character of the artist's impulse to express his feeling in artistic form
derives less, it is claimed, from the desire to communicate his feeling
to other men than from the need to apprehend it himself. By
formulating it in art he as it were digests it, makes the inarticulate
articulate and gains relief from the unassimilable pressure of the
unknown and formless. Professor Cameron says:

The rendering of a state of feeling through the complexity and inner
richness of poetic representation brings it about that the state of feeling
so rendered is itself complex and rich, and valuable on this account; or,
for we can place no limit upon the possible achievements of poetic
representation, a state of feeling which is complex and resistant to
characterisation, and on that account burdensome and frustrating, may

*be rendered clear and powerful when there is revealed to us a unity in
the complexity, a unity we should otherwise have missed.*

The theory takes account of a very general but not universal
experience of artistic creation. One remembers that Goethe in a
conversation with Eckermann said of his *Ballads:* "I have had them
all in my head for many a long year. They occupied my mind like
gracious images, beautiful dreams which came and went and with
which my imagination delighted to play. It was reluctantly that I
decided to write them and by clothing them in poor inadequate
words say farewell to these radiant images which had been my
friends for so long." Goethe's "radiant images" with which his
imagination played were the so-called formative ideas, the vague
and elusive source material, from which actual poems were eventu-
ally composed in his mind.

In the Crocean theory good art is successful expression of emotion
and expression consists in the finding of images by which the
emotion is articulated and rendered determinate for apprehension—a process which Croce called "intuition." Thus artistic creation is a mental process and the work of art is in the mind of the
artist. Its subsequent embodiment in physical form of paint or stone
or musical sound, by which it becomes a public object, is regarded
as secondary. The theory has been criticized on the ground that it
attributes too little importance to the physical medium and to the
actual manipulation of the medium by the artist in the coming into
being of works of art. Indeed criticism of this type is found as early
as 1926 by Alain in *Système des beaux-arts.*

In a more general sense art is claimed to "express" the total
personality of the artist, and works of art like handwriting are
regarded as in some sense images or replicas of the artists who create
them. This idea of art as generalized self-expression dominates
modern criticism and educational practice, in which the child is
encouraged to "express himself" rather than to learn and follow
rules of correctness. The knowledge that a work of art does inevitably reflect the personality of the artist is no new thing. Isocrates in
the fourth century B.C. repeatedly affirmed that fine writing is a
reflection of character and an outward image of inward virtues of
the soul, a view which was repeated by Longinus in his often

quoted remark that "sublime utterance is an echo of greatness of soul." The idea has become a commonplace, as in such statements as Sainte-Beuve's "Tel arbre, tel fruit," and more recently Vlaminck's "Tel homme, telle peinture." But the idea that self-expression by the artist is a central function or a sufficient justification of art did not appear in the West before the Romantic Movement. It too has since become a generally accepted assumption. In a letter published in the catalogue to his Amsterdam exhibition in 1958 shortly before his death Roger Bissière wrote: "J'ai horreur de tout ce qui est systematique. De tout ce qui tend a m'enfermer dans des barrières. Ma peinture est l'image de ma vie. Le miroir de l'homme que je suis, tout entier avec mes faiblesses aussi. Devant ma toile je ne pense pas au chef d'oeuvre . . ." When asked to talk about their work artists tend to voice the ideas which are current in their time: before the modern, post-Romantic period such an utterance by a prominent artist would have been impossible or have seemed the sheerest nonsense. Now it is taken for granted.

No one could be interested to deny that works of art are indications of the artist's character. The whole of modern biographical and sociological criticism rests on this assumption. Yet, as the French aesthetician Charles Lalo has shown at length in his two books *L'Expression de la vie dans l'art* (1933) and *L'Art loin de la vie* (1939), far from being simple and straightforward the ways in which art objects can be used as evidence for the personality traits of their creators are almost indefinitely varied and complicated. Sometimes the work of art seems to express directly the artist's character, at other times—as for example with Schubert—a man's art seems to give vent to submerged personality traits which do not find expression in his nonartistic life. It is commonly claimed that the art products of children and psychotics express their subconscious minds, have a therapeutic effect by providing release for submerged emotional stresses and also afford data whereby the trained observer can make deductions about inhibitions and complexes effectively. Yet these need not be good works of art in order to serve this purpose. There is a sense in which everything a man does deliberately and with attentive care is a "sign" of his personality and everything which he does spontaneously reveals his unconscious makeup: if we knew everything a man does we should be in a position to know all that can be known about him. Yet it is clear that sometimes (though not always) when works of art are said to be an expression of the artist's personality something more is meant than that a skilled observer can deduce from them things about the artist's mental makeup. The contact with the artist's personality which is thought to be obtained through the work of art is conceived as more immediate and direct than knowledge by inference and deduction. Yet precisely where the difference lies, the special sense in which works of art are asserted to be expressions of personality, has not been worked out in any coherent theory. From the point of view of aesthetics it is perhaps more important to understand the ways in which the post-Romantic conception of art as self-expression differs from the classical and the oriental conceptions.

In antiquity there was no theory of self-expression as such. The idea was developed in connection with the theory of public speaking and consisted, briefly, in the belief that in order to persuade his audience to take up the emotional attitude toward a situation which he wished them to take up an orator ought himself to experience that emotional attitude. This would enable him to "image" more vividly, to put the situation convincingly "before the eyes" of his audience in the light he wanted, and to find suitable words to do so. The classical statement of the doctrine is by Quintilian.

Accordingly the first essential is that those feelings should prevail with us that we wish to prevail with the judge, and that we should be moved ourselves before we attempt to move others. But how are we to generate those emotions in ourselves, since emotion is not in our power? I will do my best to explain. There are certain experiences which the Greeks call phantasias, *and the Romans* visions, *whereby things absent are presented to our imagination with such extreme vividness that they seem actually to be before our very eyes. It is the man who is really sensitive to such impressions who will have the greatest power over the emotions. Some writers describe the possessor of this power of vivid imagination, whereby things, words and actions are presented in the most realistic manner, by the Greek word* euphantasiotos; *and it is a power which all may readily acquire if they will. When the mind is unoccupied or is absorbed by fantastic hopes of daydreams, we are haunted by these visions of which I am speaking to such an extent that we imagine we are travelling abroad, crossing the sea, fighting, addressing the people, or enjoying the use of wealth that we do not actually possess, and seem to ourselves not to be dreaming but acting. Surely, then, it may be possible to turn this form of hallucination to some profit. I am complaining that a man has been murdered. Shall I not bring before my eyes all the circumstances which it is reasonable to imagine must have occurred in such a connection? Shall I not see the assassin burst suddenly from his hiding-place, the victim tremble, cry for help, beg for mercy, or turn to run? Shall I not see the fatal blow delivered and the stricken body fall? Will not the blood, the deathly pallor, the groan of agony, the death-rattle, be indelibly impressed on my mind?*

From such impressions arises that enargeia *which Cicero calls illumination and* actuality, *which makes us seem not so much to narrate as to exhibit the actual scene, while our emotions will be no less actively stirred than if we were present at the actual occurrence* . . .

Here Quintilian is developing the accepted classical theory of emotional effects. The work of art is judged by its effectiveness in producing a desired result. The result desired is a particular emotional response in an audience. The means by which it is to be achieved is by vividly picturing and representing a scene as if present before the eyes. In order to do this Quintilian thinks that the artist must induce in *himself* the emotions he wishes to produce in his audience and thus by expressing his own feelings implant similar feelings in the audience. A great deal of Western (as opposed to Oriental) theory of drama has been based on this assumption.

The expression theories which came into vogue with the Romantic ways of thought were instrumental in a different sense. It was assumed that self-expression by the artist was a good thing *either* because any extension of experience is a good thing *or* because the artist is a superior sort of man and therefore benefits others by expressing himself and communicating his superior make-up through the medium of his art. The latter view was stated by Véron when he said: "In a word, it is from the worth of the artist that much of his work derives." Similarly some more recent philosophers and educationalists, including for example John Dewey, have maintained that the worth of the artwork derives from the superior refinement, insight, or endowment generally of the artist or from his capacity otherwise to set an example to his fellowmen. The attitude most prevalent today, however, involves an unexamined assumption (instanced by the quotation from Bissiére on p. 234) that self-expression is sufficient justification in itself and needs no further excuse.

Such a view is repugnant to the Oriental habit of mind, which in this respect is nearer to medieval European ways of thought than to post-Romantic attitudes. As we saw in surveying Chinese art theories, the idea of self-expression was familiar to Chinese writers at an early date. But the artist was first required to bring himself into unison with the cosmic spirit of Tao and only then was self-expression justified when by expressing himself the artist was also expressing the Tao. Indian art theory tends to be more metaphysical and to apply to artistic activity the language of religious discipline. The Indian aesthetician K. C. Pandey is able to adopt the language of German Idealism and states that the arts, according to Indian theory, "present the Absolute in sensuous garb" and that art products serve as a medium whereby a competent observer may "get the experience of the Absolute." The Indian artist was expected to undergo a self-imposed mental discipline, a mode of spiritual yoga in some ways analogous to mystical disciplines known in the West, and only then was self-expression justified when by it the artist could also express his insight into or union with the metaphysical world beyond the world of ephemeral and passing illusion. The aesthetic pleasure obtained by contemplation of a great work of art was spoken of in terms analogous to those used to describe the bliss of the adept who achieves union with the Absolute. So far as the expression of emotion was concerned, the artist was required to bring his own emotional reactions into harmony with a universal pattern of emotion before their expression in art was admitted. Radhakamal Mukerjee of Lucknow University has put it as follows: "The Indian artist through his elevated yoga meditation, that engenders complete detachment and universality of self, and subdues the fluctuations of passing desires and emotions, evokes his own abstract or universal moods and sentiments." Difficult as such language may seem, it is at any rate plain that for Indian thought self-expression by the individual was not a function of art but was thought justified only when by it the artist could express and communicate an insight achieved into some overindividual order or reality.

The difference between Oriental and Western ideas on self-expression has been described as follows by Dr. Thomas Munro in *Oriental Aesthetics* (1965), where he speaks of the "subjectivism" of Western art and says that one of its characteristic manifestations is

> the desire for self-expression by the individual artist—an aim which Oriental and medieval Christian religion would have regarded as egotistic. The desire to express one's own personality does involve a special interest in oneself; in that which is to be expressed; in one's own inner attitudes, desires, emotions, and perhaps frustrations. Here again the Western artist, however self-conscious, differs markedly from his traditional Eastern counterpart. The latter, in theory at least, sought to achieve inner peace, serenity, and oneness with nature. Many Western artists are more eager to display before the public their moods of anxiety, frustration, discontent, mockery, rejection, exclusion, and resentment towards the modern world. Such attitudes are at the opposite pole from the Confucian ideal of inner harmony and the Taoist one of contentment with the natural course of things. The Western artist may not try to change his psychic discords into harmonies by self-discipline; he may prefer to vent them impulsively and perhaps aggressively for what they are.

ART AS EMOTIONAL COMMUNICATION

Popular wisdom believes, and most psychologists agree, that in emotional situations the act of expression relaxes nervous tension and brings relief to pent-up emotional pressure. We become less keyed up when our feelings are manifested overtly. Therefore both in connection with artistic creation and in other walks of life we commonly say that a man "expresses himself" or "expresses his feelings" when he indulges in some form of activity which derives from a deep-seated urge and leaves him soothed and fulfilled. Since men are social beings most people obtain added satisfaction if the expression conveys to other people an awareness of their emotion and induces others to share it sympathetically. The element of communication can add to the effectiveness of the expression in bringing relief; failure to communicate can bring a sense of frustration. But the connection between expression and communication is not an essential or an inevitable one. It is not nonsense to say that a man expressed himself in the creation of a work of art which was not understood by anyone until after his death or which was so idiosyncratic that it failed to communicate his emotions to others.

When writers speak of expression in art they nevertheless generally imply communication also. The sort of communication which is implied differs from that which is achieved through descriptive nonartistic language. When a man says in cold and unemotive language as a result of introspection that he is experiencing, or has just experienced, such and such an emotion we do not say that he is "expressing" the emotion but that he is reporting it. It also differs from the sort of communication which may attend natural expression of emotion. When a man displays the signs of indignation or anger, observers do not usually themselves feel anger though they may feel fear or amusement. But if a man describes or represents in some way a situation calculated to evoke indignation (e.g., a case of blatant injustice) and does so in a manner which makes patent his own feeling of indignation, then he may arouse indignation in his audience. This is the arousal of emotion by "infection," to use Tolstoy's word. Most emotional theories of art turn on this point. The naïve conception of art as an instrument of emotional arousal has been central to most discussions of art from educational or sociological points of view and was the most prevalent conception in antiquity (e.g., the foregoing quotation from Quintilian). Such theories can be classified as "contagion" theories: the artist expresses his own emotion or emotional attitude and does so in such a way as to evoke in his public a like emotional attitude toward the situation which he presents. But the intention to arouse emotion is not a necessary concomitant of expression. It would be difficult to say whether in the *Guernica* Picasso was primarily expressing his own hatred and indignation at the barbarities of war or whether his purpose was primarily to arouse such emotions in others.

Communication theories of art must be classified in general as *instrumental* theories in that they assume the central function of art is to assist a certain sort of communication among men, and as their standard for appraising particular works of art they apply the yardstick of their effectiveness in communicating emotion or experience. "Communication" is used with a different significance in different types of communication theory. Sometimes it is assumed to be a matter of causing the audience or observer actually to experience the emotion, feeling, or mood with which the artwork is concerned. And such theories of emotional inducement may envisage an ephemeral and playful experience of emotion, a not very serious interlude from the more important involvements of life, or they may envisage a permanent and important influence upon the character and personality of persons exposed to the artwork. In both types of theory, but particularly in the latter, the standard of effectiveness is usually supplemented by a moral appraisal of the effect. Such composite theories, which predominated in antiquity and have been prominent at all periods in the West, may be termed "amelioration" theories because they tend to assess works of art not by aesthetic standards, or not by these standards alone, but by their effect upon persons exposed to them. The two outstanding names associated with theories of this kind are Plato and Tolstoy.

There is another kind of communication theory, which differs from the foregoing in holding that the emotion, feeling, or mood is not communicated by inducing the observer to experience it as in ordinary life but in a special kind of way, which is said to differ both from learning *about* it and from being fully involved in it.

The most extreme form of the amelioration theory was put forward by Leo Tolstoy in *What Is Art?* (1898). Tolstoy was impressed by the amount of social and individual energy devoted to the cultivation of the arts and wanted to find out, first whether the sacrifices which are made in the service of art are justified and second how to distinguish genuine from spurious art and so avoid wastage. Therefore, he said, "it is necessary for a society in which works of art arise and are supported to find out whether all that professes to be art really is art; whether (as is presupposed in our society) all that which is art is good; and whether it is important and worth those sacrifices which it necessitates." Tolstoy was seeking a criterion of value and assumed that the pursuit of art can be justified only if some ulterior benefit can be seen to derive from it. He believed that he had found the social function of art, and hence its justification, in the transmission of emotions by "infection." He therefore defined art in terms of this function. "Art," he said, "is a human activity consisting in this that one man consciously, by means of external signs, hands on to others feelings he has lived through, and that other people are infected by these feelings, and also experience them." Having reached this conception of the nature of art, Tolstoy inevitably imported a moral criterion for its appraisal: good art was for him that art which transmits to others by infection "the highest and best feelings to which men have arisen."

The search for an external justification of art in edification or amelioration, whether in Tolstoy or some forms of Marxist or other sociological theories, is opposed to the view which is most characteristic of contemporary outlook that the cultivation of the arts is a "self-rewarding" activity needing no justification outside itself. It is also nowadays generally assumed that direct emotional response to a work of art is not consistent with a genuine "aesthetic" contact. It is not denied that works of art often have stimulated emotion, that this is one of the many purposes they may serve. But the aesthetic enjoyment of a work of art is nowadays thought to differ characteristically from the emotional response to a revivalist sermon or a political harangue, and direct evocation of emotion is not any longer regarded as a central criterion in art theory.

A special form of amelioration theory is the theory of emotional *catharsis,* which derives from Aristotle. One of Plato's objections to the arts in his ideal society was his belief that the sympathetic stimulation of emotion through poetry and drama was likely to increase the emotional impressionability which he regarded as one of the weaknesses of the Greek character. In the *Republic* (605, c–d) he said: "When we hear Homer or one of the tragic poets representing the sufferings of a great man and making him bewail them at length with every expression of tragic grief, you know how even the best of us enjoy it and let ourselves be carried away by our feelings; and we are full of praises for the merits of the poet who can most powerfully affect us in this way." Aristotle was mitigating this too drastic condemnation with his theory of *catharsis,* a word which carried associations with both religious purification and medical purging. In the eighth book of the *Politics* he said:

> Mental disturbances, which are pathological in some cases, afflict us all in reduced or acute measure. Thus we find pity and fear in the former cases and pathological disorders in the latter. Persons who are a prey to such disorders are seen to be restored when they listen to the delirious

strains of sacred song, just as though they had been medically treated
and purged. In precisely the same way pity, fear and other such emo-
tions, in so far as they affect each of us, will yield to the purificatory
effect and pleasurable relief produced by music.

Aristotle appears to regard pity and fear as forms of mental distur-
bance, which can be "purged" and rendered innocuous by appropriate kinds of art. Therefore, he concludes, music and drama do
have a useful function. He is resuscitating the homeopathic theory
which had been ridiculed by the philosopher Heraclitus: "The
blood-guilty vainly seek purification by blood as if a man should try
to wash off mud with mud." The word *catharsis* occurs twice in
Aristotle's *Poetics* (only once as an aesthetic term) and Aristotle
nowhere developed the theory. How much significance he gave to it,
and the precise significance he attached, is obscure. Different interpretations have been argued. The simplest, and the most frequently
assumed, is that expressed by Milton in the prefatory essay to
Samson Agonistes, that it was a power "by raising pity and fear, or
terror, to purge the mind of those and suchlike passions—that is, to
temper and reduce them to just measure with a kind of delight,
stirred up by reading or seeing those passions well imitated."

This theory so interpreted holds that the audience obtains relief
by sympathetic emotional release in a way analogous to the genius
or neurotic who obtains emotional release by expressing himself in
artistic creations. The theory is most plausible when applied to
drama or cinema or dance. But the view that art is justified by its
curative side effects on the audience, or that people cultivate the
arts for emotional relief, conflicts with the general outlook on
artistic matters today. The voiding of emotion obtained from
exposure to a tear-jerking film or a sentimental novel is, it is explained, a passive affect, whereas the full appreciation of a work of
art demands concentration and energy. Some writers, however, still
try to give a profounder significance to *catharsis* in explaining the
appreciation of great drama such as *Lear* or *Ghosts.*

A third form of amelioration theory, and the one most in keeping
with the new outlook which came to the fore in the Romantic
period, is the belief that works of art enable those who enjoy them
to expand and enrich their emotional experience beyond the limi-

tations imposed by the circumstances of each man's individual life. Through art, by sympathetic and imaginative self-identification, we enjoy, savor, or get the feel of, emotions and attitudes which otherwise we would not have known. Underlying this view is the assumption that the elaboration of emotional experience, its enrichment, expansion, or increased malleability are worthwhile for their own sake. The arts are held valuable as a potent instrument for achieving this and the artist's service to society is said to derive from his power to bring to others the possibility of such expansion of experience without the inconveniences which full commitment in real life situations would involve. The classical statement of this Romantic view was given by I. A. Richards in *The Principles of Literary Criticism*. In the theory of value which he there propounds he says: "The conduct of life is throughout an attempt to organize impulses so that success is obtained for the greater number or mass of them, for the most important or weightiest set." He draws the consequence that the most valuable states of mind "are those which involve the widest and most comprehensive coordination of activities and the least curtailment, conflict, starvation, and restriction." It is the peculiarity of the arts that by giving ourselves over to them we can secure the arousal of emotional impulses in ourselves and enjoy their organization into the most comprehensive and richest systems with the least interference because they do not spill over into overt action.

> *The arts* [says Richards] *are our storehouse of recorded values. They spring from and perpetuate hours in the lives of exceptional people, when their control and command of experience is at its highest, hours when the varying possibilities of existence are most clearly seen and the different activities which may arise are most exquisitely reconciled, hours when habitual narrowness of interests or confused bewilderment are replaced by an intricately wrought composure. Both in the genesis of a work of art, in the creative moment, and in its aspect as a vehicle of communication, reasons can be found for giving the arts a very important place in the theory of Value . . . subtle or recondite experiences are for most men incommunicable and indescribable, though social conventions or terror of the loneliness of the human situation may make us pretend the contrary. In the arts we find the record in the only form in which these things can be recorded of the experiences which have seemed worth having to the most sensitive and discriminating persons.*

Written in 1925 this is an early twentieth-century formulation of Romantic presuppositions. Since that time the trend has been away from an instrumental theory of artistic value, however elevated may be the definitional form it takes.

ART AS EMOTIONAL EMBODIMENT

In the course of the present century the distinctive trend of aesthetic thinking has been away from instrumental theories as also from naturalistic theories. As the Romantic notion of the artist-genius has receded, the idea that artists are primarily concerned with expressing their own superior emotions and evoking corresponding emotions in their public has lost something of its hold on aesthetic theory. At the same time a better understanding of what takes place in the appreciation of works of art has brought about a pretty general agreement that the central feature of our commerce with art objects is not represented by ordinary emotional response. There is now a healthy scepticism toward all theories based on the idea that the observer reacts emotionally toward works of art by experiencing in himself the emotion "carried" by them from the artist, and then perhaps projecting his own emotion upon the work of art. When we hear a piece of music as plaintive, we do not experience an emotion of sadness and project this into the music (we may be feeling gay and therefore regard the plaintive music as inappropriate to our mood of the moment); neither do we, as an element within the act of appreciation, infer that the composer was feeling mournful when he composed the music. Rather, it is thought, in appreciation we apprehend and as it were taste the tincture of mournfulness as an objective quality inherent in the music as heard. Appreciation is regarded as a mode of cognition, of particularly intense and often emotionally colored awareness, of the art object. And this awareness and savoring of higher order qualities is valued for itself not for extraneous advantages which may follow from it.

In view of this change of attitude modern theories in one form or another take the view that the artist somehow embodies or symbolizes an emotion in the work of art (an emotion he may either have experienced or have known by imaginative sympathy) and the observer savors and enjoys this emotion without experiencing it in the ordinary sense although in some way he achieves the distinctive flavor of its feeling tone. In a very general way T. S. Eliot described such theories by saying that the poet or artist creates in the work of art an "objective correlative" of the emotion. In his essay "Hamlet and His Problems" (1919) he said: "The only way of expressing an emotion in the form of art is by finding an "objective correlative"; in other words, a set of objects, a situation, a chain of events which shall be the formula of that *particular* emotion." Further elaboration of the way in which a situation or object in an artwork can act as a "formula" or correlate of an emotion has since been undertaken by philosophers of the Wittgenstein school.

This changed outlook led to a reformulation of the communication theory. In an interesting article entitled "The Language of Feelings" (*The British Journal of Aesthetics,* January 1962) Huw Morris Jones maintained that the several arts are languages whereby "the artist explores and exploits the changing ways of feeling, and gives them a habitation and a name." Through being embodied in the artwork the feeling becomes depersonalized as statements of belief are depersonalized when they receive logical formulation.

> *If therefore it be asked* whose *feelings a work of art expresses or embodies, it can be answered that they are those feelings known by those who speak and feel in a common language, who have learnt the rules, techniques and conventions which are features of the specialised artistic "languages" of this society. These feelings are not to be conceived of as private episodes in the biographies of certain individuals, of the artist or of the person who contemplates his work. . . . Recognising a feeling is like understanding the meaning of a statement, and the conditions of the understanding are the same as those which govern the apprehension of a feeling.*

In our enjoyment of works of art we observe, savor, and have direct perception of the emotional content in its full concreteness of feeling tone but do not fully identify ourselves with it at least in the sense that we do not respond emotionally in the way of ordinary life situations. The tendency now is to regard artistic appreciation as a mode of emotionally colored cognition, not a special form of emotional response.

A special form of this theory was put forward chiefly by Susanne K. Langer, following the German philosopher Cassirer. Her theory is not easy to summarize but can perhaps best be suggested by saying that according to it works of art are symbols or "iconic signs" of emotions. They do not directly express the artist's experienced emotions but rather his apprehension of the nature of emotions. "The function of art is the symbolic expression not of the artist's actual emotions, but of his knowledge of emotion." Art is not a language in the sense of a system of communication which is built up from elements each of which has its own independent emotional significance as words have their meaning.[2] But each work of art is a unique symbol. "A work of art is a symbol—a single, indivisible symbol; which is not saying that it is unanalyzable, but indivisible in the sense that an individual is so. . . . Every work of art is a whole and new symbolic form, and expresses its import directly to anyone who understands it at all." The peculiar manner in which works of art symbolize is by providing a sensuous analogue of the inner life. Works of art "imitate" or reproduce in themselves not the concrete emotion or situation of actuality but the pattern, form, rhythm, or *gestalt* of emotional situations. "Music," Miss Langer has said, "is a tonal analogue of emotive life." Thus a work of art is a symbol which does not symbolize anything other than itself but which reproduces in its own structural form the structure or pattern of feeling and emotion.

In a series of books, from *Philosophy in a New Key* (1942) to *Mind: An Essay on Human Feeling* (1967), Miss Langer has expounded and amplified her theories without substantial change but with a breadth of scholarship and a genuine understanding for the emotional aspects of art appreciation which have recommended her writings to many people. Her language is metaphorical as perhaps any close formulation of an Expressionist theory must be. And as she has not succeeded in rendering her metaphors fully concrete or coherent, it is unlikely that others could manage to do so. Works of art, she says in *Mind,* are "images of the forms of feeling." The artist is he who has an intimate knowledge of feeling, and by "projecting" its "forms" into the art object he "expresses the nature of feeling." By the term "forms of feeling" she means, or

2 Such a view as this was unsuccessfully propounded by Deryck Cooke in his book *The Language of Music,* 1959.

sometimes means, the ebb and flow of emotional life, "how feeling rises, develops, tangles or reverses or breaks or sinks, spent in overt action or buried in secrecy." Through his artwork the artist communicates direct awareness of this emotional life, not knowledge *about* it in the manner of the psychologist or the reporter. For an "image" is distinguished from a model: the image "sets forth what the object looks or seems like," whereas a model "always illustrates a principle of construction or operation; it is a symbolic projection of its object which need not resemble it in appearance at all." In contrast the art symbol "sets forth in symbolic projection how vital and emotional and intellectual tensions appear, i.e., how they feel." At the same time, however, Miss Langer claims that the work of art communicates not merely the private and personal emotions of the artist but the basic forms of feeling which are common to most people.

The later expositions of Miss Langer's theories do not escape a very fundamental difficulty which has made them seem implausible to many people: the current of emotional life, the flow of feeling and mood, does not display to introspection—and there is no other way of access to it—the kind of structural qualities, the coherence of formal pattern, which is the most prominent feature of works of art as perceptual objects. No felicity of metaphor can override this fact. Despite frequent and important insights which always make her writings repay careful reading, Miss Langer's theories are out of key with modern aesthetic beliefs, which are no longer content with the view that art communicates, however directly, by symbolization, by projection or by embodiment, a preexistent emotion. Emphasis today is rather upon the creative function of art. Although art springs out of life experience, it is today felt to be of central importance that the artist imaginatively constructs a new object, in the contemplation of which both artist and observer achieve a new feeling-experience inherent in the created art object alone. So fundamental is this that it seems artificial to speak of the artwork as projecting or expressing anything other than itself. The point has been well made by Louis Arnaud Reid in an article "New Notes on Langer" (*The British Journal of Aesthetics,* Vol. 8, No. 4, October, 1968), in which he says: "If art reveals human feeling it is neither (as we know) just the artist's feelings before making; nor is it even anything so general (if indeed there *is* anything so general) as 'the form' of human feeling; what is experienced is the particular individual affective import of *that* work."

Miss Langer's contribution to art theory is, in most general terms, an attempt to revive in contemporary idiom the basic attitudes of nineteenth-century German Romanticism. As such it is in some respects inevitably an anachronism. As the emotional climate of the times has changed and much of Romanticism seems overexpressive, overcharged, so a theory which makes emotional expression central to the essence of art as such rather than one of the things which art can interestingly do, is out of keeping with much of the most characteristic thinking of the twentieth century. Contrasting the Classical with the Romantic temper in music Aaron Copland wrote as follows (*The New Music 1900–1960,* 1968 edition, p. 20) :

> *In the work of the Classical composer, the musical creation gives every sign of having been conceived in a spirit of objectivity. A certain air of impersonality hovers about the music. There appears to be no undue stressing of the emotional message. To the Classic composer it was apparently axiomatic that musical sounds are, by their very nature, carriers of emotion. No need, therefore, to concentrate on anything but the manipulation of the musical materials, these to be handled with consummate taste and craftsmanlike ability. There could be no question of conscious projection of the composer's personality into the composition, making that one of its vital elements, for that was the part of creation that could be taken for granted, just as it could be taken for granted that the composer would read, think, sleep, and live in his own individual way. . . . The Romantic in music, on the other hand, worked from an entirely different premise. He began with the idea that his music was unique—unique by virtue of the fact that it was primarily an expression of his own personal emotions.*

This statement can well be generalized from music to the other arts. Today we are again more objective in our attitudes toward the work of art as a new creation to be perceived, contemplated, and enjoyed, for new emotional configurations among other things, and not—or not primarily—as an instrument for the communication or expression of an emotional state preexisting its creation. Miss Langer's writings embody the most penetrating and the most consistent formulation of Expressionist theory—perhaps the most original. As a guide to the apprehension of Romantic art they are invaluable. But considered as a general theory of art they are still one-sided and misleading.

The idea of the embodiment of emotion and its savoring in works of art has been worked out in Indian aesthetics from Anandavardhana in the ninth century onward sometimes with subtlety and understanding, sometimes with rather aridly academic classifications. Very briefly, Indian theory postulates certain "permanent emotional modes" which together make up the whole gamut of human emotions and all of which exist at all times in every human being as latent traces. These permanent modes of emotion are activated by various causes in ordinary life and have characteristic concomitants of effects (including the natural forms of expression such as those studied by Darwin), manifesting themselves from time to time in transient mental states. In art the transient emotion of the individual is not to be expressed but must first be generalized into a sentiment of universal human import and must then be presented by suggestion (*dhvani*). In appreciation the observer does not experience in himself the real life emotion which underlies the suggested sentiment, but tastes or savors it in an act of intuition which is compared with the metaphysical or mystical intuition in enlightenment. This tasting or savoring is called *rasa,* the central concept of Indian aesthetics which goes back to the *Natyashastra* of Bharata in the fourth or fifth century. It is a state of enjoyment which is often regarded as specific to aesthetic experience. In an article entitled *"Rasa* and the Objective Correlative" (*The British Journal of Aesthetics,* July, 1965) Professor Krishna Rayan says: "Eliot's central formulation—that in art, states of sentience are suggested through their sensuous equivalents—is also the central formulation of Sanskrit aesthetics." Of *rasa* he says: "It is emotion objectified, universalized; raised to a state where it becomes the object of lucid disinterested contemplation and is transfigured into serene joy."

The Indian theory became excessively complicated in some of its formulations and classifications reminiscent of medieval scholasticism. But the gist of the theory was closely in line with the modern tendency which has been adumbrated. I shall quote two contemporary descriptions to show this.

In *Sanskrit Poetics as a Study of Aesthetic* (1963) Professor S. K. De writes:

These theorists hold that the emotion itself exists in the mind of the reader in the form of latent impressions (vasana) derived from actual experiences of life or from inherited instincts. On reading a poem which describes similar emotions, this latent emotion is suggested by the depicted factors which, presented in a generalised form, cease to be "ordinary causes" but become "extraordinary causes" in poetry. . . . The emotion (bhava) is generalised into a sentiment (rasa) also in the sense that it refers not to any particular reader but to readers in general. The particular individual, while relishing as a reader, does not think that it is his own personal emotion, and yet it is relished as such; nor does he think it can be relished by him alone, but by all persons of similar sensibility. Thus by generalisation is meant the process of idealisation by which the reader passes from his troubles personal emotion to the serenity of contemplation of a poetic sentiment. . . . The resulting relish, therefore, is neither pain nor pleasure in the natural sense, which is found in the ordinary emotions of life associated with personal interests (which word should also be understood to connote scientific interest in them as objects of knowledge), a relish dissociated from all such interests, consisting in pure joy free from the contact of everything else perceived but itself. Put another way, an ordinary emotion (bhava) may be pleasurable or painful; but a poetic sentiment (rasa), transcending the limitations of the personal attitude, is lifted above such pain and pleasure into pure joy, the essence of which is its relish itself. The artistic attitude is thus given as different from the naturalistic and closely akin to but not identical with the philosophic. It is like the state of the soul serenely contemplating the absolute, with the difference that the state of detachment is not so complete or permanent.

Of the *rasa,* which is the core of the aesthetic experience so described, Professor De says: "*Rasa* is not a mere highly pitched natural feeling or mood; it indicates pure intuition which is distinct from an empirical feeling."

In his book *Indian Sculpture* (1966) Philip Rawson says:

To awaken the rasas, *as distinct from straightforward emotions, a number of conditions must be fulfilled. It is of the utmost importance that the spectator should* not *respond to the artistic activities as if they were realities. They must remain purely symbolic. The various devices of theatrical presentation—the stage sets, properties, lights, make-up, costume, gestures, dance-steps, music, eye-movements, verse with its rhythms, rhyme and assonance, even the very atmosphere of the occasion—are expressly meant to prevent the spectator reacting as he would in real life either to the actor or to the person portrayed. He must not behave as he would if he met Mr. X the actor, or as he would if he met the hero Rama whom the actor is portraying. He must not respond to the actor's apparent feelings as he would towards a real person who was actually feeling those feelings. He must not, in fact, actually fall into one of the Permanent Emotional Modes. At the same time echoes of actual feeling-responses drawn from the Modes must continually be touched by these very theatrical means. This inhibition of normal reactions combined with the deliberate evocation of a multiplicity of feeling-echoes results in the actor's expression provoking in the spectator's mind a quite unusual state. For if the mind must not be absorbed in the particular emotions, which are not the purpose of the art, it remains free to be aware of the range and sequence of responses without any one of them taking over the whole attention. . . . The mind does become conscious of that peculiar and individual psychophysical state, for which* rasa, *flavour, is the adopted term, and which we may call an image of the Emotional Mode itself.*

Common both to Indian theory and to that trend of modern communication theory which we have been describing is the belief that in appreciating works of art we do not, characteristically, respond emotionally as we respond to situations in real life or situations described in a newspaper. Nor do we *simply* reproduce in ourselves the emotional situations presented in the work of art. Nor again are we offered objective information (true or untrue) *about* the occurrence of emotional situations. In some manner we "get inside" so as to savor and enjoy, but without full commitment, emotional situations presented to awareness as embodied in the work of art. We are aware of them as "out there" in the work of art, not as emotions in ourselves, though our awareness may involve some reflected experiencing of the embodied emotion rather in the manner that we may, but need not, have visual or aural images of events which we read about. The same sort of thing occurs when we are sympathetically aware of the emotions of other people. A fully developed theory of fiction would have to take account of this characteristic way of experiencing "embodied" emotions in works of art. Both in Indian and in some contemporary Western formulations of the theory it is sometimes also assumed that the emotions "embodied" in artworks differ in a special way from the passing emotions and moods which we know in everyday life: they are in some way more "universal," more significant, than the occurrent and evanescent feelings which enter into the business of daily living.

X. Aesthetics in the Twentieth Century

Perhaps the most striking feature of the work done in aesthetics during the last thirty years or so by professional philosophers who belong to the linguistic or analytical schools of thought has been the repudiation of systematic aesthetics and a more or less dogmatic skepticism about the possibility or the value of defining key terms such as "art" or "beauty." Philosophers who think in this way regard attempts such as those of Clive Bell to discover "the essential quality of works of art, the quality which distinguishes works of art from all other classes of objects," or to find "some quality common and peculiar" to all beautiful things, as not only unsuccessful but as fundamentally misconceived. Some have argued that, understood in this way, the question What is art? is an unreal question to which no answer is possible. Others have maintained that any common feature of all things traditionally and currently held to be beautiful (any "common denominator of all works of art," to use the words of DeWitt Parker) would turn out to be trivial and not worth pursuing. Wittgenstein's writings were influential with this trend of contemporary philosophy, and philosophers such as Paul Ziff and Morris Weitz have had considerable support for their contention that general terms such as "art" and "beauty" must be elucidated by disclosing "family resemblances" among their established uses and that the work of aesthetics should consist not in vainly tracking down a mythical "essence" of artistic excellence but rather in pinpointing the overlapping and interacting criteria which are actually applied in the criticism and assessment of the various arts. Morris Weitz said: "If we actually look and see what it is that we call 'art,' we will also find no common properties—only strands of similarities." Therefore he held that, in aesthetics, "our first problem is the elucidation of the actual employment of the concept of art, to give a logical description of the conditions under which we correctly use it or its correlates."[1] W. G. Gallie has similarly maintained that "work of art" is either a "family resemblance term" or, sometimes, a sheer blanket word denoting any of a set of essentially unrelated alternatives each of which has its proponents. "The informed sceptic," he said, "will *deny* that the word 'art,' as commonly used, stands for any one thing."

These views were put forward for the most part in essays and papers and can be most conveniently studied in the anthology *Aesthetics and Language* (1945) edited by William Elton. Although some of the philosophers who were most convincing in establishing them have subsequently modified their own views, they do constitute a fairly consistent, and interesting, outlook. Later anthologies are *Philosophy Looks at the Arts* (1962) edited by Joseph Margolis and *Collected Papers on Aesthetics* (1965) edited by Cyril Barrett.

It is not without interest that similar perplexities exercised the eighteenth-century English empiricists when aesthetics was first staked out as a distinct philosophical discipline. In his *Essays on the*

---

[1] The word "correctly" in this sentence is significant of a dubious inclination of some linguistic philosophy written under the remoter or more direct impetus of Wittgenstein to seek by an examination of the ways in which a term is actually used to find and impose criteria for its correct use.

Intellectual Powers of Man, published in 1785, Thomas Reid wrote:

> *Yet of beauty there is a great diversity, not only of degree but of kind;*
> *the beauty of a demonstration, the beauty of a poem, the beauty of a*
> *palace, the beauty of a piece of music, the beauty of a fine woman, and*
> *many more that might be named, are different kinds of beauty; and we*
> *have no names to distinguish them but the names of the different*
> *objects to which they belong. And there is such a diversity in the*
> *different* kinds *of beauty as well as in the* degrees, *we need not think it*
> *strange that philosophers have gone into different systems in analysing it*
> *and enumerating its simple ingredients. They have made many just*
> *observations on the subject; but, from the love of simplicity, have re-*
> *duced it to fewer principles than the nature of the thing will permit,*
> *having had in their eye some particular kinds of beauty while they*
> *overlooked others.*

Later in the same *Essay* he explicitly says: "I am unable to conceive of any quality in all the different things that are called beautiful, that is the same in them all."

The discussion was brought squarely into the linguistic field by Dugald Stewart, Professor of Moral Philosophy at Edinburgh University, to whom Thomas Reid dedicated his *Essays,* and a man of whom Lord Cockburn said that had he lived in ancient times his memory would have come down to us as one of the eloquent sages. In his *Philosophical Essays* (1810) Stewart was, I believe, the first to put forward explicitly, in the context of aesthetics, the notion if not the name of Wittgenstein's "family resemblance term." He protests against "a prejudice which has descended to modern times from the scholastic ages, that when a word admits of a variety of significations, these different significations must all be *species* of the same *genus* and must consequently include some essential idea common to every individual to which the generic term can be applied." In lieu of this false assumption he propounded the idea of *linguistic transference.*

> *I shall begin by supposing* [he says] *that the letters A, B, C, D, E,*
> *denote a series of objects; that A possesses some one quality in common*
> *with B; B a quality in common with C; C a quality in common with D;*
> *D a quality in common with E; while at the same time no quality can be*
> *found which belongs in common to any* three *objects in the series.*

Sometimes, he goes on, the same epithet comes to be applied in the common language to all the objects in such a series. He named this linguistic phenomenon "transference" because he thought that in such cases the epithet has a primary reference to some one quality in the series, of which it was originally used; then in accordance with the principles of psychological association, and perhaps under the influence of a common emotional response, it has in course of time been transferred to other items of the series as linguistic habits change in popular idiom. Something of this sort happened, he supposes, in the case of the word "beauty." In its "primitive and most general acceptation" the word refers to objects of sight; by transference it has been extended over a much wider range; but the attempt to extract a common core of meaning from all its applications is futile because there is no common meaning but only a process of historical change in linguistic habits:

> It has long been a favourite problem of philosophers to ascertain some common quality or qualities which entitles a thing to the denomination of beautiful; but the success of their speculations has been so inconsiderable that little can be inferred from them but the impossibility of the problem to which they have been directed.

Stewart therefore proposed a radical change in the method of aesthetic inquiry:

> Instead of searching for the common idea or essence which the word Beauty denotes when applied to colours, to forms, to sounds, to compositions in verse and prose, to mathematical theorems, and to moral qualities, our attention is directed to the natural history of the Human Mind, and to its natural progress in the employment of speech.

The new way of tackling aesthetics which came into vogue from the 1930s, partly as a reaction from the residual Romanticism of Croce's followers and the Idealism of Bradley and Bosanquet, was symptomatic of a cautious, empirical, analytical but more rigorous temper, which was reluctant to generalize but more keenly alert to the special characteristics of the individual arts of music, painting, poetry, theatre, etc. Interest centered on the logical exercise of clarifying the conceptual apparatus of criticism in each of the arts severally and on rendering explicit the different criteria of valuation which are employed. In comparison the establishment of uniformities was treated either as premature or, sometimes, as dangerously obscurantist. Penetrating studies have contributed strikingly to the elucidation of particular problems and advances have been made in separating the genuine from the spurious issues involved. But over the whole field the work achieved has shown less congruence as regards the conclusions reached than in the method of fragmentation, which delights to isolate problems for anatomization by the surgeon's scalpel after they have been neatly anesthetized upon their separate operating tables.

One exemplification of this way of approach is the view that philosophical aesthetics should be kept as a "second order" discipline whose raw material is provided not by our enjoyment of art and beauty or directly by our experience of appreciation but by the descriptive categories and the criteria of judgment implicit in the language of critics and connoisseurs of the arts. Although this view has not received by any means general acceptance, it has been defended by such philosophers as W. G. Gallie and Joseph Margolis among others. It would treat aesthetics as a kind of "metacriticism," a language about language, and would restrict its useful functions to analyzing and rendering coherent the things said about the arts by a class of sensitive persons who are in direct contact with them.

Useful work has been done not only toward the clarification of more specific aesthetic concepts but also on the logic of aesthetic concepts generally. The seminal study in the latter field was a paper by Frank Sibley, *Aesthetic Concepts* (1959, reprinted in the anthology *Philosophy Looks at the Arts*). Important developments have also come from Isabel Hungerland in America and, in the phenomenological school, from Roman Ingarden, who has led the way in investigating the interrelations of aesthetic concepts among themselves. Sibley's paper divided the terms by which we refer to the features of works of art and other familiar things around us into aesthetic and nonaesthetic terms. Nonaesthetic terms (such as "red," "noisy," "brackish," "clammy") refer to features which are observable by "anyone with normal eyes, ears, and intelligence." Aesthetic terms on the other hand (such as "dainty," "delicate," "graceful," "elegant") refer to features of things where judgment requires the exercise of taste or sensibility. As Isabel Hungerland points out, aesthetic properties include "those features of everyday perception which the gestalt psychologists have called attention to." They are sometimes called "emotional" or "physiognomic" properties—"the cheerfulness of red and yellow, as well as the cheerfulness of faces, the overall pattern of faces which, once familiar, enables us to see a circle with three dots and a curved line as a face, the grace or awkwardness of certain movements, the cumulative effect of repeated patterns in music, and so on." The argument of Sibley's paper was to show that aesthetic qualities are not in a positive sense conditional upon nonaesthetic qualities. In a negative sense they may be so conditioned: for example, a picture which is uncolored or which has only a few pale colors cannot be fiery or gaudy or garish or flamboyant. But, Sibley maintains, "there are no nonaesthetic features which serve in *any* circumstances as logically *sufficient conditions* for applying aesthetic terms." Part of the importance of this paper was that it gave fairly rigorous expression to an assumption which had become almost doctrinal in recent aesthetics, namely the assumption that aesthetic descriptions or appraisals of works of art cannot be supported by or deduced from descriptions of their nonaesthetic features.

It may be remarked that if aesthetics is regarded as the investigation of aesthetic terms and concepts in the very wide sense given to these expressions in Sibley's paper, this branch of philosophy loses the very close connection which it has traditionally borne with the sorts of experience usually referred to by the terms "aesthetic experience" or the appreciation or enjoyment of beauty. The subject matter of aesthetics becomes virtually coextensive with the study of perception, since so-called aesthetic features are features of everyday observation. In the words of Isabel Hungerland, "the ordinary things of our ordinary perception present themselves to us as dismal or jolly, awkward or graceful, dainty or sturdy, and so on." Properties indicated by the terms dainty or dumpy, clumsy or graceful, enter into our ordinary everyday recognitions and descriptions of things as much as such qualities as those indicated by saying a thing is tall or short, round or square. They have no special attachment to works of art or things of beauty. In consequence of this broadening of the subject matter it may also be thought appropriate to query the sharp distinction in principle which has often in the past been thought to pertain between the kinds of verification applicable to judgments about aesthetic and judgments about nonaesthetic features. This widening of the conception of aesthetics and denial of the sharp distinction between kinds of proof were admitted by Sibley in a later symposium, where he said:

> As for the insistence upon proofs: it is not clear that we would know in detail any better how to give proofs, or what would be involved in giving a proof, that something is funny, or that two faces resemble each other, or even that something is red, than we do with aesthetic judgements. In short, the aestheticians' familiar demand for proofs is one we seldom encounter or know fully how to meet even in non-aesthetic matters of a relatively objective sort.

He goes on:

> The programme that aestheticians must face is thus a large one, the charting of huge areas neglected by other philosophers working within their customary bounds. Indeed, far from its being true that aesthetics is peripheral to philosophy, aestheticians encounter ranges of concepts wider than and inevitably inclusive of those studied by most other branches of philosophy.

Aesthetics ceases to be peripheral at the expense of changing its character and repudiating its primary connection with the appreciation of beauty.[2]

A new outlook on the philosophy of mind, stimulated partly by the *Philosophical Investigations* of Wittgenstein and manifested in recent work on ethics, has led to a growing dissatisfaction with the sharp distinction between "fact" and "value" generally and a tendency to regard "descriptions" as involving implicit valuations

---

2 In a Presidential address delivered to the annual meeting of the American Society for Aesthetics in October, 1967, Isabel Hungerland took a different line from that of Sibley. She repudiated his basis of differentiation between aesthetic and nonaesthetic properties on the ground that many of the properties which fall into the category of aesthetic do not require any special sensitivity or the exercise of taste for their detection: "It takes no special sort of training on the part of a child to get the angry or cheerful look of a face. What is required seems no more beyond the ordinary than what is required in the child's seeing that his ball is round and red." Instead she bases the distinction on a claim that aesthetic properties are not intersubjectively verifiable, or at least not in

while valuations are understood to apply to things or situations only as *seen in a certain light* or under a certain *description*. In aesthetics the breakdown of the sharp distinction between description and appraisal tends in the direction of Roman Ingarden's accounts of the *actualization* of artworks (see pp. 267–68). Descriptions involve the element of interpretation implicit in any actualization of a work of art while some appraisals at any rate are themselves inherent to the actualization. This trend leads on toward a new examination of the logic of criticism the outcome of which is likely to be rejection of the supposed gulf between the kinds of proof and verification appropriate to aesthetic appraisals and the kinds required for factual statements. This is the theme of *The Language of Criticism* (1966) by John Casey.

These new methods and preoccupations in aesthetics are to some extent an outcome or even a by-product of changes in general philosophical temper and practice rather than a direct reflection of any new outlook on art. Nevertheless there have occurred in the course of the present century fundamental changes of outlook or emphasis—or at any rate changes which are apt to seem fundamental—in the attitudes and assumptions implicit in our practical habits of appreciation of the arts. These changes have not for the most part been systematized in formal philosophy but are latent in the way we speak and act. It is never easy to diagnose and still less to assess attitudes and assumptions with which one is closely involved or to set in perspective the intimate environment in which one lives. In this case the task is made still more difficult because the changes of outlook most characteristic of our time certainly involve repudiation of some basic assumptions of both Naturalism and Romanticism, and yet by force of inertia these assumptions still

---

the straightforward way in which ascription of nonaesthetic properties are. Moreover she argues that the contrast between what a thing "really is" and what it "only looks" is not applicable to aesthetic qualities. (It makes sense to say that a thing looks red although it is not really red; but it does not make sense to say that something looks dainty but is not really dainty.) She therefore holds that statements ascribing aesthetic features to things fall into a different logical category or belong to a different "universe or discourse," from statements ascribing nonaesthetic properties and it is therefore a mistake to ask what is the logical connection between the two groups of statements.

permeate much of the language of criticism and appreciation. The same thing could be said about assumptions of Instrumental theories such as Expressionism and Moralism. As in previous periods of history, incongruous and incompatible assumptions often exist side by side in our practical attitudes toward the arts and are reflected in the language we use about them.

ART AND EMOTION

Despite the continued currency of the word "expression" in the language of art criticism, there has over the last thirty years been a significant movement away from the Romantic emphasis on emotional expression and evocation as the purpose and perfection of works of art. It is not denied that works of art may, and often do, both express and stimulate emotions. But this is no longer regarded as the only or always the most important thing they do. Indeed it is commonly held that "psychological distance" is an essential feature in the aesthetic response to a work of art. If we respond directly to a work of art as an emotional stimulus in the way in which we respond to emotional stimuli in ordinary life (to a revivalist sermon or a political speech, for example), we are to that extent not responding to it as a work of art. In aesthetic awareness we *savor* the emotional situation presented and the form in which it is presented with perspicuity and insight; we come to realize not with the understanding but directly in feeling what it feels like to take up such and such an emotional attitude in a situation, to hold such and such beliefs, and we apprehend this in feeling whether or not we ourselves do ordinarily take up that particular emotional attitude or hold those particular beliefs. The modern outlook in this regard has been well put by Professor J. N. Findlay in an article, "The Perspicuous and the Poignant: Two Aesthetic Fundamentals" (*The British Journal of Aesthetics,* vol. 7 No. 1, January, 1967). He writes:

> *Another important point must be the firm rejection of the view of emotions as playing an absolutely essential and central role in aesthetic* approfondissement, *as suggested by many forms of the expressive theory. There are of course deep and characteristic emotions excited by aes-*

thetic approfondissement, but these are the fulfilment rather than the essence of aesthetic activity. And there is further no doubt that emotions are extremely interesting objects of aesthetic appreciation, whether savoured in their misty interiority in ourselves, and whether married to gestures and facial expressions in sincere persons or actors, or in portraits or other simulacra or whether clinging suggestively to poetic combinations or words or to musical compositions and sequences of tones. But they enter the aesthetic sphere either as attendant on perspicuity, and so properly aesthetic, or as characters or features themselves rendered perspicuous, brought luminously before us and dwelt upon. And in this second role emotions are in no sense privileged aesthetic contents: a pattern of tones or colours not connected closely with a particular emotion, but clearly showing us what it is, is as essentially an aesthetic object as a pattern held together by an emotional significance which pervades it throughout. What is aesthetically important about emotions like gaiety, dreariness, scheming hatred, jealousy, etc., is not what they are but that they should be well displayed; and if this good display involves our own personal entering into them and reliving them, this is an incidental rather than an essential feature of the aesthetic situation. We have to be moved in various ways by poetry and music and architecture in order fully to appreciate what they are about, what they mean to set before us; it is, however, as an essential constituent of the aesthetic object that emotions are here aesthetically relevant. We may say, therefore, if we like, that when emotions enter the aesthetic sphere they do so in service to the intellect and to a sort of intellectual activity, and not in their own right. This is part of what Kant meant by calling aesthetic feelings disinterested. And we may say, further, that in so far as aesthetic objects take that two-tiered form called "expressive," in which a sensuous or other form is linked with an inner emotional meaning—a feature by no means essential to aesthetic enjoyment, which may be either confined within what is sensuously given, or entirely liberated from it—emotions are not the essential matters to be expressed. A complex set of numerical or quantitative relations, a contrast of qualities, a strange affinity of seeming disparates, the remarkable logic of some ingenious theory, the atmosphere of a historical period, etc., etc., may be what is well expressed in a piece of poetry or prose or music, and not any specific emotions connected with the latter.

In recent philosophy of mind emotions are not thought of as inner turbulences and agitations or throbs of feeling set in motion on the one hand by objective stimuli according to causal laws and associated on the other hand with complicated patterns of physical behavior which are their "expression." Emotions are analyzed as including complex patterns of belief involved in the way in which we describe or interpret to ourselves the situations with which they are connected and including also tendencies to expressive action, wants or valuations, all of which involve a close integration of private attitudes with public reference. It is not fully clear in what ways this model of emotion has relevance for aesthetics or for the phenomenology of appreciation. What are still commonly referred to as our emotional responses to say music or patterns of color and shape without representational significance have in some ways affinity with "objectless" moods of feeling rather than with emotions in the full sense indicated above. The following points may, however, be made.

1. Apart from the apprehension of "represented" emotional situations, the "emotional response" in appreciation of artworks is thought of as inextricably attached to the cognitive act by which we become aware of the visual or auditory pattern, not as a subjective reaction casually induced by the artwork.

2. It is nowadays recognized that the gracefulness of a vase does not depend upon this or that person's pleasure in looking at it and to this extent the gracefulness can be thought of as inherent in the vase. Similarly "emotional qualities" such as the sadness of music do not depend upon the experiencing of the emotion of sadness by this person or that—still less on the projection of such experienced emotion back upon the music—but are intimately connected with the actualization of the music in awareness, with our apprehension of the aural pattern.

3. The emotional experiences of works of art are often described as *sui generis*: by this is apparently meant either or both that they are more general than the emotions of everyday life and that they are more specific to the pattern of awareness with which they are connected.

In certain respects the contemporary outlook on emotion in relation to artistic experience may be thought to have some affinities with the Indian doctrine of *rasa*.

THE AUTONOMY OF THE ARTWORK

Perhaps the most distinctive feature of practical aesthetic attitudes today has been the concentration of attention on the work of art as a thing in its own right, an artifact with standards and functions of its own, and not an instrument made to further purposes which could equally be promoted otherwise than by art objects. It is not denied that works of art may legitimately reflect more or less illusionistically a reality other than themselves, or that they may embody and effectively promulgate social, religious, or other values. But whether or not they do these things, and how well they do them, are regarded as irrelevant to their quality as works of art. Representation and the promotion of nonartistic values have come to be regarded as incidental possibilities and no longer essential to the concept of fine art. The naturalistic types of theory, which have the common characteristic that they direct attention through the work of art upon that other reality which the work of art presents, and instrumentalist theories of art in general are not necessarily repudiated outright but tend nowadays to be set on one side and treated as of secondary importance in relation to art. A work of art, it is now held, is in concept an artifact made for the purpose of being appreciated in the special mode of aesthetic contemplation; and although particular works of art may be intended to do other things and may in fact serve other purposes as well as this, the excellence of any work of art *as art* is assessed in terms of its suitability for such contemplation. This is what is meant by claiming that art is *autonomous*: it is not assessed by external standards applicable elsewhere, but by standards of its own.

This new attitude may be considered in part a clearer apprehension of implications already inherent in the concept of "fine art" which emerged to prominence during the eighteenth century. It has seldom been worked out explicitly in theory but is implicit in most of the critical and theoretical writing about art during the first half of the present century. The idea was clearly and vigorously expressed in the writings of the French critic André Malraux. In *Les Voix du Silence* (1951), for example, he says: "The Middle Ages had no more idea of what we mean by the word art than had Greece or Egypt, which lacked the word to express it. In order that this idea could be born it was necessary for works of art to be separated from their function. . . . The most profound metamorphosis began when art had no other end than itself."

It is mainly in the last hundred years that the characteristic aesthetic way of appreciation and judgment has become dominant and the revolution of aesthetic consciousness, which had its roots in the eighteenth century, has come powerfully to fruition. Several factors have jointly contributed to the development. Partly the process has been helped by the relatively sudden opening up to a broader public of the vastly heterogeneous and hitherto largely inaccessible artistic heritage from widely separated ages and cultures. When the art products of the world are displayed in isolation from the living cultures which gave them birth and are made available in museums and galleries and books of reproductions, then their impact is the impact of works of art divorced from the social and religious purposes for which they were originally made, stripped of the extra-artistic values which they once carried. A Byzantine icon is nowadays for most people a work of art and no longer a Christian symbol or a theophany: its impact is visual and the emotional religious appeal is attenuated. We cannot most of us now recover the state of mind which was expressed by the Villeneuve *Pietà* any more than we can enter imaginatively into the world of belief which inspired the theriomorphic representations of the Egyptian gods or the Buddhist statues of India and Korea. We know next to nothing about the outlook and beliefs which lay behind Mayan art or the Harappa culture of Mohenjo-daro, or the curiously formalized figures of Chavín and Tiahuanaco. Even if we learnt what archaeology has to tell of these things, we could no longer enter fully into the spirit which inspired them or make it our own. A fetish cannot again become a fetish for us and a Gabun carving is no longer a passport to the supernatural powers. Yet we can—so it is believed—appreciate the formal qualities of these things as art objects and insofar as the aesthetic impulse has been pretty well universal among men, even when it worked blindly and unrecognized, we can thus to some extent recover and share their qualities as human products.

Deliberate concentration on formal properties and a tendency to play down the importance of subject or theme has been a feature of most contemporary movements in painting since Impressionism. Instead of the planned composition depicting a historical scene or pointing a moral the Impressionists, or some of them, sought to convey the suggestion of a haphazard slice of life—a *tranche de vie*—as if their subject were that of a snapshot taken at random. Instead of pursuing a realistic representation of objects and things they sought a different realism which was to be obtained by transferring onto canvas the optical image of light and color before it was analyzed and constructed by perception into familiar things. Though the ideal of the "innocent eye" is now thought to have been a will-o'-the-wisp inherently impossible of attainment, it had importance as a manifestation of that rejection of traditional concern with subject matter which has been one of the strongest signs of modern revolt from naturalism. The attitude which has predominated since Impressionism was summed up in a now famous statement by Maurice Denis (1870–1943): "One must remember that a picture—before being a warhorse, a nude woman or some anecdote—is essentially a plane surface covered by colors assembled in a certain order." We might describe this attitude by saying that since Impressionism artists have become more interested in making a picture than in representing some aspect of reality outside the picture or than in using the picture for the purpose of furthering any nonaesthetic values. Another way of expressing this attitude has been the reiterated affirmation by artists of their ambition to *create something new*—something new which is the work of art—rather than to reproduce or to interpret that which already exists. Gauguin, for example, remarked: "It is said that God took a piece of clay into His hand and created all that you know. The artist, in his turn, if he wishes to create a really divine work, must not imitate nature, but use the elements of nature to create a new element." And in their book on Cubism Albert Gleizes and Jean Metzinger typically said: "The painter, intent on creating, rejects the natural image as soon as it has served his purpose." One must understand that when contemporary artists speak of creation they use the word with a quite different meaning from those who at the time of the Renaissance liked to compare the creative work of the artist with God's creation. Renaissance writers had in mind that an artist may imagine, and therefore mentally create, a world more perfect than the actual world or things more beautiful than the imperfect beauties of nature. They may then make works of art which naturalistically mirror these idealized imaginary realities. The works of art are mirrors through which we see reflected the ideal realities conceived by the artist. But when the modern artist speaks of creating he does not mean that his work of art is a copy or reflection of some nonartistic reality which he has created in imagination. There is no suggestion that the statues of Henry Moore or Giacometti, or the white horses of Chirico, are representations of imagined flesh and blood figures, figures which if they actually existed in flesh and blood would be more beautiful or in any way more interesting than the figures we meet in daily life. The thing created is the work of art itself, not something else of which the work of art is a copy. The created thing could *only* exist as pigment on canvas or as stone or wood. It is *not* conceived as having another potential or ideal existence which is mimicked in the materials of art. The work of art is the created thing not a copy of a created thing.

Contemporary writing and thinking about the arts is still pervaded by the Romantic form of Instrumentalist theory which explains art as a means for expressing and communicating from man to man states of feeling and inner experience which cannot be communicated with precision in any other way. As an example René Huyghe's book *Art and the Spirit of Man* (1962) is based on the conception of art as the "other" language or the "language of the spirit." He explains his theme in the following words:

> *Its essential, unvarying role, from the very beginning, has been to serve as one of mankind's modes of expression. . . . There exists a language of the intelligence, which has come down to us as the language of the word. Art, however, is a language of the spirit, of our feelings as well as our thinking nature, our nature as a whole in all its complexity.*

There are few people now who would wish to deny that such communication of spiritual states is one of the uses which art may serve. And perhaps there are few who would deny that this function of art offers one of the more fruitful approaches to interpretation and appreciation. It is, however, more in keeping with the post-Romantic outlook that a work of art, once created, is frequently thought of as having a certain life and independence of its own not entirely bounded by the personality or intentions of the artist who created it. It is recognized that the inspiration and conception of a work of art may often derive from the unconscious levels of the artist's personality and may not lie wholly open to deliberate, conscious apprehension. Hence the created work may embody fuller wealth of import than the artist himself is aware of. Indeed it is sometimes maintained that the artist himself is not the best interpreter or exponent of his work. In his essay *Penser la musique aujourd'hui* (1963), for example, Pierre Boulez argued that the attempt to interpret a work by tracing the creative processes of the artist has the disadvantage that it

> *circumscribes the work within the limits of the composer's creative imagination: a paralysing restriction, for it remains fundamental in my view to safeguard unknown potential which lies enclosed within a masterpiece of art. I am convinced that the author, however perspicacious he may be, cannot conceive the consequences—immediate or distant—of what he has written and that his insight is not necessarily more acute than that of the analytical critic.*

Such statements are by no means isolated for indeed it fits in with the temper of our time to speak of great works of art as independent existents incorporating within themselves a hidden wealth and abundance of significance which was not fully apparent to the artists who brought them into being and which emerges only gradually to successive generations of appreciators. The relevance of the artist's conscious intentions, where these are known, has been one of the themes discussed by critics and aestheticians and it has been debated whether the understanding and appreciation of a work of art require us to have, or can properly be influenced by, a knowledge of the artist's intentions. The term "Intentional Fallacy" was coined in an article with that title by William K. Wimsatt, Jr., and Monroe Beardsley (printed in *Philosophy Looks at the Arts*). A good summary of the arguments is to be found in a paper on "The Work of Art and the Artist's Intentions" by John Kemp in *The British Journal of Aesthetics,* vol. 4, no. 2.

Some philosophers, of whom Roman Ingarden is the most important, have distinguished between the physical work of art—the carved stone or pigmented canvas—and the work of art when perceived as an aesthetic object by this or that observer. The physical object is as it were a permanent possibility for the actualization of aesthetic objects in apprehension; what Ingarden calls its *concretion*. When an observer looks at a painting in order to appreciate it aesthetically, in the aesthetic posture of attention (not, that is, in order to observe the techniques of pigments, to learn lessons of history from the garments, and so on), he actualizes potentialities within the work and apprehends an aesthetic object. But, Ingarden holds, a physical work of art is not completely determinate: it does not command one and one only actualization but contains "areas of indeterminacy" which require to be filled out by the observer. Thus the possible or legitimate concretions are negatively determined by the work of art but are never completely determinate. Some are ruled out as being incompatible with the determinate qualities of the physical work. Others, and perhaps infinitely many, are permitted in virtue of the measure of actual indeterminacy which every work contains. With those arts which are "performed"—music, drama, dance—and where there is no one physical object such as the picture or the statue, the matter is complicated by the fact that a "concretion" is required of the performers and a second "concretion" of the performed work is made by the audience. Such discussion, which becomes very elaborate, is symptomatic of the contemporary attitude toward the art object as an independently existing thing and not merely a mirror or an instrument.

A special aspect of the more deliberate concern with formal or perceptual properties of artworks instead of their thematic content has been the emphasis on what is often called the "emotional" or "expressive" significance of pictorial elements—colors, shapes, lines, masses, and their combinations. Seurat in his later years, following suggestions made by Poussin, tried ineffectually to find a scientific basis for emotional symbolism in terms of formal plastic elements. In an article published in 1891 shortly after the artist's death his friend Teodor de Wyzewa wrote of Seurat:

First of all he analysed colour: he searched for diverse means of rendering it, tried to discover the way which rendered it with the most accuracy and variety. Then it was the expression of colours which attracted him. He wanted to know why certain combinations of tones produced an impression of sadness, certain others an impression of gaiety; and from this point of view he made a sort of catalogue for himself, where each nuance of colour was associated with the emotion it suggested. Next in turn expression through lines seemed to him a problem capable of a definite solution, for lines also have an innate, secret power of joy or melancholy. . . .

What is called the "expressive power" of pictorial elements was studied on a more instinctive level by Gauguin and by the Nabis under his influence. Van Gogh was excited beyond measure by the emotional significance of color, line, and artistic calligraphy. Perhaps the most influential work of modern times on this theme was Kandinsky's essay "Concerning the Spiritual in Art," first published in German as "Über das Geistige in der Kunst" in 1912. Kandinsky earned for himself the title of founder of Abstract Expressionism, and this essay stands out as the basic formulation of the underlying principles of one school of abstract painting.

Although the word "expression" is used in this context, it carries very different implications from those which it bears in the context of Romanticism. Romantic theory pictures an emotional experience of the artist being in some manner embodied in his work of art and subsequently evoked by the work of art in the spectator. But Kandinksy and the moderns were interested rather in an "innate affinity" which they supposed to hold between certain pictorial elements and emotional states, in virtue of which combinations of pictorial elements symbolize complex emotional states directly in perception. The work of art was thought of primarily as a supreme overall combination of subordinate and contained arrangements of these elements in which innately associated emotional qualities were seen as objectively present.

In the context of the Romantic conception of art as an instrument for the communication of feeling the theory of *empathy* was formerly popular. Empathy is the sense of emotional affinity—called by Hume "sympathy"—which enables one to put oneself in the other man's place and know the emotions he is feeling and expressing.[3] In particular it is the "sympathetic" projection of human emotions and attitudes into inanimate objects which is general among primitive, prescientific peoples and which survives in popu-

---

[3] Empathy is of course distinguished from sympathy in the normal sense.

lar language and poetic imagery. When we speak of an "angry sunset" or "gay daffodils" we are (according to this theory) using animistic metaphors which derive ultimately from the habit of empathy toward inanimate nature. Shelley was indulging in empathy when he addressed the west wind:

> *Wild Spirit, which art moving everywhere;*
> *Destroyer and Preserver; hear, O hear.*

Under the name *Einfühlung* the German aestheticians Robert Vischer and Theodor Lipps worked out a particular application of the general idea of empathy to the appreciation of art in order to explain the power of art objects to serve as a medium for the communication of feeling. The observer, it was supposed, in contemplation of a work of art identifies himself with it and experiences in himself (though unconsciously) the emotions appropriate to the case. Thus in contemplating a Gothic church one experiences, it was said, the aspiring and elevated emotions appropriate to the soaring spire; in listening to sad music one experiences the mood of sadness appropriate to the slow, heavy rhythms; and so on. Then, it was claimed, the observer projects the (unconscious) emotion he has experienced and seems to see it as a quality of the work of art by which it was evoked in him unconsciously. Modern theory rejects this clumsy mechanism of occult and unverifiable mental operations and accepts quite simply that we perceive "emotional qualities" directly in the object. The latter view has been developed by Gestalt psychologists—notably by Rudolf Arnheim—within the context of a more general theory of "tertiary qualities." Tertiary qualities are, broadly speaking, qualities expressed by such words as "graceful," "dainty," "somber," "dynamic," "tragic," "austere," etc., which are seen directly in things when we look at them as a whole but which do not apply to the atomic parts into which things can be analyzed and which are therefore not measurable by ordinary methods of measurement. They are sometimes called "emergent" qualities because they characterize the complex whole but not the elements from which the whole is physically constructed. Emotional qualities such as sadness, gaiety, sentimentality, are treated as on a par with other tertiary qualities. As we

Saskia Lying in Bed *by Rembrandt, 1606–69. Pen-and-wash drawing.*
Courtesy of the Staatliche Graphische Sammlung, Munich.

have said, they are thought to be observed directly as qualities of the work of art, not first experienced by the observer and then projected into the work of art. This raises problems about the relation for example between the emotional quality of sadness in a piece of music and the absence of any actual emotion to the occurrence of which it would seem to point. These problems are dealt with obliquely but illuminatingly by O. K. Bouwsma in a paper "The Expression Theory of Art" (in *Aesthetics and Language*).

SOCIOLOGICAL AESTHETICS

The sociological study of the arts has been fostered in the main by two contrasting interests, which in particular strands of theory can often be found combined and interlocking to the detriment of clarity and consistency. On the one hand primarily art historians and theorists have been interested in tracing how social and economic conditions and the changing patterns of civilization have influenced or been reflected in the arts that have been produced from one age to another. On the other hand political philosophers, educationists, moralists, reformers, and others have shown greater concern for determining the ways in which society may be influenced by the arts and the effects they have, or might or should have, on individuals as members of a society. From whichever point of view it sets out, the sociological study of the arts may be treated either as a *descriptive* or as a *normative* discipline. As a branch of general sociology considered as a purely descriptive science the sociology of art is closely linked with the history of criticism, the history of taste, and the history of fashion according to the direction in which emphasis is slanted. But the hope of reaching an objectively valid standard of correct taste by accumulating empirical evidence about the things which at different periods and in different patterns of society men have and have not found pleasing seems unlikely to prove more fruitful under the aegis of sociology than it was amenable to the more amateurish approach of the eighteenth-century writers.

1. That taste, and therefore the production of art, is influenced by geographical, climatic, racial, and historical factors was an idea familiar enough to the eighteenth century despite the restricted

Bretonnes à la Barrière *by Paul Gauguin, 1889.*
Zincograph. Courtesy of the Bibliothèque Nationale, Paris.

The Omnibus *by Honoré Daumier, ca. 1850. Watercolor.*
Courtesy of the Walters Art Gallery, Baltimore.

Cover design by
Aubrey Beardsley for
La Morte d'Arthur, *1893.*
Courtesy of
J. M. Dent & Sons, London.

Les Demoiselles d'Avignon
by Picasso, 1907.
Collection of
The Museum
of Modern Art,
New York, acquired
through the
Lillie P. Bliss Bequest.

horizons of that time. The historical approach to literature was developed further in Germany by J. G. Herder (1744–1803) and by the Schlegels, who taught that historical conditions have no merely superficial effect on poetry and the arts but that their very essence is involved in the historical process. Their point of view was more rigorously formulated again in the Positivist philosophy of Auguste Comte (1789–1857) and to this can be traced the doctrine, which has had so important an influence in all subsequent sociological writing: that literature and the arts are human artifacts which are in principle determined by the conditions of their production and can be studied and understood only in the context of the social conditions which produced them. The relevant conditions were made explicit in a famous formula originated by Auguste Taine in the Introduction to his *History of English Literature* (1864) *"race, milieu, moment"* (the race, the social environment, and the historical epoch). Taine also formulated the task of the scientific historian: given the work of art, to discover through general laws governing cultural achievements what conditions of race, social milieu, and historical epoch must have been necessary to produce it.

A new twist was given to sociological art theory when the nineteenth-century evolutionists applied their developmental approach to the history of art. According to their view the arts do not exist outside the system of natural causes and effects, as a result of some divine inspiration or any impulse not explicable by natural laws, but evolved by natural processes along with other social and cultural developments, emerging at a late stage from prehistoric technologies and through a gradual advance in the adaptation of means to ends. Herbert Spencer was one of many who thought that the fine arts, including even music, were originally evolved to serve a biologically useful purpose and that they acquired aesthetic interest as survivals when their utilitarian functions had lapsed. The optimistic if tautological concept of progress, which was built into the nineteenth-century theory of evolution, proved, however, to be singularly inappropriate to the fine arts since the verdicts of criticism could not corroborate the supposition of a steady improvement in aesthetic quality from the earliest known artistic products up to the artistic output of most advanced societies. And even when the idea of increasing complexity was substituted for that of improvement the theory became hardly more plausible. Since about 1920, therefore, evolutionary theories of art and of culture generally have suffered a recession in popularity. An attempt by Thomas Munro to revive interest in them by his book *Evolution in the Arts and Other Theories of Culture History* has not been entirely successful.

Sociological premises have been particularly important to art history in connection with the concept of style. For it has been thought that there are in the history of art distinctive and ostensively recognizable styles, which are related in significant ways to nonaesthetic aspects of social structure. Artistic styles, it has been assumed, are not arbitrary and cannot be adopted at will. In the words of Wölfflin: "not everything is possible at all times." From the pioneer work of Burkhardt on the Renaissance a long line of historians have explored the connections between art products and changing conditions of social and economic structure. Many others, without adopting a rigidly sociological approach, have been concerned to emphasize the value of art to the general historian as reflecting the spirit of an age, national character, economic conditions bearing on market and demand, factors of religious faith, common ideals and endeavors, and in a word all that contributes to the understanding of any cultural period. Typical of this approach we may mention: Edgar Wind's *Art and Anarchy*, Erwin Panofsky's *Gothic Architecture and Scholasticism,* and Frederic Antal's *Florentine Painting and Its Social Background.*

2. Through most of the nineteenth century thoughtful minds were preoccupied with the more immediate social and economic consequences of the changes brought about by the Industrial Revolution and with their more distant spiritual and cultural effects. The factory system of production resulted in poverty, ugliness, and depression for a new class of workers along with the emergence of a prosperous middle class weak in indigenous cultural traditions. As one consequence of mass production society was geared as seldom before to standards of utility measured in economic and monetary terms, while mechanization seemed to deprive the factory worker of the opportunity for self-expression or identification with his job. Perceptive thinkers began to be aware of a growing sense of isolation and estrangement, which under the name "alienation" has come to be regarded as the chief spiritual malady of our age. It is

Composition in Red,
Yellow, and Blue
by Piet Mondrian, 1939–42.
Neo-Plasticism.
Courtesy of
The Tate Gallery, London.

Time Transfixed
by René Magritte, 1939.
Courtesy of
The Tate Gallery, London.

seen both as a metaphysical isolation of the individual in the post-Christian world of thought and as psychological alienation in the depersonalized world of technological culture.

Creative artists had their own reasons for feeling themselves to be social outcasts and functionless in an alien society. The termination of traditional sources of patronage put them in the ranks of the unemployed, if not unemployable, and made it necessary for them to seek a living in an open market constituted by the new middle classes whose philistine taste conflicted with their own aesthetic convictions. In the second half of the century the official art of the academies had sunk to a very low ebb and the industrial or "applied" art exemplified in The Great Exhibition of 1851 had as yet nothing new to offer. In the economic sphere social criticism and programs of reform go back to Robert Owen and to the Swiss writer J. C. L. Sigismondi. Inevitably sociological thinkers and those interested in the arts asked themselves these questions: How can the arts contribute to rescue society from the grave perils by which it is beset? What is the true function of the artist in an ideally organized society? How can a reformation and renovation of the arts be brought about?

In France the Positivist school founded by the Comte Saint-Simon adopted an ambivalent attitude toward the arts. On the one hand they regarded the arts factually as a product of society, reflecting its present state with all its inherent defects—and in his later years Saint-Simon himself advocated suspension of artistic activity until the perfected society had been realized. But on the other hand the arts were spoken of as an instrument for social reformation. The philosopher-scholar was to draw up plans for the rationally perfected society, the industrialist was to bring these plans to fruition, while to the artist fell the duty of creating enthusiasm for the ideal by representing it in an attractive light and the duty, too, of strengthening the bonds of sympathy between man and man which are the cement of all social organization. In deliberate repudiation of the isolationist idea of "art for art's sake" the socialist reformer Pierre Joseph Proudhon (1809–65) defined art as "an idealized representation of nature and ourselves, its end being the physical and moral perfection of our species." The sociological aesthetician Jean-Marie Guyau (1854–88) in his book *L'Art au point de vue sociologique* (1887) evolved an aesthetic which was designed to break down the barriers which separate art from the other aspects of civilization and represented aesthetic experience, with its culmination in artistic enjoyment, as a restoration of harmonious living and a sense of belonging which is the denial of estrangement and alienation. Art is identified with the sense of beauty and the sense of beauty is expanded to become an ideal of all healthy and harmonious life-experience. The feeling for beauty was explained as "the higher form of the sentiment of solidarity and unity in harmony; it is the consciousness of a society in our individual life." Fifty years later the American philosopher and educationist John Dewey wrote with a very similar outlook and aim—though with very different philosophical presuppositions—in *Art as Experience* (1934). He defines the work of art as not the actual product but "what the product does with and in experience." And he gives it as the primary task of anyone who writes about the philosophy of the fine arts "to restore continuity between the refined and intensified forms of experience that are works of art and the everyday events, doings, and sufferings that are universally recognized to constitute experience."

In England the outstanding thinkers in the second half of the nineteenth century on the social aspects of art were John Ruskin and William Morris, certain aspects of whose aesthetic have already been discussed. Ruskin held a no less fervent belief than Kant in the moral aspects of beauty; but whereas Kant thought that only a taste for natural beauty has moral implications, Ruskin extended this belief to the arts. In his early works on architecture he argued that great works of art reflect the moral character of the men who make them and the society in which they are made: in their turn they wield a potent influence for better or for worse upon the social milieu. Both Ruskin and Morris thought that mechanized labor takes away from men their natural right to creative self-expression, both disliked the division of labor and both desiderated a reformed system of production which would allow the workman to enjoy the advantages of creative craftsmanship. Both thinkers combined a sentimental longing for an idealized medievalism—which in Ruskin accounted for his support of the neo-Gothic taste—with utopian schemes for the future.

The belief in art as a potent factor for social reform was not confined to sociologists but spread widely among artists and writers themselves. It was one of the convictions of the Pre-Raphaelite school; it was the inspiration of Wagner at Bayreuth; it impelled Courbet to join the Paris Commune in 1870; and it was voiced in Victor Hugo's statement that the ideal of "art for the sake of progress" is more beautiful than "art for art's sake." The dual and often contradictory beliefs that art reflects social conditions and that it is an instrument for social amelioration were everywhere prevalent, but were nowhere more central than in Marxism, which for political reasons if no others must be regarded as the most important of contemporary sociological aesthetic theories. To this we now turn.

MARXISM

Neither Marx nor Engels wrote a formal treatise on aesthetics, although as young men they shared a common interest in literature, and neither worked out a systematic theory of the functions of art in society. Their views must be pieced together from passing remarks and occasional literary criticism, mainly in the early works. During the 1930s, when the need for formulating an official policy toward the arts in the U.S.S.R. stimulated a lively interest in the views of Marx, the youthful works *Economic and Philosophical Manuscripts* (1844) and *The German Ideology* were published with partial Russian translation. The former is available in English in a translation by T. B. Bottomore under the title *Early Writings* (1963). The aesthetic aspects of Marxism underwent further development at the hands of Lenin in 1905 and 1909.

One of the best known of Marx's views about art is his doctrine that art and literature, together with other aspects of culture, are shaped by social conditions. As we have seen, this was not a novel conception but was pretty widely current at the middle of the nineteenth century. As taken over by Marx the doctrine was colored by his emphasis upon economic conditions, in particular by the importance he attached to the control of the means of subsistence, and by his materialistic interpretation of history, which caused him to represent existing social organizations as stages in a dialectical historical process which would necessarily culminate in the Communist Utopia. Yet his views fell short of complete economic determinism and are better expressed by his metaphor of an economic base and a cultural superstructure. In *A Contribution to the Critique of Political Economy* (1904) he stated: "It is well known that certain periods of highest development in art stand in no direct communication with the general development of society, or with the material basis and the skeleton structure of its organization" and he pointed out that Greek art and poetry "still constitute with us a source of aesthetic enjoyment and in certain respects prevail as a standard and model beyond attainment." Thus he rejected the view that aesthetic value is purely relative to the economic system and allowed some scope for the arts to wield an influence, if a minor one, on the process of historical development.

Marx was also deeply conscious of a sense of alienation resulting from conflict of man's profoundest spiritual needs with his actual physical condition. He attributed this to industrialization, which turns man from an individual to a cipher—a factory hand, to factory production, which "degrades him to the level of an appendage to a machine" and "destroys every remnant of charm in his work and turns it into a hated toil," to specialization and the class system, and to the monetary economy, which falsely reduces qualitative values to homogeneous quantitative measure. About the function of art in society he had little specifically to say and he does not expressly look to the arts to bring about a cure for man's sense of alienation and estrangement. But in his conception of the ideal Communist state he believed that alienation would be eliminated and man's aesthetic faculties freed. When in a mature Communist system the means of production are owned and controlled by all, he thought that leisure and opportunity would be provided for every man to achieve an all-around development of personality. Art would be open to all and the artist would no longer be a specialist but a "complete man" who indulges in the arts as a form of self-expression. "In a communist society, there are no painters, but at most men, who among other things, also paint." His conception of life in the socialist Utopia had much in common with William Morris' "joy in labor" and his idea of the artist as a romanticized all-around craftsman held affinities with the Arts and Crafts Movement.

The two aspects of Marx's thought which have persisted most prominently as rather uneasy yokefellows in official Marxist doctrine are the conception of art and literature as a socially conditioned reflection of the actual state of the society in which they are produced and the conception of art as a social force for the promulgation of revolutionary ideas and an instrument for furthering the cause of Communism in its historical battle against capitalism. In both these developments the influence of Lenin made itself powerfully felt.

In *Materialism and Empiriocriticism* (1908) Lenin laid the basis of dialectical materialism with his epistemological theory that all thought is socially conditioned and all knowledge is a "reflection" of reality, and specifically of social reality. Lenin developed his theory primarily in relation to scientific knowledge and seems to have envisaged a possibility that despite social conditioning there might be some principles of objective validity in the aesthetic sphere. Later exponents of Marxist dialectical materialism, however, have applied the theory more rigorously to art as a completely determined form of cognition wherein the world in its actuality is reflected. Thus Boris Meilaj states in *Lenin and the Problems of Russian Literature* (1954) that from Lenin's conclusions about aesthetic problems it can be clearly deduced that the general Marxist theories of "reflection" are immutable also for art. Linking with pre-Soviet Russian realists such as N. G. Chernyshevski, who in *The Aesthetic Relation of Art to Reality* (1855) explained all art as essentially a reproduction of reality, this more rigorous application of dialectical materialism provided a theoretical basis for the official support given to realism both as a critical method and as a directive to artistic practice. But realism has proved a protean concept. Interpreted most narrowly it has justified the official backing for a conventional (and therefore broadly acceptable to the aesthetically untrained masses) form of representational art with an innocuous social content together with the official condemnation of avant-garde and experimental art (Joyce, Proust, Kafka, nonfigurative painting, etc.). It was a weakness even of the theories of Proudhon and Guyau that their logical tendency was to assign the highest value to those art products which appealed most widely to the untutored masses and this tendency has been practically demonstrated in some phases of Marxism. But realism has also been understood to mean the reflection of the true hidden "essence" of reality and in particular of human nature in its social setting. And this has allowed much greater flexibility and breadth of vision.[4]

There is a certain contradiction between the belief that art is fully determined by historical conditions of time and place, a faithful reflection of the actual social state, and the belief that it is a propaganda instrument which can be molded in the service of revolution. To some extent this conflict was bridged by Lenin's doctrine of the Party. Bringing to prominence the Hegelian aspect of Marx's materialistic interpretation of history, Lenin represented the historical process as a transcendent development of inevitability, in which the clash of warring ideologies contributed as thesis and antithesis toward the ultimate goal of self-realization of the human spirit in perfected Communism. The true nature of this process, and of its goal, emerges to consciousness, he taught, only in the Communist Party and only the members of the Party know what is conducive to and what in opposition to the course of historical inevitability. Therefore, he claimed, the Party is justified in imposing control upon cultural manifestations as it exercises control in the economic sphere. In an influential article on Party Organization and Party Literature (1905) he repudiated bourgeois theories which claimed the right to freedom of thought and freedom for artistic creation, arguing that the true freedom of the artist and writer lay in subordinating himself to those social forces which were struggling toward the goal of true social and spiritual liberation of man in the Communist state. Upon these grounds it was possible to justify state control in all branches of culture and the imposition from above of a programmatic art. Despite this argument Lenin himself was alive to the advantages of a measure of liberalism and tolerance, declaring in the same article that literature lends itself least of all to regimentation and to the domination of the minority by the majority. He drew this distinction between imaginative literature on the one hand and educational and scientific writing on the other. After the October Revolution of 1917 Lenin himself supported the Commissar for Education, A. V. Lunacharsky, in a relatively liberal regime, but later his doctrines were interpreted

[4] See in particular Adolfo Sánchez Vásquez, *Las ideas Esteticas de Marx* (1965).

more restrictively to justify the notoriously oppressive control imposed on the arts under Stalin and Zhdanov. In 1925 the fourth point of a Resolution of the Bolshevik Party on policy to be adopted toward literature declared that "the party character of art in general and literature in particular expresses itself in forms infinitely more varied than is the case, for example, in politics." But at the First All-Union Congress of Soviet Writers in 1934, at which socialist realism was proclaimed as the aesthetics of Marxism-Leninism, Zhdanov defined this concept in the following terms:

> *Socialist Realism is the fundamental method of Soviet Literature and criticism. It demands of the artist a true, historically concrete representation of reality in its revolutionary development. Further, it ought to contribute to the ideological transformation and education of the workers in the spirit of socialism.*

Outside Soviet territories also Marxist principles have often been regarded as synonymous with an art which actively propagates Communist revolutionary ideals, and Communist ideological content has sometimes been treated as either the only justification for art or even as the criterion of excellence, aesthetic standards being subordinated to or confused with political criteria. As an example of this I may refer to the manifesto of the Mexican Syndicate of Technical Workers, Painters, and Sculptors, organized by the painter David Alfaro Siqueiros in 1922, which contained the words:

> *We proclaim that this being the moment of social transition from a decrepit to a new order, the makers of beauty must invest their greatest effort in the aim of materialising an art valuable to the people, and our supreme objective in art, which today is an expression for individual pleasure, is to create beauty for all, beauty that enlightens and stirs to struggle.*

The efflorescence of Mexican mural painting is the only movement of professedly Marxist and nationalist inspiration which has achieved general recognition on aesthetic grounds.

ORGANIC UNITY

The concept of "organic unity," or more loosely "unity in variety," is commonly traced back to classical antiquity, though there is in fact little about it in the surviving literature. The not entirely happy metaphor which compares the unity of a work of art with the functional unity of a living organism goes back to a casual remark in Plato's *Phaedrus* (264c), which may not warrant the burden of significance which has in later ages been read into it. In discussing the art of rhetoric he makes Socrates say: "Any discourse ought to be constructed like a living creature, with its own body, as it were; it must not lack either head or feet; it must have a middle and extremities so composed as to suit each other and the whole work." Plato himself in the dialogue draws from this no more recondite conclusions than that a good speech must have a beginning, a middle, and an end and that these should fit together coherently. The concept is further developed by Aristotle.

In the *Metaphysics* (1024a) Aristotle distinguishes between a "whole" and an "aggregate." Collections "to which the position of the parts in relation to each other makes no difference are 'aggregates,' those to which it does make a difference are 'wholes.' " Aristotle further adds that a genuine part of a "whole" cannot retain its own character except in the whole of which it is a part. He also says that removal of a part is apt to make the whole mutilated and any transposition of the parts will damage or even destroy its unity. The last statement is both important and obscure. It is, of course, the case, as McTaggart showed, that any change in any of the parts of an *aggregate* changes the whole aggregate. What Aristotle appears to mean when he advances this as a point of difference between an aggregate and a unified whole is that in the case of the whole but not in the case of the aggregate any change in any part produces changes in the nature and relations of all the remaining parts as parts of that whole. This idea is very important to the modern notion of an organic unity as applied to works of art.

In the *Poetics* Aristotle applies his concept of unity to drama (chs. 7 and 8). The plot, he says, must represent an action which is "whole and complete and of a certain magnitude." A whole is "that which has a beginning, middle, and end." In discussing magnitude he assumes the very important principle that a beautiful thing must be a thing which can be apprehended in a single act of "synoptic" perception, *seen* as a single thing or unity, and not seen as an aggregate of parts which are connected by theoretical reason, discursively.

Furthermore since a beautiful thing, either a living creature or any structure made of parts, must have not only an orderly arrangement of these parts but a size which is proper to it—for beauty lies in size and arrangement, hence neither a very tiny creature can be beautiful, because our view of it is blurred as it approaches that instant where its perceptibility ceases, nor an enormously big one, because then the perception does not take place all at once and the sense of oneness and wholeness is gone from the viewers' vision, as for example if it were a creature a thousand miles long—hence as in the case of bodies, i.e. living creatures, a certain size is required but one which can easily be taken in by the eye as a whole, so in the case of plots: they must have a certain length but such as can be easily grasped in memory as a whole.

One may compare the statement in *Metaphysics* 1078a 36: "The chief criteria of beauty are order and symmetry and determinate bounds."

The classical statement of the principle of aesthetic unity comes in the next chapter.

Hence, just as in the other mimetic arts a single representation is a representation of one thing, so too the plot, being a representation of an action, must be a representation of a single unified action which is also a whole; and the component elements of the plot must be so fitted together that if one of them is changed around or removed the unity of the whole is disturbed or dislocated. For if the present or absence of a thing makes no difference to the clarity, it is not an integral part of the whole.

Through the Middle Ages, following ideas suggested by St. Augustine, beauty was thought of as a combination of unity and variety as when diverse and varied parts are combined into a unified whole so that the congruence of the parts in the whole is immediately perceived. The key concepts were proportion and congruity among the parts in a heterogeneous or composite whole. The result was called "concinnity." This line of thought was summed up by Alberti at the outset of the Renaissance. Asking what is the property that by its nature makes a thing beautiful, he suggests that *congruity* is the source of all beauty and grace.

The business and office of congruity [he goes on] is to put together members differing from each other in their natures in such a manner that they may conspire to form a beautiful whole: so that whenever such a composition offers itself to the mind, either by the conveyance of the sight or any of the other senses, we immediately perceive this congruity.

He therefore says: "I shall define Beauty to be a harmony of all the parts, in whatsoever subject it appears, fitted together with such proportion and connection that nothing could be added, diminished, or altered, but for the worse."

The principle of "unity in variety" became very popular in the centuries following the Renaissance. The principle was supposed to be exemplified in such mathematical formulas as the Golden Section (see pp. 102–03) and in Hogarth's lines of beauty and grace. J. P. Crousaz in his *Traité du Beau* explained that the human mind has a need for variety as a relief from dullness and monotony but unless balanced by unity, variety will lead to confusion and fatigue. Sir Joshua Reynolds argued in a similar vein in his *Discourses*. Hutcheson stands out as the chief theoretical exponent of this principle. He defined beauty as a compound ratio of uniformity and variety and enunciated the general rule: "Where the Uniformity of Bodies is equal, the Beauty is as the Variety; and where the Variety is equal, the Beauty is as the Uniformity." His "internal sense" of beauty was described as a "passive Power of receiving Ideas of Beauty from all Objects in which there is Uniformity amidst Variety." In the 1930s George Birkhoff proposed an ingenious method of *measuring* aesthetic value in works of art by means of a formula relating order to complexity (*Aesthetic Measure*, 1933).

This interest in unified diversity as a signpost of the beautiful helped to keep alive the idea of "synoptic" awareness, the perception of large and manifold wholes, which otherwise was threatened with extinction by the new scientific ideal of "atomic" perception. The scientific ideal of perception, which was fostered by British associationist psychology, emphasizes the qualities of acuity and precision, sacrificing richness of content to exactness. Its logical extreme is the "pointer-reading." It was this scientific ideal of atomic percipience which provided the paradigm for Hume's "delicacy of taste." He describes it in terms of acuity and precision: "Where the organs are so fine as to allow nothing to escape them, and at the same time so exact as to perceive every ingredient in the composition, this we call delicacy of taste, whether we employ these terms in the literal or metaphorical sense." He uses the analogy of those kinsmen of Sancho Panza who detected a taste of leather or of iron in a hogshead of wine in which there was afterward found a key with a leather thong attached to it. But precise and exact discriminations of individual sensations are not in themselves sufficient for aesthetic awareness. The person with the most exact ear for pitch is not necessarily a good critic of music. With Hume's analogy we may contrast that of the Abbé Dubos who in his *Reflexions critiques sur la poésie et sur la peinture* compared our feeling for a work of art as a whole with our enjoyment of a ragout: in neither case do we analyze and apprehend the various sensory elements and ingredients in isolation from each other, but savor and give our verdict on the taste as a whole. Yet when we are aware of the "emergent" qualities, what is often called the expressive character, of a whole we are more than usually alert to any small incongruence among the constituent parts—anything which, in Wittgenstein's words, "doesn't make the right gesture." The same point has been ably demonstrated by Anton Ehrenzweig in his posthumous book *The Hidden Order of Art* (1967).

The contrary ideal of perception was fostered in the tradition which goes back to Leibniz. In contrast with the psychologists who regarded perception as the passive receiving of impressions from outside to be worked up by associative processing into a coherent world of things, for Leibniz perception was the central activity and as it were the very core of being in every monad; it was the point at which the potentialities of its nature are realized, its own "being" is crystallized into actuality and the universe reflected in it. Perfection, he said in an early paper *Von der Weisheit,* is the actualizing of potentialities over and above normal healthy functioning; and the perfection of the perceptual faculty consists in the maximum of *content* as well as clarity. It was this notion of perception which was implicit in the work of Alexander Baumgarten (1714–62), who first coined the word "aesthetics" and first put forward the idea that the current rationalistic classification of philosophical studies needed to be rounded off by a science of the so-called inferior cognition which is mediated by the senses. In his early work *Meditationes philosophicae de nunnullis ad poema pertinentibus* (1735) Baumgarten contrasted the "extensive clarity" of the scientist, who by conceptualization and generalization reduces the intuited content of perception to its elements and classifies these into a system, with the "intensive clarity" of the poet and artist, who sees things whole and retains the full richness of the intuited experience in a single undivided glance. His maturer theory repeated the contrast between the vital fullness of perceived reality which is caught and communicated by the artist in all its richness and the discursive analytical processes of science. By breaking down experience into its elements, searching for laws and physical causes, analyzing and generalizing, scientists gain much useful knowledge; but the original vital richness of the experience is dissolved and lost. The geologist can tell us much in a scientific way about the landscape we see: but in his explanations the landscape itself disappears. Conceptualization, Baumgarten argued, sacrifices the life of experience by reducing it to an aggregate of features in which only the common and repetitive aspects are retained, letting slip the original and the unique.

In Chapter xii of the First Treatise in his *Inquiry* Hutcheson showed himself also aware of this difference.

> *Let every one here consider how different we must suppose the perception to be with which a Poet is transported upon the prospect of any of those objects of natural beauty which ravish us even in his description, from that cold lifeless Conception which we imagine in a dull Critick or one of the Virtuosi without what we call a fine Taste. This latter class of men may have greater perfection in that knowledge which is derived from external sensation; they can tell all the specifick differences of trees, herbs, minerals, metals; they know the form of every leaf, stalk, root, flower and seed of all the species, about which the Poet is often very ignorant. And yet the Poet shall have a vastly more delightful perception of the whole; and not only the Poet, but any man of fine taste. Our external senses may by measuring teach us all the proportions or architecture to the tenth of an inch, and the situation of every muscle in the human body; and a good memory may retain these. And yet there is still something further necessary not only to make a man a compleat master in architecture, painting or statuary, but even a tolerable judge in these works or capable of receiving the highest pleasure in contemplating them.*

Hutcheson accepted the "passive" notion of perception common to the psychology of his time. Therefore, since the external senses receive particular sense impressions, he had to postulate an "internal sense" to receive the impressions of the whole as a combination of unity and variety. Baumgarten, however, inherited the active notion of perception which was current in the Leibnizian tradition and he was therefore able to define beauty as the expansion and perfection of ordinary perception. "The object of aesthetics," he says, "is the perfection of sensory cognition as such. And this is beauty" (*Aesthetices finis est perfectio cognitionis sensitivae, qua talis. Haec autem est pulchritudo*). Where he might have been expected to have attempted a psychology of perception, he produced instead a theory of art and beauty, equating the "theory of the liberal arts" or the "art of thinking beautifully" with the science of sensory cognition (*Aesthetica—theoria liberalium artium, gnoseologia inferior, ars pulchre cogitandi, ars analogi rationis— est scientiae cognitionis sensitivae*). This follows from the notion of beauty as the perfection of sensory awareness.

Interest in pursuing the study of internally complex perceptual experience, which in their several ways Dubos, Hutcheson, and Baumgarten had connected with the artist's method of coming to grips with his world, remained submerged for more than a century under the growing prestige of associationist psychology, which favored the "scientific" model of atomic sensory elements. The emergence to importance in modern times of the concept of organic perceptual wholes owed something to Gestalt psychology, when toward the end of last century it revived the idea of perceptual configurations with configurational properties which cannot be reduced to or built up from more simple "atomic" elements of sensation combined according to external relations which leave them internally unaffected.

From the first aesthetic objects were recognized as good examples of the kind of configurations which the Gestalt psychologists were interested to demonstrate. In his essay "Über Gestaltqualitäten" (1890) Ehrenfels, one of the founders of the school, instanced a melody as an example of a configuration which has an "emergent" character in that its quality in perception cannot be constructed theoretically by adding together the perceptual qualities of the individual notes from which it is formed and the relations in which they stand to each other. You can change every component in it by playing it at a different pitch or on a different instrument, but it remains the same melody. But it must be apprehended as a single impression. If you play the ten notes of a melody to ten different hearers, or if you change the order of the notes, the melody is lost. If you play it in bits to a hearer who knows it, he will hear the bits *as fragments of a melody* not as several small melodies. The melody as a whole has a character of its own distinct from that of the notes or fragments which compose it. Yet the notes and fragments, *heard as parts of that melody,* acquire a perceptually different character from the character which they possess if heard in isolation or as parts of a different melody.

The modern conception of an artistic unity combines the old Aristotelian concept of a whole with the *gestalt* idea of a perceptual unity displaying emergent or "field" qualities which belong to the whole but not to the parts. In aesthetic appreciation the art object is isolated from its environment and framed apart in attention as a single individual, apprehended as a single complex impression and not as an aggregate. For when we apprehend something as an aggregate we apprehend it discursively; we are aware of a manifold of interrelated parts, and we recognize each part for what it is independently of the whole to which it belongs. We do not become directly aware of any properties of the whole which are not constructed from our prior knowledge of the parts. But in aesthetic appreciation we become aware of the object in its internal complexity by a direct act of synoptic perception; we do not "construct" it in thought by discursive reason, though of course the final appreciative awareness may often be *prepared* by much preliminary study. Ideally, in aesthetic contemplation, we become aware of a total presentation manifesting qualities which are not built up from, or fully analyzable into, the properties and relations of the constituent parts. The whole in apprehension is more than the sum of the parts. Although the contained parts may be attended to separately in the perhaps lengthy process of becoming acquainted with the total work of art, they become fully articulate only when they are perceived as parts of the particular whole in which they occur, in the completed act of appreciation. We cannot know the parts as they are without knowing the whole. Although the whole is composed of its parts, the qualities of the whole permeate and determine the parts and the parts are what they are only in the context of the whole in which they are apprehended. It is, in the words of Coleridge, "a whole that is presupposed by all its parts."

A major problem has been to pinpoint the difference between aesthetic objects and other sorts of configurations. It has been pointed out that what has been said about organic wholes in general could also be said about nonaesthetic wholes, such as human faces. We recognize a face by a certain overall configurational character which makes it unique, not by adding together an assemblage of remembered features. We can also recognize a likeness in profile though turning it from full face to side view causes every feature to change beyond recognition in terms of abstract form. Faces also display "expressive" properties which are also configurational but are not identical with the configurational characters by which we recognize them. We can recognize the face of a friend whether it is angry or sad, calm or convulsed. Contrariwise we can "read" the expression on a face whether it is the face of a friend or of an unknown person. These gestalt properties have nothing directly to do with aesthetic enjoyment: we perceive them whether the face is beautiful or plain and our perception of them does not provide a basis for an aesthetic judgment. These are practical everyday acts of perception not perception in the aesthetic mode. When on the contrary we contemplate a work of art (or for that matter a face for its beauty) we do not simply recognize it by some overall configuration or "read" its expressive features as a piece of information about it: we dwell upon it, hold attention deeply with it and concentrate our energies on actualizing it in perception. One can take up an aesthetic attitude of "disinterested" attention to anything at all, fixing it in awareness not for the sake of recognition or any other practical purpose. But some objects—and these we call aesthetic objects—favor disinterested contemplation, while others repel it and are too jejune to sustain it. Not all organic wholes in perception are meet for aesthetic contemplation. Aesthetic objects are organic wholes which in suitably conditioned persons are able to attract and sustain intense, prolonged or repeated, and fruitful perceptive attention in the nonpractical aesthetic mode. It has not been easy to explain the qualities of "organic unity" which successful works of art and other things of beauty possess and which nonaesthetic configurational wholes do not possess. Aesthetic unity would have to be understood in such a way that it could serve as a criterion of excellence in judging artworks yet without favoring some art styles above others. It should not, for example, lead to the ascription of superior excellence to works manifesting formal classical proportion over those which have greater Romantic freedom and asymmetry or demand a preference for the Neoplasticism of Mondrian rather than the apparent randomness of Action Painting. For to do so would conflict with accepted critical verdicts. In practice it has proved so difficult to render the notion of aesthetic unity concrete while keeping it free from stylistic bias that some philosophers have despaired of using it profitably. (The whole question is discussed in a symposium published in *The Journal of Aesthetics and Art Criticism,* vol. XX, No. 2, Winter 1961.) On the other hand it has been suggested that works of art tend to differ from other perceptual configurations in that the qualities of artistic wholes are not only "emergent" from the parts in the way which has been described but are to some extent reflected back upon the parts so that the parts of an artistic whole themselves display something of the distinctive aesthetic character of the whole. This is why, for example, a torso or even an isolated limb reflects something of the beauty of the whole statue from which it came. It is not certain, however, whether this feature applies generally to all art objects and much work remains still to be done on the elucidation of the concept of organic unity in relation to aesthetic objects.

AESTHETIC VALUE

Two revolutionary developments came to fruition in the first half of the twentieth century and in virtue of them we are inclined to say that a new outlook on art and a new conception of aesthetic value have emerged in our time. The first, which we have spoken about already, is connected with the assumption that works of art are new creations with autonomous criteria of value specific to themselves. With it goes the possibility of emancipation from the presuppositions of Naturalism and all forms of Instrumentalism which have dominated art theory in the West until now. This change of outlook applies not only to our commerce with the new schools of art in our own time but colors our enjoyment of the artistic heritage of the past. Because of this we are learning to appreciate the art products of past ages as things which carry their own aesthetic value not entirely dependent on the diverse extraneous values which they were originally made to serve. Because of this we can admire one fetish as a fine work of plastic art while remaining indifferent to another, although both were equally potent with magical *mana* for the people who made and used them. We are no longer bound to the anecdotal interest of pictures or their power to elevate, edify, or amuse. The second revolutionary change of outlook was mentioned briefly by way of contrast in the chapter on Eighteenth-Century British Aesthetics (pp. 150–54). It is the belief, tacit or affirmed, that the enjoyment of aesthetic experience, the cultivation of aesthetic sensibility, and the training of the capacity to appreciate fine works of art are one of the ultimate values of human life, valuable for their own sake and not in need of justification from any extrinsic benefits which they may confer. This belief has sometimes been formulated in terms of the sociobiological notion of a "self-rewarding" activity (see Appendix 1) and sometimes in the context of a theory of "play" in a special meaning of that word perhaps first clearly expressed by Kant (see Appendix 2).

These new assumptions and changes of outlook are still operative rather in our practical commerce with the arts and in the literature of criticism and appreciation than in philosophical theory. Insofar as they have achieved philosophical expression they are reflected mainly in what is called the "formalistic" theory—or group of theories. It is characteristic of such theories to maintain that there exist certain properties called "formal" (or sometimes, confusingly, "expressive") which are necessary and (probably) sufficient to render any natural thing or set or sequence of things meet for successful aesthetic contemplation and to constitute any human artifact a work of art. In one form of theory "organic unity," which we have discussed, is held to be the special form of arrangement which sustains aesthetic contemplation. A formalistic theory does not bind one to believe that only formal properties of things or artworks are of interest and importance or to value them necessarily above other features. But those who adhere to a formalistic theory will maintain that although works of art in common with other artifacts may be valued for many other reasons, and properly so, they are said to be good or bad *qua* works of art—that is, aesthetically—in virtue of their formal properties only. There is a proper excellence of art, the formalist holds, which derives in most cases from the way in which a theme is presented rather than from the theme itself. A simple nude may be a better picture than an imaginative mural of the Creation of the World. One painting of the Crucifixion is not better than another as a work of art because it puts the religious beholder more vividly in mind of the historical scene depicted or even because it makes more real to him the redemptive significance of a crucified God. A picture glorifying the socialist Utopia is not necessarily more valuable as art than a still life of a jug and a bottle. To the modern idea which we are concerned with artifacts are to be judged good works of art only to the extent that they are suited for aesthetic appreciation, adapted for contemplation and concentrated "disinterested" awareness apart from considerations of function and purpose. This is sometimes expressed by saying that art is *autotelic*—that it has its aim and object inherent in itself.

It would be a mistake, however, to confuse this position with the "art for art's sake" doctrine which orginated within the Aesthetic Movement in the closing decades of the last century. In its most characteristic form this doctrine maintained that works of art *must not* serve as vehicles for any other values except aesthetic values, that any extraneous function or usefulness is a defect in a work of art. In the words of Théophile Gautier: "Il n'y a de vraiment beau que ce qui ne peut servir à rien; tout ce qui es utile es laid" (Nothing is truly beautiful except that which can serve for nothing; whatever is useful is ugly). "Art for art's sake" was a slogan of extremists who made a religion of beauty and wished arrogantly to belittle all other aspects of life. Nowadays few people would be interested to maintain anything of the sort, or to deny the patent fact that throughout history many of the finest works of art *have* been made for ulterior purposes and *have* served as vehicles for nonaesthetic values. But apart from exaggeration the hard core of truth in the "art for art's sake" doctrine, the truth which has persisted and become a commonplace of contemporary criticism, lies in the recognition that the cultivation of the fine arts not with a view to usefulness or propaganda but for their own sake is one of the ultimate values of this life along with such values as knowledge for its own sake, religious experience, human affection, and so on. It was this recognition which inspired the famous "trinity" of values— truth, beauty, and goodness—which finds expression in countless poetic statements and some as banal as the following from Emerson's *Rhodora:*

> *That if eyes were made for seeing*
> *Then beauty is its own excuse for being.*

Formalistic theories of art are still sometimes accused of being trivial and jejune, of concentrating on the superficial if keen pleasures some people derive from the game of attending to sensory patterns at the expense of neglecting the important "human" values embodied in great works of art. Without belittling the importance of these other values formalistic theories do invite the *philosopher of aesthetics* to give special attention to the class of formal values even though in the act of appreciation no artificial barriers are drawn between formal values and the "human" values which the forms contain. Therefore formalistic theories need to be underpinned by recognition of the intrinsic value inhering in aesthetic appreciation as a self-rewarding activity, a basic human drive in whose very appeasement its own sufficient justification lies. This assumption is fundamental to the outlook from which formalistic theories stem. The value ascribed to aesthetic experience becomes the source and fountain of so-called aesthetic values. Individual works of art are said to have aesthetic merit insofar as they are fitted to evoke and sustain aesthetic contemplation: this is the basis of their appraisal as aesthetic objects. Works of art are, of course, rightly and properly valued for other reasons than this: they are also carriers of nonaesthetic values. But aesthetic value means—or should mean—something different from the total value of a work of art. When we attribute aesthetic value to anything at all we judge about its suitability to sustain the self-rewarding activity of aesthetic contemplation. To ascribe this value is not to deny that the object may have other values or that these other values may be fairly intimately linked with the aesthetic values it has. But if beauty is a value, it is a value derivative from the ultimate value presupposed for appreciation. It is not a part of aesthetics to institute comparisons between the intrinsic value of aesthetic experience and other ultimate values such as those of morality, goodness, knowledge for its own sake, the love of God, human affection, or sensual satisfactions. Such comparisons, or their possibility, may offer problems which the branch of philosophy known as axiology must skirt. In daily life we may look for guidance to those mentors of the modern world, the schoolmaster, the parson, the judge, and the psychoanalyst. The artist and the connoisseur may find enthusiasm a more than adequate substitute for reflection. The student of aesthetics will look to his textbooks in vain for an answer.

APPENDIX 1

APPRECIATION AS A SELF-REWARDING ACTIVITY

The notion, if not the name, of a self-rewarding activity can be traced back to ancient Greece. It was inherent in the aristocratic culture which supplied the background for Aristotle's social and moral philosophy and which had certain features in common with the modern idea of the "affluent" society. For Aristotle a self-rewarding activity was one which served no ulterior or utilitarian purpose but could properly be indulged by a free man in the occupation of his leisure. "It is not derogatory to the dignity of a free man," he says, "to do something for his own sake or for the sake of his friends or for the virtue that is in it, but a man who does the same thing for others may well be regarded as behaving in a menial or servile way." The supreme example of a self-rewarding activity was held to be philosophy or the pursuit of wisdom, since this was regarded as an end subservient to no other purpose than satisfaction of the instinctive desire for knowledge which exists in all men.

For since the object of philosophy is to escape from ignorance, it is evident that men pursued knowledge for its own sake and not for any utilitarian end. And this is confirmed by the facts; for it was when almost all the necessities of life and the things that make for comfort and recreation were present that such knowledge began to be sought. Obviously, then, the pursuit has no ulterior motives. But as we call the

*man free who exists for himself and not for another, so alone of the
sciences we consider this free since it alone exists for itself.*

The notion of self-rewarding activity has recently been formulated by C. A. Mace with illuminating parallels and differences in
connection with art appreciation.

*What happens when a man, or for that matter an animal, has no need
to work for a living? On the genetic approach the simplest case is that of
the domestic cat—a paradigm of affluent living more extreme than that
of the horse or the cow. All the needs of a domesticated cat are provided
for almost before they are expressed. . . . What then does it do? How
does it pass its time? . . . It prowls the garden and the woods killing
young birds and mice. It* enjoys *life in its own way. The fact that life
can be enjoyed, and is most enjoyed, by many living beings in the state
of affluence (as defined)* draws attention to the dramatic change that
occurs in the working of the organic machinery at a certain stage of the
evolutionary process. This is the reversal of the means-end relation in
behaviour. *In the state of nature the cat must kill to live. In the state of
affluence it lives to kill. This happens with men. When men have no
need to work for a living there are broadly only two things left for them
to do. They can "play" and they can cultivate the arts.*

The basic idea is this. When man achieves a stage of social and
industrial organization which enables the individual to sustain life
without exercising his capacities to the full for the production of
the means of life, he does not just allow these capacities to atrophy
from disuse but continues to exercise them for their own sake—as a
form of enjoyable game. When this stage is reached society sets an
ultimate value on the exercise of such capacities for their own sake.
In the case of fine art the capacity to which such value is ascribed is
the direct nonutilitarian perception or the immediate awareness of
our environment for the sake of such awareness. This theory of art
explains the contemporary change of attitude toward aesthetic
experience and is a useful guide to the significance of that change in
our appreciation of art and in the role we ascribe to it. Nowadays
the cultivation of the arts is valued generally, if vaguely, as an
activity extending our powers of perception, often with the corollary that traditional education carries a bias, which ought to be
corrected, toward purely intellectual skills. The reason why correc-
tion of this imbalance is thought to be necessary is not in the last
resort utilitarian, or not primarily so, not for any side effects it may

be expected to have on the social structure, but because the revival and development of atrophied powers of perceptiveness is regarded as valuable for its own sake and conducive to a more complete and rounded personality.

The Greeks of the classical period did not rise to the idea of ranking the fine arts among self-rewarding occupations; they were interested in them either as approved recreation (as music and song in Homer) or for their moral influence on character and disposition. Yet to this too there is the hint of an exception in Aristotle, who may reflect a change of outlook at the beginning of the Hellenistic era. Discussing in the Eighth book of the *Politics* the reasons that music was traditionally included in the educational curriculum, he concludes that its uses as recreation or for the improvement of character are not sufficient or its only justification.

For the educational processes and the subjects studied must have their own intrinsic merit, as distinct from those necessary professional subjects which are studied for reasons outside themselves. Hence, in the past, men laid down music as part of the curriculum of education, not as being necessary, for it is not in that category, nor yet as being useful in the way that a knowledge of reading and writing is useful for business or administration, for study, and for many civic activities, or as a knowledge of drawing is useful for the better judging of artists' works, nor again as gymnastics is useful for health and strength; for we do not see either of these accruing from music. There remains one purpose—to provide an occupation for leisure; and that is clearly the reason why they did introduce music into education, regarding it as a fit occupation of free men.

On second thoughts he is prepared to allow a relative independence even to the study of the visual arts: although he will not go so far as to say that their appreciation is of itself self-rewarding, he allows that the study of painting can predispose us to appreciate natural beauty. "Similarly the art of drawing and design is not only useful in preventing our being cheated when we buy *objets d'art* or handicrafts but more particularly because it makes us observant of beauty in natural things."[5]

This almost casual anticipation stands isolated in classical litera-

5 Τοῦ περὶ τὰ σώματά χαλλονς may perhaps more probably mean "the beauty of human bodies."

ture and awoke few echoes down the centuries. Through the Middle Ages appreciation of sensuous beauty was subordinated to intellectual apprehension of cosmic concinnity as reflecting the nature of Diety. The medieval attitude to natural beauty is aptly summed up by the words of Scotus Erigena: "It is not creation that is bad nor yet the knowledge of it; but the perverse impulse which leads the reasonable mind to abandon the contemplation of its author and turn with lustful and illicit appetite to the love of sensible matter." There is in the writings of the early Church Fathers more incidental evidence of an appreciation for scenic beauty than we find expressed anywhere in classical poetry. But this feeling was held suspect and any allurement of delight in sensuous enjoyment of natural things was condemned both upon moralistic and upon theological grounds. True beauty belonged to God and could be apprehended only through the rational intellect as proportion and concinnity or, more perfectly, through mystical exercises. The natural world was generally thought of as a veil cloaking God from man and the enjoyment of natural beauties for their own sake was discouraged. For the medieval philosophers the idea of beauty had lost the incipient connection with the arts which it acquired during the period of connoisseurship under the Roman Empire. The arts, held in suspicion at first as the relics and depositories of paganism, were accepted only gradually and on sufferance as their capacity to add luster to the dignity of the Church was realized and their usefulness for educating a rude and illiterate populace in ecclesiastical doctrine became apparent. Painting, sculpture, drama, and the rest of what we now call the fine arts were ranked with the "mechanical" crafts because they operate in a material medium and rely for their effect on appeal to the senses—and "mechanical" was sometimes fancifully derived from the Latin *moechor* (to commit adultery) on the supposed ground that the human intellect, created for spiritual pursuits, was lured to adultery by such involvement with the material. When at the Renaissance the fine arts emerged from the vulgar and banausic crafts to take their place among the liberal professions so that the painter and the sculptor and the poet could sit beside the scholar and the gentleman, their "scientific" character was strongly emphasized, and for this reason it was a favorite topic of debate at this time whether painting or poetry is the more "philosophical." It was not until the idea of "fine art" emerged (see p. 157) that the cultivation of the arts and aesthetic enjoyment in general could gradually come to be ranked among the self-rewarding or self-justifying values.

APPENDIX 2

ART AS PLAY

The changed attitude toward appreciation and cultivation of the arts which has emerged alongside modern aesthetics owes rather little to formal philosophy and is not the prerogative of any particular school. It colors a great part of contemporary critical and casual writing about the arts and has colored a good deal of aesthetic theorizing in the last fifty years. Perhaps the nearest it has come to explicit formulation has been in the context of the theories, presaged by Kant, which seek to explicate our traffic with the arts on the analogy of play.

Plato on various occasions spoke of the arts as a frivolous and not very important duplication of or relief from the serious business of life (see for example, *Republic* X, 602b; *Phaedrus* 276 c-e; *Sophist* 234a; *Statesman* 288c). He also argued in the *Laws* that the undisciplined play or gamboling of young children, like the gambols of young animals, develops into an art form only when it is subjected to the discipline and order of ceremonial activity, dance, or drill. The former view of art as a nonserious occupation, a pleasant and innocuous amusement, persisted without being formalized into a set theory. For example Jacopo Mazzoni in his *Della Difesa della Comedia di Dante* (1587) classified poetry on the one hand under the rational faculty "which was called sophistic by the ancients," and on the other hand under the "civil faculty." In the latter capacity it is explained as a kind of game, a cessation or privation of serious activity. Thus "the civil faculty should be divided into two highly important parts, one of which considers the proper form of activity, and was called by the general name of politics, or the civil faculty. The other considers the proper form of the cessation of activity or the proper form of the activity of games, and was called poetics" (Part 1, sections 66–67). The idea that the arts are a frivolous form of indulgence separate from the serious affairs of life and justified only by the pleasure they give has not disappeared in our own day. But the serious philosophical theory of art as play can justly be said to begin with Kant.

Distinguishing fine art from handicraft, Kant wrote:

> *We regard the first as if it could only prove purposive as play, i.e. as an occupation that is pleasant in itself. But the second is regarded as if it could only be compulsorily imposed upon one as work, i.e. as an occupation which is unpleasant (a trouble) in itself, and which is only attractive on account of its effect (e.g. the wage).*

He goes on to differentiate fine art from entertainment, which he calls "agreeable (pleasant, or charming) art." In the latter class he puts those arts which "have mere enjoyment for their object" and every kind of play "which is attended with no further interest than that of making the time pass unheeded." Fine art, on the other hand, "has the effect of advancing the culture of the mental powers in the interests of social communication." Among the moderns Collingwood has most expressly distinguished the enjoyment of art from amusement though on a principle somewhat less pedantical than Kant's. Kant has also a secondary sense of "play" in which it is close to the modern concept of "artistic illusion" or imaginative pretense which is not intended to be taken seriously or to deceive. Contrasting poetry with oratory (which does aim seriously to convince), Kant says that poetry "plays with illusion, which it produces at will, but without deceiving by it; for it declares its exercise to be mere play, which however can be purposively used by the Understanding."

Schiller took up the analogy in both senses of the word "play," gave it a metaphysical flavor and made it central to his aesthetic theory. Kant's idea of man as a being with a foot in two worlds was particularly congenial to the conflicting impulses in Schiller's nature and he elaborated it in his own way. By the sensuous instinct *(Stofftrieb)*, he maintained, man is bound to the world of appearances and emotional drives. As a moral agent he moves in the unknowable world of absolute reality and is subject not to the contingencies of sensible experience but to the impulse to reduce them to orderly form. This impulse he called instinct for form *(Formtrieb)*. But it is intolerable that human nature should be ultimately cleft between its two aspects, and therefore the sensuous and the rational interpenetrate and are unified in the play instinct (*Spieltrieb*), which Schiller identified with the aesthetic impulse to make and enjoy works of art. With eloquence he pleads his conviction that only in his commerce with beauty is man completely himself, because this alone heals the fundamental conflict between the two aspects of his nature and serves as a cement to society. "All other forms of perception divide the man, because they are based exclusively either in the sensuous or in the spiritual part of his being. It is only the perception of beauty that makes him an entirety, because it demands the cooperation of his two natures." But in the development of his theory Schiller, as so often with Germanic writers, gives his words a new meaning and by using "play" as a technical term applicable *only* to aesthetic appreciation he destroys the value of the analogy with which he started. In Schiller "play" becomes a form of activity which is directed only toward beauty. "Reason also utters the decision that man shall only *play* with beauty, and he shall only play with *beauty*. For . . . man only plays when in the full meaning of the word he is a man, and he is only completely a man when he plays."

The modern form of the play theory was articulated in the context of the evolutionary ideas of the seventies. It was characteristically formulated by Herbert Spencer and elaborated by his follower Karl Groos, who wrote *The Play of Animals* (1898) and *The Play of Man* (1901). In the atmosphere of Victorian complacency Darwin's principle of the survival of the fittest was often mistakenly understood as guaranteeing that features of structure or behavior which exist, since they have proved capable of surviving in the struggle for existence, must be profitable either for the preservation of the individual or for the maintenance of the species and of society: for only by subserving these ends could they have made good. In *The Principles of Psychology* (1870–72) Herbert Spencer argued that art and play are the two grand exceptions to this rule. Neither has survival value. Both are luxuries from the evolutionary standpoint. Spencer does indeed suggest that both art and play may result from a need to work off superabundance of vital energy, a harmless indulgence which may even bring the benefit of relieving the tension of unexpended vitality. He also suggests that exercise of the faculties beyond the serious requirements of life may serve to keep them in good trim and prevent the danger of atrophy. In a short essay on *Use and Beauty* (1852) he argued that things which have once been useful may survive and acquire a decorative value when their utility is over. "Equally in institutions, creeds, customs, and superstitions, we may trace this evolution of beauty out of what was once purely utilitarian." But the main position he advocates is that both art and play, and they alone, are a biologically and socially useless expenditure of energy, both are luxuries from the evolutionary and sociological point of view, and therefore art may be regarded as a kind of play.

Groos developed the view that play is an unconsummated exercise of instinctive modes of behavior, serving the purpose of training the faculties and perfecting skills. He based his argument on the typical case of dogs at play which bite one another but without driving the teeth home. McDougall, taking the gamboling of lambs or puppies or kittens as "the purest examples of play," follows Spencer more closely and argues that the corresponding instincts (combativeness, etc.) are not really at work, but that play is "activity for its own sake, or, more properly, it is purposeless activity, striving toward no goal." There is no doubt that this random, purposeless frolicking exists and has always been recognized, as by Plato in the *Laws*. But there exists also directed play. The cat which plays with a mouse and *almost* kills it, *almost* allows it to escape, is not gamboling quite at random. William James notices but does not analyze the element of *pretense* which enters into games. "All simple active games are attempts to gain excitement yielded by certain primitive instincts, through feigning that the occasions for their exercise are there." He connects children's games with the love of festivities and ceremony, which he regards as "another sort of human play, into which higher aesthetic feelings enter."

In modern times the idea of play has been associated with that of a "self-rewarding activity." They have in common that both are activities engaged in for their own sake and not for any ulterior benefit or reward deriving from them. But the association is apt to be misleading if the implications of frivolity and lack of seriousness which attach to the idea of play are carried over into the notion of art as an ultimate and self-sufficient value.

Conclusion

In the foregoing pages I have traced two main strands in the complicated tangle of man's thinking about the arts. Assumptions deriving from divergent interests have been manifest in many different guises, sometimes formulated into articulate theories and speculations, sometimes latent in the standards of critical judgment which have been used. Contrary and even conflicting assumptions have frequently been admitted conjointly. Outside these ways of thinking about the arts there is evidence of an aesthetic impulse which has emerged to consciousness only comparatively recently but which has operated for the creation of works of art with aesthetic qualities beyond the requirements of current theories and for their valuation and consequent preservation in accordance with aesthetic standards not wholly derivable from the theories professed.

Mimetic theories arise from the assumption that art is man's own substitute for reality, whether it be a replica of the actual or a blueprint of the ideal. In the West speculations of this sort began in association with a striking development of naturalistic art in Greece during the fifth and fourth centuries B.C. and naturalistic assumptions were dominant in theory at most periods until the middle of the nineteenth century. In China and India mimetic assumptions have occupied a less central position and have often been transformed by the context of special religious or metaphysical contexts. In contemporary aesthetic thinking mimetic doctrines have once again become peripheral, but they still play some part in theories of illusion, in the belief that art must be "rooted in experience," and so on. Mimetic ways of thinking are important in enabling speculation to keep a firm grip on the essential continuity between man's aesthetic experience of the arts and life as a whole.

Instrumental theories derive from interest in the functions and uses of art activity. The concepts of art and craft were not clearly differentiated in theory until in the course of the eighteenth century there emerged the notion of fine arts as the crafts whose function it was to subserve appreciation; and craftsmanship was synonymous with manufacture almost until the emergence of the factory system of mass production in the nineteenth century. These things caused what have proved little short of revolutionary changes in aesthetic thinking. Interest in the educational, ameliorative, and propaganda functions of art in society was dominant in classical antiquity and has remained one of the more prominent motives of instrumentalist thinking. Other forms of Instrumental theory came to the forefront during the Romantic period and still exercise strong influence on popular thinking in the twentieth century. Most important among these are the theory of art as a means of self-expression, the conception of art as an instrument or language for the communication of feeling and emotion, and the view that art functions as a means for the expansion of experience through the imaginative prehension of attitudes, beliefs, judgments, valuations to which in ordinary life a man would not subscribe.

In the twentieth century a good deal of useful spadework has been done toward the conceptual clarification of aesthetic thinking and over and above this a new group of "formalistic" theories has been aired. Formalistic theories are linked to a new interest in the course of the eighteenth century, from which time the unconscious aesthetic impulse has gradually emerged to awareness as a deliberately cultivated value. It is the claim inherent in formalistic theories that neither mimetic nor Instrumental theories of art provide aesthetic standards of judgment. There is no kind of imitation in virtue of which it is possible to say "the better the imitation the better the art," and a criterion derived from the nature of the reality imitated is not an aesthetic criterion. Nor are any of the functions attributed by Instrumental theories to works of art functions that are exclusive to art. In contradistinction to this it is claimed that certain qualities which are comprised under the term "form" *are* distinctive of aesthetic value.

Despite the work which has been done on formalistic theories, however, and despite a massive development of sociological aesthetics since the middle of the nineteenth century, what is most characteristic of the twentieth-century outlook in aesthetics must be sought in the practical attitudes of criticism and appreciation rather than in formal philosophy. Ideas of self-expression and the communication of unverbalized feeling and emotion have been inherited from the Romantic era and their influence has strongly persisted. But alongside them and partly in conflict with them one may discern a new conception of art as creative. By this is meant on the one hand that a work of art is looked upon as a new created reality; whether or not it is also mimetic of a preexisting reality is a matter of indifference. On the other hand its purpose as art is conceived to be that it should afford occasion and scope for satisfying aesthetic contemplation; whether or not it serves any of the other purposes in which Instrumental theories have been interested is a matter of indifference to its existence and quality as art. Linked with this conception of a work of art as a new created reality subserving the purpose of appreciation there is apparent in contemporary writing about the arts a new seriousness attributable to conscious or unconscious recognition of the autonomous value of aesthetic experience. These two assumptons—that aesthetic values take their source from the ultimate value of appreciation and that works of art are new creations appraised aesthetically in relation to their value for appreciation—have become more dominant and more general through the first half of the present century and are mainly responsible for the distinctive tone of nonphilosophical aesthetic writing today as compared with critical writing in the past.

Selected Reading List

General

BEARDSLEY, M. C. *Aesthetics from Classical Greece to the Present: A Short History.* New York: Macmillan, 1966.

———. *Aesthetics: Problems in the Philosophy of Criticism.* New York: Harcourt, Brace, 1958.

CARRITT, E. F. *The Theory of Beauty.* London: Methuen (1914), 1962.

GOMBRICH, E. H. *Art and Illusion.* 2d ed. London: Phaidon Press, 1962.

OSBORNE, H. *Aesthetics and Criticism.* London: Routledge & Kegan Paul, 1955.

SPARSHOTT, F. E. *The Structure of Aesthetics.* London: Routledge & Kegan Paul, 1963.

STOLNITZ, J. *Aesthetics and Philosophy of Art Criticism.* Boston: Houghton Mifflin, 1960.

Anthologies

BEARDSLEY, M. C. and SCHUELLER, H. M. *Aethetic Inquiry: Essays on Art Criticism and the Philosophy of Art.* Englewood Cliffs, N.J.: Prentice-Hall, 1967.
GAUSS, C. E. *The Aesthetic Theories of French Artists from Realism to Surrealism.* Baltimore: Johns Hopkins Press (1949), 1966.
HERBERT, R. L. *Modern Artists on Art.* Englewood Cliffs, N.J.: Prentice-Hall, 1964.
HOFSTADTER, A. and KUHNS, R. *Philosophies of Art and Beauty: Selected Readings from Plato to Heidegger.* New York: The Modern Library, 1964.
LANGER, S. K. *Reflections on Art: A Source Book of Writings by Artists, Critics, and Philosophers.* New York: Oxford University Press, 1961.
MARGOLIS, J. *Philosophy Looks at the Arts: Contemporary Readings in Aesthetics.* New York: Scribner's, 1962.
OSBORNE, H. *Aesthetics in the Modern World.* London: Thames & Hudson, 1968.
PHILIPSON, M. *Aesthetics Today.* New York: The World Publishing Company, 1961.
SESONSKE, A. (ed.). *What Is Art? Aesthetic Theory from Plato to Tolstoy.* New York: Oxford University Press, 1965.

Classical Aesthetics and the Classical Tradition

BRUNIUS, T. *Inspiration and Katharsis.* Stockholm: Almqvist & Wiksell, 1966.
CARPENTER, R. *Greek Art: A Study of the Formal Evolution of Style.* Philadelphia: University of Pennsylvania Press, 1962.
ELSE, G. F. *Aristotle's Poetics. The Argument.* Cambridge: Harvard University Press, 1957.
HOUSE, HUMPHRY. *Aristotle's Poetics.* Rev. C. Hardie. London: Rupert Hart-Davis, 1956.
LONGINUS. *On Great Writing (On the Sublime).* Trans. G. M. A. Grube. New York: Bobbs-Merrill, Library of Liberal Arts, 1957.
———. *On the Sublime,* ed. D. A. Russell. New York: Oxford University Press, 1964.
PLATO. *The Collected Dialogues.* New York: Pantheon Books, 1961.
ROWLAND, B. *The Classical Tradition in Western Art.* Cambridge: Harvard University Press, 1963.

SCRANTON, R. L. *Aesthetic Aspects of Ancient Art.* Chicago: University of Chicago Press, 1964.

SÖRBOM, G. *Mimesis and Art.* Stockholm: Svenska Bokförlaget, 1966.

VERMEULE, C. *European Art and the Classical Past.* Cambridge: Harvard University Press, 1964.

VITRUVIUS. *The Ten Books on Architecture.* Trans. M. H. Morgan. London: Constable (1914); New York: Dover Publications, 1960.

Chinese Aesthetics

GOEPPER, R. *The Essence of Chinese Painting.* London: Lund Humphries, 1963.

SZE, MAI-MAI. *The Tao of Painting, with the Mustard Seed Garden Manual of Painting.* London: Routledge & Kegan Paul, 1957.

ROWLEY, G. *Principles of Chinese Painting.* 2d ed. Princeton: Princeton University Press, 1959.

LEE, S. E. *A History of Far Eastern Art.* London: Thames & Hudson, 1964.

SIRÉN, O. *The Chinese on the Art of Painting* (1936). New York: Schocken; Bailey Bros., 1963.

MUNRO, T. *Oriental Aesthetics.* Cleveland, Ohio: The Press of Western Reserve University, 1965.

SULLIVAN, M. *A Short History of Chinese Art.* London: Farber & Farber, 1967.

WALEY, A. *The Way and Its Power.* London: Allen & Unwin, 1934.

WILLETTS, W. *Foundations of Chinese Art.* London: Thames & Hudson, 1965.

Middle Ages and Renaissance

ALBERTI, L. B. *On Painting.* Trans. with Introduction and Notes by John R. Spencer. London: Routledge & Kegan Paul, 1956.

ASSUNTO, R. *Die Theorie des Schönen im Mittelalter.* Köln: Verlag M. Du Mont Schunberg, 1963.

BLUNT, A. *Artistic Theory in Italy 1450–1600* (1940). New York: Oxford University Press, 1956; paperback, 1962.

DE BRUYNE, E. *Études d'esthétique medievale,* 2 vols. "De Tempel," Tempelhof, 51, Brugge (Belgii), 1946.

———. *L'Esthétique du Moyen Age.* Louvain: Éditions de l'Institut Supérieur de Philosophie, 1947.

KOVACH, F. J. *Die Ästhetik des Thomas von Aquin.* Berlin: Walter de Gruyter, 1961.

LEONARDO DA VINCI. *Paragone: A Comparison of the Arts.* Trans. with Introduction by Irma A. Richter. Oxford: Oxford University Press, 1949.

MATHEW, G. *Byzantine Aesthetics.* London: Murray, 1963.

MICHELIS, P. A. *An Aesthetic Approach to Byzantine Art* (1955). London: Batsford, 1964.

PANOFSKY, E. *Gothic Architecture and Scholasticism.* London: Thames & Hudson, 1957.

SIMSON, O. VON. *The Gothic Cathedral* (1956). 2d ed. London: Routledge & Kegan Paul, 1962.

SVOBODA, K. *L'Esthétique de Saint Augustin et ses sources.* Brno, 1933.

Eighteenth Century

BATE, W. J. *From Classic to Romantic: Premises of Taste in Eighteenth-Century England* (1946). New York: Harper & Row, 1961.

BURKE, EDMUND. *A Philosophical Enquiry into the Origin of Our Ideas of the Sublime and Beautiful,* ed., with Introduction and Notes by J. T. Boulton. London: Routlege & Kegan Paul, 1958.

HIPPLE, W. J. *The Beautiful, The Sublime, and The Picturesque in Eighteenth-Century British Aesthetic Theory.* Carbondale: Southern Illinois University Press, 1957.

MONK, S. H. *The Sublime* (1935). Ann Arbor: University of Michigan Press (Ann Arbor paperback), 1960.

THORPE, C. DEWITT. *The Aesthetic Theory of Thomas Hobbes.* New York: Russell, 1964.

Immanuel Kant

KANT, I. *The Critique of Judgment.* Trans. J. C. Meredith (1928). New York: Oxford University Press, 1952.

———. *The Analytic of the Beautiful.* Trans. W. Cerf. New York: Bobbs-Merrill, Library of Liberal Arts, 1963.

Romantic Age; Imagination

ABRAMS, M. H. *The Mirror and the Lamp: Romantic Theory and the Critical Tradition.* New York: Oxford University Press, 1953.

BUNDY, M. D. *The Theory of Imagination.* London: Routledge & Kegan Paul, 1938.

CLIVE, G. *The Romantic Enlightenment.* New York: Meridian, 1960.

DOWNEY, J. E. *Creative Imagination*. London: Kegan Paul, 1929.

FURLONG, E. J. *Imagination*. London: Allen & Unwin, 1961.

HOUGH, G. *The Romantic Poets*. London: Hutchinson University Library, 1953.

NEWTON, E. *The Romantic Rebellion*. London: Longmans, 1962.

PRAZ, M. *The Romantic Agony* (1933). New York: Collins (Fontana), 1960.

SARTRE, J.-P. *Imagination*. Trans. F. Williams. London: Cresset Press, 1962.

TUVESON, E. L. *The Imagination as a Means of Grace*. Berkeley: University of California Press, 1960.

Theories of Expression and Communication

COLLINGWOOD, R. G. *The Principles of Art*. New York: Oxford University Press, 1938; paperback, 1963.

CROCE, B. *Philosophy, Poetry, History: An Anthology of Essays by Benedetto Croce*. Trans. Cecil Sprigge. New York: Oxford University Press, 1966.

DE, S. K. *Sanskrit Poetics as a Study of Aesthetics*. Berkeley: University of California Press, 1963.

DEWEY, J. *Art as Experience* (1934). New York: Putnam, 1959.

KRIS, E. *Psychoanalytic Explorations in Art*. New York: International Universities Press, 1953.

LALO, G. *L'Art loin de la vie*. Paris: J. Vrin, 1939.

LANGER, S. K. *Mind: An Essay on Human Feeling*. Baltimore: Johns Hopkins Press, 1967.

READ, H. *Education Through Art*. 3d ed. London: Faber & Faber, 1958.

REID, L. A. *Ways of Knowledge and Experience*. London: Allen & Unwin, 1960.

RICHARDS, I. A. *Principles of Literary Criticism*. 2d ed. London: Routledge & Kegan Paul, 1926.

RICHARDS, I. A., OGDEN, C. K. and WOOD, J. *The Foundations of Aesthetics*. London: Allen & Unwin, 1921.

TOLSTOY, L. *What Is Art?* The Walter Scott Publishing Co., 1899.

Twentieth Century

ARNHEIM, R. *Art and Visual Perception*. London: Faber & Faber, 1956.

BELL, CLIVE. *Art*. London: Chatto & Windus, 1914.

BULLOUGH, E. *Aesthetics*, ed. with Introduction, by Elizabeth Wilkinson. London: Bowes, 1957.

CASEY, J. *The Language of Criticism*. London: Methuen, 1966.

DUFRENNE, M. *Phénoménologie de l'expérience esthétique.* Paris: Presses universitaires de France, 1953.

ELTON, W. (ed.). *Essays in Aesthetics and Language.* Oxford: Blackwell, 1954.

EMOND, TRYGGVE. *On Art and Unity.* Lund: Gleerups, 1964.

HOOK, S. (ed.). *Art and Philosophy.* New York: New York University Press, 1966.

HULME, T. E. *Speculations.* London: Kegan Paul, 1924.

KANINSKY, W. *Concerning the Spiritual in Art.* Eng. trans. New York: George Wittenborn Inc., 1947.

MUNRO, T. *The Arts and Their Interrelations* (1949). Indianapolis: Liberal Arts Press, 1967.

OSBORNE, H. *Theory of Beauty.* London: Routledge & Kegan Paul, 1955.

OZENFANT, A. *Foundations of Modern Art.* London: Rodker, 1931.

VALENTINE, C. W. *The Experimental Psychology of Beauty* (1913). London: Methuen, 1968.

WITTGENSTEIN, L. *Lectures and Conversations on Aesthetics, Psychology and Religious Belief,* ed. Cyril Barrett. Oxford: Blackwell, 1966.

Index